Nick Munier with Esther McCarthy
BOILING POINT

Adventures in the Restaurant Game

Nick Munier with Esther McCarthy

BOILING POINT

Adventures in the Restaurant Game

Y BOOKS

First published in 2010 by
Y Books
Lucan, Co. Dublin
Ireland
Tel/Fax: +353 1 6217992
publishing@ybooks.ie
www.ybooks.ie

ISBN: 978-1-908023-09-4 (paperback)
ISBN: 978-1-908023-10-0 (ebook: mobi format)
ISBN: 978-1-908023-11-7 (ebook: epub format)

A CIP catalogue record for this book is available from the British
Library.

10 9 8 7 6 5 4 3 2 1

Typeset by the Little Red Pen
Cover design by Graham Thew Design
Front and back cover images courtesy of David Bentley Photography
Printed and bound by CPI Mackays, Chatham ME5 8TD

For my three loolas and my queen of calm.

Nick Munier

To my mammy, Kathleen, for everything.

Esther McCarthy

CONTENTS

ACKNOWLEDGEMENTS

Little did I know that I would ever be in a position to tell my little story about my years in the hospitality trade. So, how do I begin to express my gratitude to the countless people who have helped me over the years?

I am very grateful to Chenile Keogh and Robert Doran, who came knocking on my door to ask if I would write a book about my experiences. At first it seemed like an odd idea to me – why would anyone take an interest? But, of course, me being me, I eventually leapt at the chance and gave a year and a half to the amazing Esther McCarthy, who listened, questioned and drew out of me moments that I had forgotten or that lay hidden in the recesses of my memory. Without her and her endearing patience and friendship, this book would not be filled with the candid recollections that I hope make it special. I would also like to thank Elizabeth Hudson for her wonderful editing and vision.

Warmest thanks to my family, especially to my mum and dad, Jean and Elaine, for always being there with their support and encouragement and for imparting their invaluable expertise. I will always have special memories of my wonderful French grandparents, who I still speak to every day. Thanks to my brother Pascal for being a great listener … and for living in a wonderful village in France!

Stephen Gibson, you help my dreams come true every day – I thank you. Alan Barclay helps steer the ship. Katrina McBrien, you calm me down. Helen Egan, you dance around our café with such grace. Eoin Tyrrell, you guide me away from trouble. Robert Scanlon, you are a legend and a true friend. Mary Wedick, thank you for your astuteness. Mark Huberman, you make me laugh. To all the Pichet crew who have joined the ship along the journey, thank you.

Thanks to Ben Frow, the master; Fintan McGuire, who captured my dreams on film; and to all at TV3 for your loyal support.

Harry Crosbie is my rock 'n' roll hero, and Rita Crosbie is the celeriac queen who brings us plums and pears – your support is endless and is hugely appreciated.

Thanks to: Susan Hunter for flying the Pichet flag worldwide; John Banville for the words; Tom Dunne for the tunes; Gerry Ryan for the memories; Gino D'Acampo for making the girls swoon; John Flanagan and Fran McGrath for believing in my art life; the Terracher family for helping me decide to go front of house; Gerry Purcell and Ashling Gleeson for the big hugs and smiles; the Kennedys for writing our menus; Victoria and Pauleen for the very long lunches; the two Ritas, who bring laughter to the café every day; Don Buckley and Joan for your eagle eyes; and all Pichet's loyal customers – you make me get out of bed every day to do a job I love.

Jean Cottard, you put me on my course and I thank you dearly. Marco Pierre White, you gave me some of the best experiences of my life, and I admire you. Albert and Michel Roux, my respect for you is endless. Declan Maxwell, you are the best dinner companion. Thanks also to Kevin Watson, my best man, and to the Kemp ladies, who inspire me every day.

Kathleen McBrien, you are the mother ship. Gerry McBrien, you are my wisdom. Emma, Anthony and Dylan Roberts, you make my heart smile. Christy and Mary Balfe, we have to go fishing. Linda, Conor, Orlagh and Bronagh, you have entered my life and are safe in my heart. Thanks to all the Balfe and McBrien family, for always being proud of me.

Thank you to: the Muldowney family, who nurtured my art life; Antony and Claire Ely for the Oasis moments; Nick and Sue for my first art exhibition; Sheerin Wilde for jogging my memory; Frank Gleeson for understanding me; Dave Bentley, whose talent behind the lens made me look good; Barbara Corsico, for the pictures; Ian Hyland, for the Catch 22; Tomas Rowley, for keeping me in the black; Catriona Kelly and Neil McKenna at Ulster Bank, for getting us started; all at ITV, for an amazing experience on *Hell's Kitchen* and *The Great British Feast*; Guillaume Le Brun for respecting front-of-house staff; Matt Brown, Roger Pizey and Tim Payne for taking the piss out of me every day on *Hell's Kitchen*.

To all those I haven't named, please know that you are in my heart and that without your friendship and guidance I would not be here.

Last but by no means least, thank you to my wife Denise – an amazing, strong and beautiful woman – and to my three princes, Conan, Luc and Alex.

Nick Munier

The management and staff of Ireland's happiest and most dynamic newspaper, *Sunday World*, have been an enormous support throughout the writing of this book. Thanks to Editor Colm MacGinty and Managing Editor Neil Leslie for their encouragement and to all of my colleagues and friends in the office for the endless ideas, interest and enthusiasm. As a panic-stricken first-time author, the support was hugely appreciated, especially from those of you who are already fully-paid-up members of the organisation known as SWAG (Sunday World Authors' Group)!

The passion, dedication and hard work that Chenile Keogh and Robert Doran of Y Books have put into this project have made my job so much easier. I appreciated the free counselling service you both provided when, having agreed to write the book, I realised that I had to actually write the book. Thanks, too, to editor Elizabeth Hudson for providing structure and dewaffling (is that a word, Liz?!).

Thanks to my hubby, Eoin O'Neill, for his constant support and for looking at the text with fresh and smart eyes when that was exactly what was needed.

I am indebted to Des Ekin for the wisdom and advice he shared with me at a crucial stage of this project, and, indeed, throughout my career, and to Siobhán Farrell for her boundless energy and her proofreading skills. Thanks to my pals Moira Hannon and Annette O'Meara for their valuable input and for allowing me to hog endless nights out with my manuscript melodramas. Indeed, thanks to all of my family and friends for lending an ear and giving practical suggestions.

I am also grateful to Margot Doran, whose transcription skills helped me to reach my deadlines.

Writing a book is much tougher than it seems, and I now realise how fortunate I was to be gifted with a subject as on top of his game as Nick Munier. Over dozens of hours of my nosy, probing interviews, he engaged with and embraced the process with courtesy, wit and honesty. Best of all for a journalist, he did not duck a single question. Thank you Nick for being an absolute gentleman, for being such brilliant company and, of course, for bringing cake.

Esther McCarthy

PHOTO CREDITS

Every effort has been made to contact copyright holders in order to obtain their permission. The publisher would like to thank the following images:

David Bentley Photography: pp. 200, 242.

Bigstock: pp. 37, 41, 61, 64, 77, 80, 83, 89, 92, 97, 105, 117, 124, 138, 139, 140, 145, 154, 155, 158, 162, 166, 168, 173, 174, 177, 181, 184, 208, 215, 222, 235, 238, 240, 247, 263, 281.

Collins Photo Agency: p. 133.

Gallery 23: p. 230.

The Mirror Group: pp. 74, 123, 243.

Nic McInness: pp. 16, 158, 258, 268, 271, 273, 278, 282, 284, 285, 286, 287, 288, 291, 292, 296, 298, 300.

Nick Munier: pp. 1, 24, 26, 27, 28, 29, 31, 32, 33, 44, 46, 48, 49, 50, 51, 53, 54, 57, 58, 63, 66, 70, 81, 86, 114, 115, 165, 186, 188, 191, 193, 194, 196, 227, 231, 255, 262, 277, 303.

PROLOGUE

It is 1 July 2009. Opening night. Show time. I am standing on the shop floor of my new restaurant, Pichet, mentally willing the people passing by to come in. I am hoping that if I send enough positive vibes, they will come dine with me. After months of planning, and a lifetime of dreaming, I have finally fulfilled my ambition to open my own restaurant. How does that make me feel? Proud, overjoyed, renewed ... and absolutely terrified. As I look out the window of our shiny new premises on Dublin's Trinity Street, I'm wondering if I've just made the biggest mistake of my life. I've opened for business just as the diners of yesterday have decided to stay at home and cook pasta to reflect their new economic reality.

We have gone for what the marketing people would describe as 'a soft opening'. As if we had any other choice. We have already run way over budget. Other than taking a stand at the Taste of Dublin festival, we have had no public-relations activity to speak of. And while we talked the talk and presented well-thought-out business plans to get the finance together (with some difficulty), we have absolutely no idea how many people will come through the door tonight.

I would love to tell you that there are queues of customers at the door, that the room we have lovingly created is bulging with people adoring what we have done. I'd love to tell you that. But tonight, on our first night in business, we welcome twelve customers. I know the number, because I have counted them, several times. My attempts at hypnotising people into entering are not working.

We have poured everything we are and have into this enterprise. We have devised menu plans, picked colour schemes, thought about the vibe we want to create, the music we want to play. No matter how much my first twelve customers are prepared to splash their cash, the sums are not going to add up. While it's just the first night, the pressures of opening a restaurant in a torrid financial climate mean that my business partner and chef, Stephen Gibson, and I don't have the luxury of wriggle room. The stakes are high. We are in debt. We already know from doing the maths that we need to make €26,000 *every week*, just to break even.

Turning from the window, I look around our spanking new room with our Parisian-blue seating and silver-and-white colour scheme. There's my partner in life and in business, Denise, organising the sparsely filled reservations book. Over at the pass stands Stephen, cooking up a storm and peering into the room to see whether our handful of diners are clearing their plates. And our new staff, who have come on board for our start-up, are working the room and putting our many training sessions into practice.

The happy voice in my head is saying, 'Well done. This is what you've always wanted, and you've made it a reality.' My dark voice is booming, 'Twelve customers?! Nick! What the fuck were you thinking?!' Though I keep my thoughts to myself, I think we've blown it. We have staked our cash, our reputations, our hearts and souls, on this new business. And we are quiet.

Despite all of that fear, there is a huge amount of positivity on that first night – from the customers. There are only twelve of them, but they are all very enthusiastic. They tell us they love the place and enjoy giving feedback because they are first in the door. Their compliments are very reassuring. Some of them have become loyal customers – and they do love to remind us that they found us first.

That opening night was the strangest experience, and one which I will never forget. It was exhilarating in the sense that we'd finally opened those doors despite all the challenges. We were upbeat, and we were certainly ready. But no matter what we'd put on the menu, no matter what the decor was like, we couldn't make the people come in.

And that's how it was every long night for the first week. We later heard that people wanted to give us a week to find our feet. I really, really wish I'd known that in those first frightening nights. After service, we would sit in the coffee-shop area of the restaurant, collectively wringing our hands. Had we got it right? What did we need to tweak? What did we do now? The logical me was reassuring: 'It's OK. We've only just opened. Give people a chance to find us.' But that was being drowned out by a feeling of panic, screaming like a fire alarm: 'We've blown it! We're all doomed!'

Then something quite spontaneous happened. People started to come through the doors, in a trickle at first, but the number of patrons steadily grew.

I knew that first night there were going to be testing times ahead, yet this was what I'd always wanted: to work on my own terms. For when it comes to the restaurant trade, I really have seen it all. As the front-of-house man who's worked in dozens of your favourite eateries, I've witnessed the greatest of chef hissy fits and have catered for the craziest whims of customers. I've been the bridge between the person who creates the meal and the person who eats it. And often, while carrying armfuls of trays, I've fallen over. Unfortunately, some of those tumbles were on national television, in front of millions of people.

I've learned to read the mood changes of volatile chefs such as Marco Pierre White and have witnessed the dramas of the gifted but troubled Conrad Gallagher. I've totted up the eye-wateringly high bills of expense-account businessmen in the boom times and have watched as they drifted away come a downturn. I've served fish and chips to Madonna and vodka ice cream to Ronnie Wood.

I've witnessed the gruelling lifestyle and long hours that see many who aspire to work in this often insane business quitting within months, while some of those who stay succumb to heavy drinking and burnout.

After more than two decades of cleaning toilets, serving food, greeting customers and ducking the flying pans of enraged chefs, I am finally running my own business. I have fallen back in love with what I do. It's a euphoric and scary feeling to be here. But how did it happen?

Step inside, take a seat – your table's ready.

ARE YOU SITTING COMFORTABLY?

After twenty years of totting up the tills for other people, why the hell did I decide to finally open my own restaurant just as the downturn kicked in?

Anyone who has worked in this business for a long time has a dream of opening their own little place and working for themselves. It's always the way. But for years, for me, it just didn't materialise. I'd get stuck into a job. I'd get made redundant. I'd have the energy but not the finance. I'd have the ideas but too many responsibilities to take a risk. I'd get waylaid. But in my head, I was always looking for the right moment.

Opening a restaurant is something that many people dream about, talk about and then don't follow through. I have been close before – through a colleague, through a friend. We'd meet up and we'd be talking, *really* talking, about going for it. But so many factors would work against us. We'd get cautious, we'd do the maths, and we'd put the idea aside.

That's why I kind of stopped musing about it after a while, because I thought it was never going to happen, especially when I hit my forties. I had put it to the back of my mind. But I didn't want to end up regretting that when I retired, and in the end it was just a question of kicking myself up the arse and finding like-minded people who wanted the same thing. When Stephen

Gibson and I set up Pichet I was forty-two. I'm not saying that's old but you need to be so motivated to open a restaurant and at that age I was pretty settled. I had kids and a mortgage and had to think about what I was putting at risk.

The economic climate was the least of my worries. I've lived through two busts already and was made redundant twice due to various downturns. I was convinced that if we kept things simple and gave customers what they wanted, it would be possible to suc-ceed no matter what else was going on in the economy around us.

I grew up with this business – my parents have worked in the service industry all of their careers. And because I am half French, I used to spend a lot of time in Paris and holidaying in France with my family. My father's parents used to take me to these little family-run restaurants and hotels where I got to see how the French do business. They just open a little bistro here, a little café there, and cater for their core local trade. It always seemed very romantic.

When you compare Dublin to, say, Paris, where you can eat very casually and very well from restaurants that offer good cook-ing and set menus, a lot of the French restaurants here tend to be quite upmarket and highly priced. Stephen and I felt that there was definitely a niche in the market. It's all about how you define yourself. If you call yourself a restaurant, it can conjure up the notion of fine dining in people's minds. But the word 'restaurant' simply means a place to eat and restore yourself. A 'bistro' means a small quality inn that serves good food at reasonable prices, and that seemed the right word for what we were trying to do.

When you've worked in high-end establishments for years – as Stephen and I did – you start to crave unfussy food. You yearn for a great salad, followed by a perfectly cooked steak and chips and finally a big slice of apple pie. Yum. Most chefs and waiting staff don't actually eat Michelin-star food. We cook it, prepare it, taste it and serve it, but we don't get to tuck in. Michelin-star grub is essentially butter, cream, reductions, sauces – heavy-duty stuff that you couldn't get away with eating every day of the week. It's food that takes a lot of work to create and serve. We eat staff food, not the high-end, expensive stuff that's brought to the customers' table. Still, when you're surrounded by elaborate food all day, eating simply is actually a refreshing change of scene. So my favourite thing is to go to a good French brasserie and to have escargots (snails with garlic) as a starter, maybe a steak for main course and *îles flottantes* (meringues on a little custard) for dessert. Give me that and I am the happiest man alive. It's really simple food, the opposite of the labour-intensive cooking done in an upmarket restaurant.

Restaurants are like theatres: there are two shows a day. And you are only as good as the performance your 'audience' experiences. That has always been a core belief of mine. Each performance has to be as good as the last. That's the difficulty most restaurants have: they start well and then fall backwards slowly, usually because of the little things, things they mightn't even notice if they started getting smug about themselves. That's why we've got to keep our eye on the ball. If our service slips because a member of staff rings in sick or if we can't get what we need from a supplier, it shouldn't matter to you, our customer. The show must go on.

Successful, good restaurants are closing in Dublin every week. Having finally opened my own place, I don't want to go back to working for others, looking for jobs here and there. That fear, to a certain extent, never leaves me. It's what motivates me to get up in the morning. Keeping ourselves in there, working our arses off and hopefully having that hard work pay off. On to the next performance.

So this is where I am. *Maître d'*. Restaurateur. The guy you might recognise off the telly. Crazy enough to open my own restaurant in the middle of the bust but smart enough, I hope, to make it a success. I'd better explain how I got here.

23

I was never camera-shy! Me and Mum in 1967.

I DO LIKE TO BE BESIDE THE SEASIDE

GROWING UP IN A GUESTHOUSE

I can't tell you whether I chose restaurants as a career or whether they chose me. The trade was what I knew. I was born into the service industry, and, from my childhood on, I got to see the upsides and downsides of that life. I grew up in a guesthouse run by my parents, who were both from a catering background. Actually, they met and fell in love in the kitchen.

My dad, Jean Victor Ernest Munier, was an only child. He grew up in Paris, in the Pantin district in the 19th *arrondissement*, during the post-war years. When the war and the Nazi occupation ended, my dad was still a small boy. Incredibly, that was when he saw his father for the first time as he had been a prisoner of war since being captured on the beach at Dunkirk in 1940. My grandfather spent almost five years at Stalag 6 in Dortmund and Bochum. Dad still remembers the joy on his father's face when he returned to his family and his excitement at being able to go down to his beloved wine cellar and see his treasured collection again. Dad also talks about how Paris quickly regained an air of relaxation and joy after the war and how he was able to sleep in his bed in peace without having to get up in the middle of the night to rush into the bomb shelters. For a lot of families, it brought a new beginning – not always easy as family life had to be rebuilt after years apart.

Dad started work as a waiter before he was even out of his teens. His restaurant manager thought it would be a good idea for him to work abroad for a while to improve his English and arranged for him to take up a one-year position at the Turnberry Hotel in Scotland. It was important to learn English, even if you intended to stay in France, as many tourists do not speak French, and English is used worldwide.

Dad was a very handsome young man with movie-star looks, not unlike the famous French actor Alain Delon. He was just nineteen years old when he arrived at the hotel, a stunning period building set against the dramatic backdrop of the Ayrshire land-scape – the perfect setting, as fate would have it, for romance.

He intended to spend a year in the UK, but forty-six years later he is still there, because he met the love of his life that summer in Scotland. My dad loves to tell us that he had already been engaged four times but that after he met my mum he was forever smitten. My mother, Elaine Rosemary Prideaux, had worked as a receptionist in Liverpool's famous Adelphi Hotel before moving to the Turnberry.

Mum always says that when she first met my father it was quite simply love at first sight. They got married

Dad (on the right) looking dashing at the Turnberry. My mother couldn't resist his charms!

in the beautiful Ayrshire town of Girvan in November 1964 and moved down to London the following month to start a new life. Dad first worked at the Charing Cross Hotel. After a few years, they sold their house in East London and used the proceeds to set up their own guesthouse in Kent.

The Normandy was an eight-bedroom guesthouse in Folkestone, which they decorated in a French style.

Our guesthouse in Folkestone, where my training began at a young age.

It's a seaside town, and Mum and Dad took their inspiration from their surroundings. The house had a blue and white façade, and the dining room had Toulouse-Lautrec wallpaper which I absolutely loved. It was a Victorian house with a big staircase in the main hall and very attractive cornicing and period features. The bedrooms were simple but nice and very comfortable, with lots of bright colours: there was a yellow room, a green room, a floral one.

Because cash was tight, Dad continued to work as a restaurant manager at the nearby Forte hotel. He took the breakfast–lunch shift so he could be at home with his family in the evenings. Mum had her work cut out for her too, doing all of the cleaning and cooking in the guesthouse as well as looking after my older brother Pascal (born 7 May 1965) and me (born 4 August 1967). I can still vividly picture her running up and down the three flights of stairs, racing from dressing the beds to answering the phone. Only now can I fully appreciate how hard she worked, and it must have been difficult with us two boys running around the place.

27

There were eight bedrooms so on a busy evening there could be up to eighteen people staying with us. It was always a bit strange to live in a place where everyone else was having their holidays. As children we did learn a certain amount of discipline. We were brought up to be well behaved and to be aware of the customers. We had to watch the noise levels and always be properly dressed and polite. We really couldn't run riot, because there would be guests staying and because Mum always had so much work to do.

It was like having visitors all of the time. Even the lounge would be shared with guests. We would watch television in the evenings with the people who were staying with us. Sleeping arrangements were bizarre. I didn't have my own permanent room like you would in a typical family home. My parents swear to this day that this isn't true, but I remember sleeping in the conservatory because they had to use my bedroom as a guest bedroom. It was a case of them taking the business when they could get it. Then, during the quiet season, I would have my choice of bedroom in the house. By the time I hit my teens I had become quite obsessed by the fact that I didn't have my own bedroom, because at that age your room is your den, your hideaway, and you get quite territorial about it. I'd go to my friends' houses and I used to envy that they would have their bedrooms the way they wanted, with posters up on the wall. I learned to accept it for what it was but I used to really long for my own

Butter wouldn't melt. Me (on left) and my brother Pascal in 1975.

space. Storage space was an issue too because we didn't have anywhere to put our stuff. My brother and I had just a tiny amount of wardrobe space in a little box room where we did homework and listened to music. That was our escape.

As the house was often full, it was difficult for us to bring back friends and to enjoy the freedom of a family home as others do. On the upside, we spent an awful lot of time outdoors, playing football and riding our bikes in the park so we weren't under Mum's feet. As a kid I was always into football. I didn't follow a particular team, I just loved the game. I played from the age of eight until I was about seventeen, with a team called Martello Minors. I played towards the front, loved playing centre forward, and also played on the wing and midfield. I won fourteen trophies, and my dad still has them in the attic. I was very passionate about football. I also played for Shepway County. Folkestone wasn't the sort of place where there were many opportunities to play beyond local level, much as I enjoyed it, and I never really pursued it further. Then I went to catering college and work in my late teens and that was the end of that.

My mum would describe me as a restless child and a bit of a comedian too. She often tells me I was very determined, always looking for different things to do, rarely sitting still, wanting to play outside at kicking a ball or climbing a tree. Mum also remembers how I used to go down to the joke shop with my pocket money

Can you tell what it is yet? My first art exhibition.

and come home all excited to show off my new jokes or tricks. Pascal and I also used to put on a Christmas show for our parents every year.

I used to keep to myself a lot, I was a bit of a thinker. I was actually quite nervous and never liked groups of people or large crowds. At school I would never have been the kid who could stand up and start talking about a subject. I would be just bricking myself. I have overcome that through years of working a restaurant room day in, day out.

Growing up in a guesthouse that was very much a family business meant that we were working there from a very young age. From about the age of ten I was helping out. It wasn't a matter of choice, really. Mum was running the place single-handedly when Dad was out at work during the day. Then he would help when he got home – they both worked very hard for us, and it was a tough life for them.

My parents never wanted me to follow them into the world of service. They knew what hard work it was and wanted something else for their boys. But when they started telling stories they would all be about the good times rather than the tough ones, and I would listen to their tales of hotels and kitchens and be completely absorbed. Mum and Dad were very sociable people – an essential quality for the job they did. There would be many dinner parties with friends, and sometimes I'd be allowed stay up late and join them. Even when I was supposed to be in bed, I would sneak out of my room and sit at the top of the stairs, eavesdropping on the laughter, gossip and music before being spotted and shooed back to bed.

Having a French heritage meant we were immersed in the Gallic way of life throughout our childhood. We had wonderful family breaks in France with my grandparents, and my parents would talk to us in French. The other great tradition – sitting

En famille. The epitome of seventies chic!

down to dinner together every evening – was always adhered to, no matter how busy Mum and Dad were. Even now, whenever I visit, we take time over dinner to discuss the world over a nice bottle of wine with cheese.

When Pascal and I were young we would be sent to our grandparents for holidays just so Mum and Dad could have a break away together on their own. My French grandparents were the most wonderful people in the world, and I miss them dearly. Because we spent summer holidays with them they were very much part of the fabric and culture of my childhood. Even now, when I'm

under pressure or trying to make a tough decision, I will have a little conversation in my head with my grandfather and imagine what advice he would give me.

We went to the traditional seaside resort of Luc-sur-Mer in Normandy for several summers in a row, making great

Cannes 1971. Summers in France, where my love affair with restaurants began.

31

friends there. We used to sit at brasseries on the seafront grazing on fantastic seafood platters, and it was there that I got a taste of how a well-run restaurant can be a huge feel-good factor in someone's life.

When I was in my teens, I hadn't a clue what I wanted to do as a job. I sort of fell into catering college. That often surprises people because when they hear that my father was a restaurant manager and my mother ran a guesthouse, they tend to assume that I followed them into catering as though it was some kind of family vocation. For me it was more of a safety net, a way of buying some time, because it was a world I knew already and one within which I had grown up. I was a natural at it but I worked hard too because I wanted to be the best – I was always competitive in that way. I studied General Catering Advanced Craft, a City and Guilds qualification, at the West Kent College of Further Education in Tonbridge, Kent, in 1985.

In the 1980s, if you qualified for a third-level degree course you took it because the employment market was so uncertain. I would say that fewer than half of those I went to college with ended up working in the business. The subjects I took included food preparation, food service, housekeeping and reception, communication skills and cookery for the catering industry. The course wasn't really important to me. It was just a qualification, and college life was a way of avoiding worrying about the real world for a while. The curriculum was quite theory-based, and I suppose I learned some things – but, like most education, it doesn't really prepare

Following in my father's footsteps. At catering college in 1985.

Top of the class. Every kitchen needs a carriage clock!

you for doing the job. I got to know how to pour a glass of wine correctly, how to fillet a fish or whatever. It did give me a bit of training, but the best place to learn a trade is in the workplace. College, I would discover, won't teach you what to do if you have an awkward customer, or if you've overbooked and a member of staff rings in sick, or if the ovens aren't working properly.

I did have an interest in learning to be a chef during this period, and, while it was never really something I pursued in a big way, I think it has helped me to be successful in my career as a *maître d'*. After all, you need to know your grub. There's nothing worse than asking a waiter a specific question about a dish and them looking back at you, clueless. If you're serious about 'front of house' as a career, you need to know the menu and the food inside out because you're the link between the kitchen and the customer.

The course I did was for cheffing and waitering, but I noticed even then that the waitering element was regarded as the sidecar attached to the motorbike. We did a lot more cooking than service.

The chefs who taught us were good. They drummed in the basics: how to make a roux, how to cut a piece of meat while keeping your fingers intact, what to do if you burned yourself.

However, the college didn't really go for career guidance in any depth so in the summer of 1985 I went to work in a fish restaurant in Germany to see if I was really cut out for the job. My dad arranged the work placement, as the owner was a friend of his. I was also very much undecided as to whether I wanted to work on the restaurant floor or in the kitchen.

The Neptune restaurant overlooked Lake Constance. It was a very beautiful, opulent, modern-looking restaurant, with a busy dining room that catered for about sixty covers. Its special quality was not so much the room itself but the view: a huge glass frontage which overlooked the vast, still lake. In the summer, the room was filled with light.

I spent just a couple of months there, working in the kitchen, and immediately I knew something was missing for me. While people who become great chefs tend to prefer being creative on the plate, being in the kitchen never felt fulfilling for me.

I have one very distinct memory of those weeks in Germany. I used to look through the porthole in the door between the kitchen and the restaurant and gaze at all those glamorous people in the dining room. Beautiful women dressed up for a night out, elegant men in their company. I'd be wondering what they were choosing from the menu, what they were gossiping about, who was connected to whom, and I'd find myself thinking, *I'd prefer to be in that room, soaking up the atmosphere than sweating my butt off in the kitchen, listening to people screaming at each other.*

It just seemed like another world. While I did like the elements of preparing and presenting food, and appreciated how creative it could be, what was going on in the restaurant seemed much more exotic from that window. I was looking out at a world

I wanted to be a part of. I think those weeks were when I decided where I wanted to be – and it wasn't in the kitchen.

Gliding around the front of house greeting customers may seem very glamorous, but that's not how you start off. To work your way up to *maître d'* is rather like becoming a chef in that you begin very much at the bottom. I started off as a commis waiter. In theory, the commis is a deputy, an assistant to the waiter. But the reality of being a commis is that it's shit. It's a simply horrible job. I spent most of my time cleaning toilets and ironing linen, doing all the crappy little jobs that my superior didn't want to do. These days nobody wants a position as a commis – everyone wants to be a restaurant manager on their first day. But you have to learn somewhere. You've really got to climb from the bottom up when it comes to the restaurant industry. It's not just a tradition or a pecking order, it's all part of the training.

What was very fortunate for me was that I picked up commis work with some of the most revered people in the restaurant industry. The Roux brothers, Michel and Albert, are French-born restaurateurs who revolutionised cuisine in London. I mean, these guys are the godfathers. They were born into a family of French *charcutiers* and cooked for wealthy private clients, the Rothschilds, before setting up their first restaurant in London in the 1960s. They helped put Britain on the culinary map when it didn't really have an international reputation. They raised the bar for food in the UK, and many of today's great chefs learned their craft working in Michelin-starred Roux restaurants such as Le Gavroche in London and the Waterside Inn in Berkshire. In 1982, Le Gavroche became the first-ever UK restaurant to hold three Michelin stars. The Roux brothers also opened up a world of knowledge to others through their books and TV series in which they passed on their skills with warmth, humour and a complete lack of elitism.

Many of today's more egotistical chefs could well learn from their attitude as well as their skill.

If I was going to be a toilet-cleaning commis, the best place to do it was in a Roux brothers restaurant. At this time Albert was at Le Gavroche and Michel was at the Waterside Inn. They were also running a French restaurant in London called Le Poulbot. I was very fortunate that the restaurant manager was a friend of my father from their days in the French army: Jean Cottard.

One day when they were on duty in Algeria the jeep my father was in ran over a mine. Jean secured the wound in Dad's leg with his belt to prevent him from losing too much blood. From that day on they were very close friends. They went their separate ways after the army but when Dad heard there was a job going at the Turnberry he recommended Jean, adding that he could speak perfectly fluent English. Big lie. Dad attended the interview and answered all the longer questions while Jean nodded wisely and said, 'Yes, yes. No, no.' They had it all set up between them.

Jean stayed in England and ended up working for the Roux brothers for seventeen years, which was how I got the opportunity to work with them. I was a young, naive eighteen-year-old, and Jean took me under his wing. In some ways he became my second father, teaching me everything I needed to know in my early career. I wanted to emulate him, and lots of times I would try to act like him, which I think actually helped me. Jean would have been in his fifties then, a genial man, quite flamboyant, always immaculately dressed. He was regarded by people who knew the restaurant business as the best manager in London, and here I was getting the chance to work for him.

I started at the bottom, as was very much the Roux method. My work involved doing all the shitty jobs that were going. The benefit was that I got to be a bystander in one of the best-loved restaurants in London, and, by watching and observing, I got to see how all the experienced guys worked. I would count and prepare the dirty linen for the laundry, make the tea, organise breakfast for the waiting staff and serve their meals. I'd clean and maintain the customer and staff toilets. It was motivating in many ways. Nobody wants to do that work for long, and I thought the best way of moving up the ranks as quickly as possible was by being good and by showing interest and ambition. I used to go to the other waiters' houses when we were off work and pester them all for information: 'How do I get out of this? How do I improve?' So they used to give me tips and would tell me what was involved in running their sections of the restaurant. I have to say, they were very supportive, and there was no snooty bullying. I think because I was interested and passionate about wanting to do better they responded well to me. They had all been there themselves – everyone goes through that process. So they understood that I wanted to get to the next level.

I started coming in before everyone else, preparing the tables and laying out the tablecloths. To this day, I still love the ceremony of preparing a room, when it's quiet, before customers arrive. I adore that feeling of anticipation. Nothing pleases me more than preparing a room in advance of, say, a wedding. I suppose it's like a designer getting the props in place before the curtain goes up in a theatre. Yet often when it comes to show time itself I can quite easily get bored. It's the preparation I like, even though it's when the restaurant is full that you really get the adrenalin rush. There's something quite luscious about the anticipation. The ritual of polishing glasses in an empty

room, getting the cutlery perfect before anyone else gets to it. My favourite thing is hoovering a restaurant – nobody can bother you when you're hoovering.

I'd race around ironing the linen so that when the other waiters came in everything would be done and I'd be sitting there nonchalantly with a cup of coffee. I used to get a kick out of bemusing them like that. It made them realise that maybe this guy was serious about a restaurant career.

Armed with a little knowledge, I used to wreck poor Jean's head every week asking him, 'Can I have a chance? Will you let me work a section?' Be careful what you wish for. One day, after about three months, I drove him so crazy that he said, 'OK, here's your chance,' and gave me the biggest section in the room. It involved looking after eight tables. I nearly passed out. Here I was, aged eighteen, in a Michelin-star restaurant, with eight tables to look after. I took a deep breath and reminded myself of what was essentially involved: Take the orders. Collect the food. Clear the plates. What made it tricky was that I had to multiply that process by eight. My mind had to be organised, because if panic set in I would lose control.

When waiting tables, you have to have the confidence to prioritise, to say to yourself, 'Who do I want to take the order from first? Who will be in more of a hurry, or more irritated by a delay? That table for four? Or the couple?' You quickly learn to read people's body language because it helps inform your approach. It's key in any good waiter's mind: does everybody have a drink and their menu? Where can I cut corners if I need to?

Remember, the customer is only part of the equation. You have to balance and time the arrival of orders for the kitchen too. Is anyone starting to look a little impatient? Does that couple want to be left alone to talk for a bit? Some people get upset if they feel they've been moved down the pecking order, if they've been left waiting. It's not splitting atoms, but some people just cannot manage the job. You've got to have an instinct – it's a huge part of the profession. It can't be taught, and if you don't have a feel for it, you're never going to be able to do it. My first night as a waiter at Le Poulbot was successful because I was ready for it and because I was able to judge the tables, and hold my nerve.

From that night I didn't look back. I got moved up a level to 'station waiter'. I had been a commis for three months and was ready to move on. Best part of all? No more cleaning toilets. The other good thing was an increase in income. On top of my £80 a week in wages, I was now averaging £25 a week in tips. This was the 1980s, and I lived in a bedsit that cost £18 a week, so now my tips were covering my rent.

I cannot credit Jean Cottard enough for his guidance and friendship in my early career. He is one of those old masters, and I think he taught me class as well as craft. Jean has a lovely manner – the way he conducts himself and carries himself was very influential on me as a young man. I was inexperienced and unsure of myself and hadn't developed that way of almost performing that you need to work a restaurant floor. I owe him a lot because he pushed me in certain directions in terms of how to deal with people – not to be scared or worried, just to do my thing and to be myself.

Jean was a phenomenal restaurant manager. He was in the industry for forty-five years and that's because he was a natural. He taught me to be myself, to be courteous, to have a sense of humour and to be relaxed at service. He had that special rapport with customers, who adored him – I mean, he knew *everyone*. Le Poulbot *was* Jean in many ways. He had some good chefs with him, but he was a huge part of the personality and character of the place. For me, he was the master of managers. Even Marco Pierre White, who worked with Jean, would say he was one of the best. He was very quirky, eccentric, funny, yet very efficient. He had a great ability to make people feel at ease, knew when to act silly and when to act seriously. I admired that, and I tried to emulate him when I was starting off. It always helped me, especially when I was honing my instinct.

Jean looked like Roger Moore, and in fact was mistaken for the James Bond star when he worked at the Waterside Inn in his younger days. He was standing at the bar, and Moore's wife at the time actually mistook Jean for Roger. He had a very strong French accent, and was offbeat to boot. He used to love chatting to the customers, but they didn't always understand him. He'd be going, 'How did you enjoy your food, *uh huh huh*?' and then they would look at me and say, 'What did he say?' and I would say, 'He said, "Have a good evening."'

Jean instilled a mantra in me: 'Work, work, work. Save, save, save.' It was something that was going to cause me problems further down the line as I became fixated with money. (Indeed, I became quite obsessed with it.) Jean was professional but didn't take things too seriously. Very efficient, a great character on the restaurant floor and not somebody who liked to cut corners.

He used to be a chain smoker, and before and after service he always had a cigarette on the go. He would leave them all over the place. He would light one, put it down, walk off somewhere, take a phone call, and light another. But he wouldn't actually smoke it. One day, I found ten cigarettes burning at various locations around the restaurant. I said, 'Jean, what's going on?' and he shrugged and answered, 'I'm lighting them for my staff.' I can still picture him at Le Poulbot, which was a basement restaurant, smoking in the upstairs reception area after service. The cigarette would be in the ashtray, and you would see the smoke wafting up while he was saying goodbye to the customers.

Jean was fanatical about cheeseboards and would go to great lengths to make the board look fabulous. And if that involved furniture polish, so be it. He used to spray a little polish on the apples to shine them up. I used to think to myself, *If somebody asks me for an apple don't take one off the cheeseboard.*

Jean gave me a lot of opportunities and had great regard for me. Once, when he went on holidays for two weeks, he left me in charge. It was a huge compliment – I was just nineteen. It was very daunting, but I got through it and enjoyed it, and that gave me confidence. He's now retired, and we remain good friends. He is such an exuberant, extravagant character, and he absolutely lived for his job, but he's having a quiet retirement. He just wants to talk about the old days. For me, it's a shame that he hasn't been recognised for his contribution to the trade. I am sure there are many unsung people who keep the cogs turning in every profession, but if you have been at the top of your game, as Jean was, for more than forty years, you should be celebrated for that.

The Roux brothers used to come in a lot, maybe twice a week. If I was doing service and they came in I would be terrified because their restaurants were the best in London, and they were kings. I went on to get to know them quite well because on the odd occasion I would be asked to do extra shifts with them in Le Gavroche and in the Waterside, and then I worked at Albert's fiftieth birthday party in his home.

They were both nice guys, very relaxed, and while they enjoyed their success as legends in food circles, they weren't at all egotistical about it. They were very proper people, decent men. Albert was always very respectful of his staff, and he would always ask how you were getting on. But they were my employers and that was really as far as the conversations were taken. The same thing with Michel. He would show respect to his staff and had an awareness of the importance of having good front-of-house people as well as everything being perfect in the kitchen.

It was a very professional environment, and I think that was the key to their success. They were at the top of their game but they always expected professionalism from their staff, and because they led the way in that regard, you behaved as they expected. I definitely think that London's reputation as a modern dining mecca started with them.

You were never just working for the sake of it if you worked with the Roux brothers. There's a very simple purpose: to feed paying customers in the correct manner. It was an important learning base for any aspiring chef, and many of the best chefs in the world started with the Roux brothers. They also instilled a strong philosophy – that of hard work and respect – in many of the people who worked for them and who went on to open their own restaurants – people such as Paul Rankin, Pierre Koffman, Marco Pierre White and Gordon Ramsay.

They created a glamorous vibe, too. Their restaurants were always immaculate and never faddy or reliant on trends. And a Roux restaurant wasn't just a place to eat: it was a way of life. It was all about entertainment. In those days, a cigar and a cognac after dinner were the norm. The customers were all *bon vivants*, for whom money was no object. We used to get celebrities in there, people like Sophia Loren, elegant folk.

The well-known faces we got in Le Poulbot wanted to be recognised, to be served with a smile. Celebrities I've served over the years generally tend to be quite well behaved, which often surprises people. That they would get good service is a given, because everyone does when they go to a restaurant like that. Believe it or not, there really wouldn't be a buzz in the kitchen just because somebody famous had come in. Le Poulbot was too posh for those vulgarities, and everyone was treated like it was just par for the course. I tend not to get star-struck anyway. My concern is how to cater for these people, how to make sure they have a good time. The people who impress me more are people like Albert Roux.

I will never forget how fortunate I am to have worked for Michel and Albert Roux at such an early stage in my career. Not only did they teach me skills I will have for life, they also showed me that waitering can be fun when it's done with some pizzazz. I made the most of that time because I was very hungry for success. I left Le Poulbot after two years, feeling more assured about my career and more certain about what it was I wanted to do.

><

I have had a fair few service disasters in my time. Opening champagne always makes me a tad nervous. With all of that fizz pushing to get out and a cork ready to pop, the potential for things to go wrong is always there if it's not done properly. In general, if champagne is not allowed get too cold, it won't explode. I used to get the shakes serving it but I've gotten over that now. A lot of it comes down to the confidence that you get with experience.

My first champagne disaster was when I worked for the Roux brothers and we used to do private parties. At one, there was an outdoor hot tub, and I had to serve the guests drinks there. I also lit them a fire – it was quite decadent. There was an angry dog in the garden, and he didn't like me. I was trying to get the logs for the fire and keep away from the dog, making sure that he was on his lead. I felt like I was in a Tom & Jerry cartoon. We were serving osso bucco, a traditional Italian dish of braised veal shanks. It was for a party of five so we decided to do it as silver service. It was in this massive, heavy dish and I was trying desperately to be professional. By the time I got to the champagne I was feeling a bit flustered and nervous. And the dog was still glaring at me as though he wanted a taste of my ankle. When I went to open the champagne, it just went *pheeeew!* and sprayed everywhere. Some of it landed on an expensive-looking pair of leather gloves. I can still hear the voice of an angry Russian millionaire going ballistic and screaming, 'You've *ruined* my gloves!'

That was awful, but not nearly as bad as the time I toppled fizz all over a bride's dress on her wedding day. That was a disaster, that was. From the wedding party's perspective, it was an idyllic day. Everything was perfect: late summer, romantic setting, beautiful gardens and a loved-up couple who had just committed to spending the rest of their lives together in the company of their closest family and friends. Then I came along.

I had poured several flutes of champagne and was carrying them on a tray. Unfortunately, just as I approached the bride, one of the flutes toppled, and it created a domino effect. They all spilled over the bride's dress. She didn't respond very favourably, and why would she? The biggest day of her life, she's looking beautiful in her white dress, then this idiot comes along and pours about ten glasses of champagne over her. Thankfully the champagne didn't stain, but her dress was soaked. I still cringe just thinking about it.

Cool, calm and collected ... as long as I don't spill a tray of champagne on the bride.

IN THE ARMY NOW

MILITARY SERVICE IN FRANCE

How does somebody register for military service only to be thought of as a deserter? How do you sign up for a parachute regiment when you can't cope with heights, let alone the idea of leaping from a plane? And how on earth do you get a job teaching English to your fellow soldiers using the little-known David Bowie approach? I'd better explain a few things about my year of military service in France.

France suspended peacetime military conscription in 1996, but those born before 1979 had to complete their service. I had been registered as a French citizen at the French Consulate soon after I was born. It meant I had dual nationality and that in due course I would get my serving papers. My father and brother had both done their military service and had both adored it. Pascal had started his two years before me and was actually still in the army when I signed up. It was my turn. I was quite happy to do it – in any case, I didn't know any better – and I have very fond memories of that time.

I joined the French National Service in 1987, at the age of twenty, applying for the *Chasseurs Alpins* (the Alpine Hunters) –

a tough corps. This was a terrible mistake and made for an inauspicious start to my army career.

How did this all come about? At the time I was seeing a girl who was going to work in a new job in Lausanne, inside the Swiss border with France, and the practical way of being closest to there was, obviously, to join the paratroopers. All I can say is that it seemed like a good idea at the time. I went for my medical and passed it, and when they asked me in the interview where I would like to be stationed, I requested that corps. It was only afterwards that I thought to myself, *What the fuck am I doing?*

The *Chasseurs Alpins* is a very elite division of the French army. The people who successfully trained there were like the guy in the Milk Tray adverts: they parachuted out of planes with skis strapped on and then booted it down mountains. There were a couple of problems: I am absolutely terrified of heights. And I don't like skiing very much either. So, joining that regiment wasn't the best idea I've ever had. I was to be stationed in Pau, in the south-west of France, where they teach the parachutists to jump out of planes, but I managed to spend my time there without ever making the leap.

My army career didn't get off to the best of starts. There was confusion about my registration, which led to the Consulate briefly thinking I was a runaway, that I had gone AWOL (absent without leave). I had actually set the ball rolling and had moved to Bayonne in south-western France, because I was expecting to be called up and was just waiting for my papers to arrive. I gave the local *gendarmerie* (the police station) my address but they never forwarded it to the French Consulate.

Back in Kent my parents were also concerned because the army was on to them wondering where I was. Going AWOL from the army is a very serious crime. The police will come after you, and, if they catch you, you face a tribunal where a judge will decide your fate, which could even be imprisonment. In my case they were very lenient as I was coming from abroad and came forward myself. I went to the police station in Anglet, in Bayonne, and explained that I was present, willing and ready to go. So that was a bit of a tense situation and a bit nerve-wracking, although it was quickly resolved.

It wasn't a great beginning: first they think I'm a deserter and then I have to explain to them that I am scared of heights. I have to say, the military was very, very good about it. I went to the hospital to tell them I had this fear and that I had made a mistake in my application. They took it on board. I think the fact that I came forward when they had initially thought I had gone AWOL made them think, *At least this guy's being honest.*

I did think about going for it while I was there and jumping out of a plane but I don't think I would ever have been able to manage it. The worst thing is that the parachutes were those old-fashioned, military-style ones with all the strings, like tents. Some days I would go down to the canteen and I'd see one of the sergeants hobbling along, and he'd say, 'Oh, I've just broken a leg on a parachute jump.' It used to terrify me. So I felt blessed that day when I was transferred.

Once you join an army and enter a barracks, your life as you know it is gone. As soon as I walked in, I was part of the French military. I went and got my uniform and my gear. It was quite a conveyor-belt process, lining up to hand over my personal effects and to receive my kit. I put my two hands out, and my boots, my uniform, my beret and my tin hat were all piled up. I could only keep one bag of my own items, and I had to keep it in a lock-up. You could say going into the army is a bit like going into *Hell's Kitchen* really.

*Armed and dangerous ...
watch out GI Joe!*

I was living in a dormitory with seven other lads. We were taught how to dress our beds in this perfect envelope shape – a skill I've held on to for life. I had one locker, and if I lost something I had to buy it back. You can probably guess what that led to: things used to be taken all the time. What happened was that stuff would get nicked and then the guy who took it would sell it back to you. If your T-shirt or helmet were missing, you then had to go and buy them back or buy yourself new ones. And if you had no money you would have to use your own savings. (I had saved some money, about £1,000, from my time at Le Poulbot, by living in a tiny bedsit and surviving on pancakes and Black Tower.)

But that's just how it was, especially if you were new to the army. The bigger guys used to come in and taunt you, and if you were asleep they would try to nick your stuff – then the next morning you would have to buy it back. It was all quite irritating, but it taught me pretty quickly to be vigilant and to watch out for my gear.

The French language uses the *vous* form for politeness and is commonly used when speaking to people you don't know, people who are in authority or those who are older than you. The more informal *tu* form tends to be used by the younger generation, especially if you're talking to your peers. But in the army it was very formal. It was *vous* all the way, even for young guys who were my own age.

There was one female sergeant who used to do the line-up and check how clean our dorms were. We would have to stand in the corridor to attention, and whilst the officers inspected us, this sergeant would count the men by touching all their balls: *un, deux, trois.* If anyone flinched, she would go back to the beginning of the line and start again. She was followed by a male sergeant who would deliver a thump in the stomach to anyone who flinched. If you giggled, you were fucked. The motivation? They were enjoying that we were the new recruits, and we just had to put up with it.

There were some awful cases of people who just couldn't cope with army life. I will always remember one guy who was in my dormitory in the training camp in Pau. He was terribly depressed about leaving his girlfriend, civilian life and his job, and he just felt unable to manage. One day he slit his wrists, and he was found in the showers. Thankfully he survived, and he was treated in the military hospital for a time. But he wasn't discharged. That was a very traumatic time for everybody. I remember he was a big stocky guy – to look at him you would think he was perfect for army life. But mentally he wasn't prepared for it because he was

Only four months, ten days, two hours and forty seconds to freedom. ———→

missing his girlfriend and because he was in a family business and didn't want to leave his job. It was very sad. Coming from where I had into a new environment and seeing that was quite scary.

We were all very young. I was still a kid, and, while I didn't realise it at the time, in hindsight I was as naive as it's possible to be. I had some confidence after working in London with the Roux brothers, but then suddenly my life had changed and I was working for the army in France for a year. It was quite a surreal experience.

When we were allowed to go on weekend leave, we would be looking forward to it for ages, but on the day the officers would challenge us by getting us to do the impossible and we couldn't go until it was done. I remember one occasion when each of us had to clean a section of a marble tiled floor, perfectly, with a toothbrush. I was rushing to finish so I'd have time to catch my train home, wondering if I'd make it, or if I'd miss it, anxiously think-ing, *I'd better fucking hurry up here.* These were the kind of little mind games they would play. It annoyed me rather than upset me – it's just how it was.

Action man ... as long as my feet remained firmly on the ground.

I got the impression that because I was half English, the French respected the fact that I was doing my national service. It was regimented, certainly, but I didn't have a hard time. In fact, I loved my time in the army. I learned an awful lot. Maybe it was an advan-tage that I went into it young and didn't know any better. Because of the confusion that caused me to join three weeks late, I felt I had to get into the swing of army life quickly, and I hit the ground running.

In principle, military service means that you're trained to go and fight for France in the event of a war, but in practical terms it is more like the National Service in England used to be. If at all possible, they like you to go and work within your skill base. You would work in the army, contribute to the army and learn a skill there. The military in France tends to place you based on what you do. You apply, they see that you are physically fit, and they put you into a position they think would suit them and you. For instance, you could do a photography course, or you could get a truck-driving licence. I think it's a very good policy, and it is a shame that they no longer have military service.

The skills I had developed up to then were in the catering industry, of course, and after realising that I was no Jason Bourne, the army decided to make the most of that. They transferred me to another military base, in Dax, also in the south-west of France. It was the happiest day of my life. I thought, *I actually don't have to jump out of a plane.*

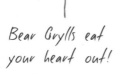

Bear Grylls eat your heart out!

When I first arrived in Dax, the army decided that the fact I was bilingual could be useful to them. They gave me a job teaching English to the helicopter pilots. The international language of aviation is English, so my job was to teach them 'Hello, my name is …' and so on. I hated that position because I have never been a natural teacher. The only way I could think of getting them interested was by playing my David Bowie tapes. So that's what I did: I played Bowie as a way of teaching them English, and they would listen on their headphones for an hour. They absolutely loved it because they had just come off their gruelling flight-training sessions and were getting to listen to some music.

We didn't last very long because I got told off and was moved to another post. I think a French chap who could speak English replaced me. My language-teaching days were very short-lived, but I like to think there is a whole generation of senior French military men out there who know all of the words to 'Starman' and 'Ziggy Stardust'. You never know, one day Bowie could prove crucial to military negotiations.

After that, I was given the task of translating a French documentary into English. It was just impossible because I am no translator, and I just got completely confused. I pretty much gave up, and they must have thought to themselves, *This guy is obviously not going to help us at all here. We will just put him back to doing what he knows best.*

When I began working as head waiter to a top-ranking French colonel, army life really looked up for me. I used to be paid what would amount to about €40 a month. The incentive was to move up and get an extra stripe, and then I would get an extra €10 a month. It was motivating – just like earning tips would become later in life, really.

I worked as a barman in the barracks for two weeks a month. There was one bar for the sergeants and lieutenants and another

Cocktail hour in the officers' mess.

officers' mess for the hierarchy. We took it in turns to work in each bar, but the officers' mess was the best one. It was comfortable and relaxing, and I could get away with murder – sometimes I'd see my colleagues marching and I would be in the mess waiting for the colonels to come down and have their breakfasts. I could get up a bit later and was allowed to grow my hair a bit longer, so, while I was still in a very disciplined post, it was slightly more relaxed than other areas.

As time went on, I ended up working solely for Colonel Labadie – the top dog and a very nice man. I was his personal head waiter, and when he went on holiday or trips away I would travel with him as a sort of butler. I even went skiing, would you believe?! On a typical day, I would organise his breakfast in the morning, his lunch and dinner, clean his boots, get his suit pressed and arrange his cars. I was like a personal valet.

We had a very professional relationship. This was the army, and he was a colonel, so there wasn't really any chit-chat – it was a case of 'Get on with it.' It was tough. Don't get me wrong, it was a lot better than jumping out of planes strapped to a parachute, but it was demanding in its own way. I would be up at 6 a.m. doing breakfast and then working late if there was any entertaining planned. I would have to prepare everything with a team of waiters.

On the face of it, this definitely was the more glamorous end of army life. Because these were very high-ranking army people, there was a certain amount of entertaining which was part and parcel of their roles. In those days there was money in the French army, and you had to be able to entertain really well. I remember one New Year's Eve when there was a grand gala. It was very formal service, a real 'white glove' night, with loads of dignitaries.

All the guests were enjoying themselves, but it wasn't a great New Year's Eve for the staff. At 5 a.m., as tradition in France has it, we served the guests French onion soup. All the staff were tired and pissed off. As a joke, some of the chefs started dropping cigarette ash into the soup and even spitting in it, which I then had to serve to the party. Everyone commented on what wonderful onion soup it was.

I would still maintain that a stint in the army can be of huge benefit for most people. I was already developing a career, but,

At the officers' New Year's Eve ball.

even if you weren't, going into the army could be really worthwhile in terms of your development. My experience, I must say, has made me a fan of national service. They don't have it any more in France but I think they should bring it back. I learned an awful lot during a very formative time in my life. I made great friendships and learned to understand the importance of camaraderie. Was it glamorous? Yes and no, because ultimately I was still in the army. But I was very happy, I liked that kind of work, and there were an awful lot of benefits to that year once I could put up with the regimen of army life and get the right perspective. I had none of those typical personal problems for a year – finding a job and a place to live, having to pay the rent and the bills. I was away from the outside world so was sheltered to some extent. Best of all, I really did get fit. I was up every morning running; I used the gym. If you embraced it and made the most of all the benefits, army life was actually quite good.

I have always been the type of guy who, when a chapter in my life is finished, just moves on to the next stage. I've always thought, *There are so many things happening in the present, how can you think about what happened in the past?* So I tend to move on, and that's the way I've always been. But I tried to keep that sense of camaraderie that I developed in the army, and, indeed, working with the Roux family before that, throughout my life. It has stood to me well in many respects, especially when I'm working with a team of people in a packed restaurant on a busy night. If you don't have that sense of involvement with the people you're working with, especially in a pressured environment, the service can quickly fall apart. And when you're working up to twelve hours a day, most days of the week, with the same team of people, it's really important to get along and to be able to address problems if they arise. So I would say that my experience in the army was great because it formed me and it allowed me to be a different person in the real world.

On the face of it, army life and restaurant life look very different, but I can say I still use skills from the military in my career to this day. It taught me discipline, that's for sure. It taught me efficiency and self-sufficiency and not to worry too much about material things. There is a work ethic in the army where everything is all structured – not unlike running a restaurant where everyone has their role to play and where organisation is key.

I quite liked that in my army days I knew exactly what time I was going to breakfast, what time I was doing sports, what time I was training. Everything was a chain, a list of events that I did day in, day out. I know that would drive some people crazy, but the structure worked for me. I got used to a certain way of life and it actually became quite enjoyable.

If I have any regrets about this time it would be that I didn't travel more and use my job to see more of the world. There was a period after I completed my year of military service when I should have made more of the possibilities. For example, there was an opportunity to stay in France and work in a really cool hotel, but my mum asked me to come back to the UK. There was a job going as a wine waiter in a restaurant in Ashford – not an area I've ever been particularly interested in, but I listened to my mum. I'm sorry that I didn't go further afield. And the girl from Lausanne? I broke up with her by telephone, but subsequently I had to go to her house and collect my things. It was not the most convivial of meetings.

Doing my best Che Guevara impression.

Dining in style at the K Club.

CULTURED CLUB

IRELAND AND THE K CLUB

People are always amused at how I ended up coming to work in Ireland. It was a completely random decision. I had just been made redundant from a restaurant called Le Talbooth in Colchester. I had to go back to living at home and had no income, a victim of a recessionary downturn. It's never a good feeling to be made redundant, and I was in a fatalistic mood, eager for a new beginning and a bit of adventure. My mind was open to choosing this in a completely random way. I was sitting on the stairs at home, leafing through *The Egon Ronay Guide*. Sticking a pin in a guidebook seemed as good an idea as any, and the pin landed on the K Club in Straffan, County Kildare, Ireland. I rang them up, and, very fortunately, they were in the market for a restaurant manager and were doing interviews in London. I quite fancied the idea of going to Ireland for a change of scene, and, as fate would have it, that was exactly what happened.

In the job interview, the only question I was asked was who was my favourite actor. I was interviewed by a man named Ray Carroll, who was the head honcho at that time and, I assume, a Robert De Niro fan. Ray had been in the trade a long time and was a very professional man with a heart of gold. He was hugely respected and very personable, very much a people's man. I have to say I did enjoy working for him.

I set off from home, with my belongings packed into the car, but instead of going to Holyhead in north Wales I went to a port in south Wales, got completely lost and missed my boat. I got the next ferry and arrived at the K Club at about 10 o'clock that night, many hours later than I'd planned.

The morning after I arrived I walked up the driveway to the hotel. It looked amazing. The K Club is an enormous country house and estate about forty minutes outside of Dublin, very much in the old-school style of grandeur, with a state-of-the-art golf course, set in over 500 acres of parkland and with its own private mile-long stretch of the river Liffey. The golf course was designed by Arnold Palmer, the American golfer widely regarded as one of the greatest players in the history of men's professional golf. Numerous prestigious competitions have been hosted there, including several European Opens and, most famously, the Ryder Cup in 2006.

When I arrived there, in 1993, at the beginning of the now-famous boom in the Irish economy, the K Club was the best hotel in Ireland. Money was no object. Indeed, there was a serious whiff of cash around that corner of Kildare. People would arrive for dinner by helicopter. We used to get a lot of old money – people in suits, businessmen, doctors, lawyers, that sort of ilk. The clientele tended to be much older, and we would get a lot of people in their fifties and sixties – a lot of nice people. I remember there was this lovely customer who used to come over regularly from England with his family to play golf and have dinner. A decent man. He owned his own company in Sheffield and could afford this indulgent treat for himself and his family once a month.

Michael Smurfit was the sole owner when I worked there and would come in fairly frequently. He used to have an apartment within the grounds. I don't really recall that much about him but I do remember he was a creature of habit with fairly uncomplicated tastes. Bizarrely, sometimes he would come round the room checking the windowsills for dust and things like that. I used to think, *What is he worrying himself about that for?* But perhaps it's that attention to detail which has made him successful.

Sometimes he would come in with fellow businesspeople from the Smurfit Group. I would have cigars ready, rolled in tinfoil to keep them fresh, next to his place setting. There was a big circular table in the restaurant that he liked to sit at. He would always take the same place, with his back to the window, facing the room. It was like the Knights of the Round Table. While his associates would have wine from the menu, one of his own favourite wines – a Château Lafite Rothschild or a Château Margaux – would be decanted especially for him. I think it gave an air of 'I am in charge', which is fair enough; he is an extremely rich man. He was a very simple eater – he liked garlic prawns, that sort of thing – and if what he wanted wasn't on the menu it would be prepared for him. He did own the hotel after all.

I was in charge of the restaurant, called Byerley Turk after a well-known racehorse. We had the best of everything: the finest silverware, linen and fittings. It was good for me at first because I was able to put my stamp on the service in the way I wanted. We did breakfast, too, and people would come in for afternoon tea, a tradition which is almost lost now, so from a service point of view it was all very top notch, and I loved that. Beautiful grounds, piano playing in the restaurant … the whole nine yards. It was such a refined environment.

But that refinement could work against you as well. The etiquette in the restaurant at that time was that gentlemen had to wear a jacket and tie. We used to keep spare jackets and ties in the cloakroom. The Rolling Stone Ronnie Wood lived nearby and used to come to the restaurant regularly. While he would abide by the dress code, he used to have a bit of good-natured fun with it. On occasion, Ronnie would show up, happily go to the cloakroom, pick out a jacket for himself that was too big and the silliest tie he could find and do it up like you would at school. He gave it the rock 'n' roll treatment, and it was quite funny. Ronnie was drinking at that time and used to have a customised dessert after dinner. It was his own unique recipe. He would order vanilla ice cream and a shot of vodka, and when we brought them to the table, he would pour the vodka on the ice cream himself. I loved that!

I will never forget the night we turned away one of the other most successful rock stars of all time because of the dress-code policy. Mick Jagger had come over to Kildare to see Ronnie, and they had booked the restaurant for a party of ten. When they turned up tieless, I had to offer them ties from the cloakroom. They would have been aware of the K Club's dress policy – I think Jagger had been in before with Charlie Watts, and that time they were wearing ties so it had been fine. But this night none of the group were wearing ties, and when I asked them to, they refused. They said they just didn't want to. They left very quietly and very politely but it was incredibly annoying that I was told not to take them in. It was pathetic when you think about it now. Very short-sighted. I mean, these were the type of guests that any restaurant would be delighted to have – a supergroup, polite, good spenders … but that was the way it was in the K Club at the time. It left a really sour note for me. What impressed me was how gracious Mick Jagger was about it. The worst part was the restaurant was quiet that night.

It has always made me cringe having to impose a dress policy in any restaurant I've worked in. To me, it's like turning a kid away from a nightclub because he or she is wearing trainers. It wasn't just about special treatment for rock stars – I've never liked imposing it on any-

Dressed to impress ... the customers had to be dressed as well as the tables.

one. Most people would succumb and wear a jacket or tie from the cloakroom, but it must have been simply mortifying for them – wearing a jacket that's maybe the wrong size, or a tie that didn't match their shirt. How uncomfortable would *you* feel, sitting down to a £55-a-head meal wearing a jacket or tie that's not your own? When you look at the way the catering business has gone in Ireland now, since the downturn in the economy, any restaurant should be delighted to have customers filling their tables, even if they are wearing shorts and flip-flops.

To be fair to the K Club, sometimes it's the other customers who can be funny about how their fellow diners are dressed. Naturally, it is more likely to be an issue in a posher establishment. People think that because they're paying a premium for their meal, it'll be like going to the opera, where you're expected to wear black tie or an evening gown. I've just never seen the sense in allowing your business to turn away people because of what they wear. And I tell that story because I think it underlines for me how staid the K Club was and why, while they have every right to have whatever policy they like, it just wasn't for me.

I lasted in the K Club for just under a year, and during that time it got a Michelin star, which caused a lot of excitement. The chef was called Michel Flamme – he was like a character straight out of the Pixar movie, *Ratatouille.* Michel was an extrovert, full-of-himself man who used to love coming into the room to talk to people. We got along OK. I worked hard to make sure there was a good camaraderie between the restaurant and the kitchen. Everyone thinks it's easy to be a front-of-house person but that couldn't be further from the truth. You are the crucial link between the customer and the kitchen, and I was always conscious of that fact.

The funniest thing about getting that Michelin star is that the restaurant served a very traditional sort of Irish cuisine. You know, coddle is a wonderful dish, but it's not particularly good-looking. What's more, it's basically a stew made of sausage, rashers, potato and onion. I used to say, 'Jesus, we got a Michelin star for doing coddle.' But, to be fair, it was a very refined coddle.

People always ask me how you twig that a food critic or a Michelin inspector is in your restaurant. Actually, it's pretty straightforward. Think smart clothing, flat shoes and lots of questions about the food. 'Can you recommend an aperitif?' 'What ingredients do you use in a Bloody Mary?' 'Do you use fresh orange juice?' 'Who supplies your lamb?' Not normal customer questions, and things that ring little alarm bells. And – how can I explain it? – Michelin inspectors just have a look about them. They generally either dine alone or with just one companion. The type of credit card they use to pay for the meal is the clincher, a dead giveaway. It's usually only valid for six months to one year – much shorter than your average credit card. That would be something that's commonly known in this business and that every restaurateur looks out for.

If you reckon there's an inspector or a food critic at a table, you always tell the kitchen, because it's much better for them to be aware than not. Suspecting there's an inspector in the restaurant usually brings on feelings of mild panic. The chefs will be eagerly peeking out through the cubbyhole to see who it is, what they've ordered and if they're enjoying it. They will dive on the plates when they come back to the kitchen to check that they are empty – always a good sign if they are. You are always very tempted to provide special treatment; however, sometimes you can make a royal mess of an inspector's meal by fussing over them too much. There has to be consistency, and it has to look natural.

The night the Michelin inspector came in, I twigged when taking her order who she might be – but I couldn't be sure. I wasn't going to be able to see the credit card until the end of the meal, after all. We were having an awful service – I mean a shit service. It is a delicate process, and it's very easy for things to go wrong. In a busy restaurant, just a couple of simple elements falling down can cause the entire house of cards to collapse. A member of staff may ring in sick, leaving everyone else under pressure. An incorrect order could be put through to the kitchen, leaving the chef having to prepare another dish and causing delays.

Running a successful service is like sitting in an air-traffic control tower – if a couple of arrivals or departures miss their time slots, it has a knock-on effect. We did about sixty people that night, which was unusual because we would normally have had about thirty to forty people at the most on a busy night. Fortunately, the inspector sat behind a column and couldn't actually see the chaos

Who knew a pillar could help you get a Michelin star?

that was developing around her, because she didn't have a clear view of the rest of the room. People were waiting ages for their food, but she obviously got pristine service because we had copped on to her.

In a business where new guides and awards are created all of the time, Michelin remains the Oscars of the restaurant industry, and, for a chef, getting a Michelin star is like winning an Academy Award is for an film actor or director. As well as the feel-good factor of your hard work being rewarded, it can be a huge benefit to a chef in terms of securing sought-after positions or career opportunities. The stars are published in *The Michelin Guide* every January and is eagerly awaited by everyone in the restaurant world. Because Michelin stars rate service as well as what is on the plate, they are very important to restaurants and hotels who can then put the coveted star on their websites and marketing material. They also generate a lot of media buzz in terms of who's the hot new kid on the culinary block or who has just lost a star.

The expectation after getting a star becomes huge, and this can be the biggest problem, especially in a hotel, where you have a shoestring staff. You want the same experience all the time, and that's what it's all about. Michelin stars are all about consistency. It is much harder for a hotel to achieve Michelin-star status because it's open seven days a week, there's breakfast involved as well, and there are different members of staff, depending on the shift.

For the K Club, it was a massive achievement. Getting into the red-and-white guide got them a place on the map. It was especially good for American tourist business, because *The Michelin Guide* is the USA's foodie bible. And if you're anything of a gourmet, you would go where the Michelin stars are, so it worked for the hotel by turning it into a bit of a destination.

A Michelin star can be good for business, but it can also have the opposite effect, especially, say, in a recession, because it can put customers off. Think about it: who wants to eat in a Michelin-starred restaurant when they're watching their budget? In those days we were charging £55 for three courses, and the wines were also very expensive. That said, the K Club attracted the kind of customers for whom money was no object.

I was doing a job I liked but I didn't really get fanatical about the ins and outs of the K Club. What I did enjoy were the service requirements and techniques for dealing with customers, the attention to detail. But eventually I started to get bored even with these things because I could do them with my eyes closed. I need to feel busy and fulfilled at work, and that wasn't happening.

I think part of the problem was that we didn't open for lunch and that the dinner service in the restaurant, though popular, wasn't very busy. It didn't have that buzz of a packed restaurant that I've always loved in other places. I had to be able to talk about politics, sport and other things that I had no interest in. It was the same with wine; I had to be able to talk about it because that was part of my job. I know about wine but have no real passion for it.

I've always been the type of person to get bored very quickly if my creative mind is not being exercised. I did get bored in the K Club because I felt as though I was just going through the motions. Working in a restaurant is fine, but sometimes I used to frustrate myself, thinking, *Am I wasting my time? Is there more to life than what I'm doing?* I could never relax once my mind started thinking along those lines. I was always on the lookout for the next thing to do.

There were some minuses to working at the K Club. I didn't get on so well with some of the managers because I felt they didn't always help me. For example, in the evenings I always used to go to reception to get a printout of how many guests were staying in the hotel, to gauge how busy the restaurant was likely to be.

One night, the receptionist mistakenly gave me the wrong number of people who were staying in the hotel. I rostered a shoe-string staff for the following morning's breakfast but what I didn't know was that there were sixty-five people staying as opposed to thirty. When I said there was a problem, I was told by one manager, 'It's not my job to help. If you have a problem it's your own because you should have put enough staff on your roster.' It was infuriating. I would always be the first person to help somebody if they were in the shit – that's just the way you have to operate in this business. Stuff like that used to upset me.

That breakfast was a nightmare, as you can imagine. One of the duty managers just stood there and watched us try to cope. People had to wait a long time for their breakfasts. The K Club was a unionised hotel in those days, so staff would only work eight hours – to the minute. That was difficult for me, as Restaurant Manager, because, say, come coffee service, staff might say, 'Right, I'm off now.' You'd be left with maybe one other member of staff to finish everything. It used to really piss me off, but that's how it was. The hotel business in Ireland was quite unionised at that time. There's a certain pool of restaurants which are still unionised, but it has changed of course. It's a good thing that things have moved on a bit from the times when people would down tools at 11 p.m. when there were still coffees to serve and customers to look after. Who suffered? The person who wasn't in the union, and the customer.

For my first few weeks in Kildare I lived in a coach house in the grounds of the estate, which I shared with another member of staff and his wife. I'd hear the headboard banging when they were getting along well. After that, I lived out in a stable house near Friel's pub in Straffan village.

I was earning about £20,000 a year. I wasn't aware of the tax system when I moved to Ireland, and I used to cry when I got my pay packet. I paid about 40 per cent in tax! Everyone else was in the same boat, but it was a horrific rate of tax to pay, especially when I was on £20,000 a year. It meant that everyone was fighting for their tips and service charges. We used to get good tips, I have to say. One night, we got £800 from a customer. That wasn't a regular occurrence. He had enjoyed a good day out golfing and came in with a party of ten people.

Tipping systems can vary hugely from restaurant to restaurant. I introduced a points system whereby tips were allocated by the number of shifts staff did combined with a hierarchy scheme. Staff were rated from a commis waiter, to a *chef de rang*, to a head waiter. One point was worth, say, £10, and if you did five shifts you got £50, so it was an incentive for everyone to work harder. Room-service guys used to keep their own tips.

A lot of customers are very anxious to know whether staff get their tips, especially if they're added on to a credit card total rather than given in cash. It's a common concern, and, unfortunately, in Ireland it's a grey area. In England it's accepted that if a tip goes on the credit card it goes to the staff, but it also means that the tip goes into the employer's bank account – the employer can do what they like with it. Some restaurants use tips as part payment towards their staff's wages, which is just wrong. If you want a waiter to get a tip, my advice would be to leave it in cash.

One of the oddest personalities I've come across is the guy – it's nearly always a guy – who gives me a tip before I even begin service. He's hosting a group of people, he wants to impress, and he hands me a twenty when he comes in and asks me to look after them. I'm wary of it. It makes me think, *Hang on, don't put pressure on us before we've even started. What if you hate it?* So I'm cautious of people who hand me a tip as they come in. It usually means they have a showy-offy agenda. They want to be looked after and appear to be a special customer of ours, to make it look like we would dance on our heads to please them.

You do have to earn your tip, and a lot of staff forget that. They think there's an automatic obligation on the customers. When I was growing up in the trade there was always an etiquette that you had to work for your tip. It's a token of the customer's appreciation. I would say, at the end of the meal, tip if you think it was worth the tip but also tip according to the service you got. It should be between 10 and 12½ per cent of the bill – that's the accepted guideline. If you have really exceptional service from a member of staff, then you could tip on the card at the table, then go up to the waiter who served you and give him or her a tip with a

Hanging at the K Club.

handshake. It's a way of letting that person know you appreciated them and they can keep that tip for themselves.

During my year working at the K Club I fell into the habit of drinking every night. Friel's pub, which was about half a mile away in Straffan, was also known as 'The Geraldine House'. We used to call it 'The Office'. I would go to Friel's every night after service then head back to my house nearby and party until 5 in the morning. I did go up to Dublin quite a few times when I had a day or two off, mostly to go partying. But during the week we would go drinking locally after service. They were quite mad times. I have to be honest, we had some great fun.

Throughout my years in the restaurant trade, I've seen a lot of guys drinking to cope with the business. The pressure-cooker environment of working in a kitchen or a restaurant – if you're not equipped for it or cut out for it – can be very stressful. Some people can cope with it; some can't. Then you factor in the long shifts and the anti-social hours. If you're going in to work those chaotic hours and then have had an argument with your girlfriend or your wife, if your kids are playing up or are sick, whatever it is, those personal problems are difficult to blank out.

Over the years, practically everywhere I've worked, I've seen how people fall into habitual drinking. A lot of guys drink to cope. Or they are all finishing work late in the evening, and the first thing they turn to is a drink. It's funny, I never fell into that trap – and a trap is what it is. Yes, I drink, but I don't drink to the extent that others do, always going down to the pub after service. I think I have been lucky in that respect because in most places I've worked, and because of the type of job that I do, I have had to close up most of the time. If I do the close it's much easier not to fall into the habit of going to the pub. I always had great discipline too. Maybe it's my personality, maybe I learned it in my army days, maybe it's because I've always been quite driven in work.

Having said that, during my time at the K Club there were many late-night sessions, but I got away with it. While I would do the odd breakfast, I would try to avoid the early breakfast roster when I was out late, and I could sleep into the afternoon. But it was affecting my work because sometimes I would show up exhausted. Even though that is fairly common in the restaurant industry because of all the crazy characters and anti-social hours, I never wanted to do it. I always hated when people turned up for work not at their best.

The drinking started to get out of hand – I mean, one night we almost burned my house down out of complete and utter messing with fire and drink. It was the culmination of a wild night out with fellow staff where we ended up at my place after drinking at the local pub. We thought it was a fabulous idea to throw whiskey on a lit AGA stove, just to see what would happen. It was a science experiment that almost went very badly wrong! That was a wake-up call – I needed to calm everything down. It was all very well enjoying myself, but at some point I had to think about my career. The K Club had been good to me. I'd learned a lot there and had enjoyed some fun times. But I was tired and I had lost interest in my work. I started to come around to the idea that I'd like to get back to London. I needed to get back into the reality of things because I was drinking too much, partying too hard.

I was only in my early twenties when I worked at the K Club as Restaurant Manager, and, looking back now, maybe I was a little young for the job. The surroundings didn't suit me. The K Club was in a rural setting and Kildare was a complete fish tank. Everyone knew everyone and what everyone else was doing. Because I didn't feel fulfilled in the day-to-day routine of managing the restaurant, I had become extremely unmotivated, which was quite out of character for me.

I have mixed feelings about my time at the K Club, but to this day I do think that the pin landing on that page in the *Egon Ronay* guide happened for a reason and was a real step towards opening my own restaurant years later. The time I spent working in Kildare was a solid grounding for me in getting to know the Irish way of life. That was something that definitely worked in my favour. Even now the fact that I worked there stands to me.

I really loved it there at first and felt it was the right move for me at the time. But, as fate would have it, London came calling. One day the phone rang, and on the other end of the line was my good friend and mentor, Jean Cottard.

Marco Pierre White. The Don.

DUCK AND COVER

MARCO AND THE HYDE PARK

I was at work – of course – when Jean rang.

'How's it going Nick? There's a job going with Marco Pierre White. Assistant Manager at this new restaurant he's opening in the Hyde Park Hotel. Do you fancy it? Give him a ring.'

Jean had been engaged to work at the new restaurant and had told Marco about me. I was already well aware of Marco's growing reputation in food circles. While he hadn't yet become the big-brand celebrity chef that he is today, he had already attracted some notoriety in the restaurant industry, both for his natural talent with food and for his temperamental attitude. His name was a rising one among foodies in London, and working with him was an asset to have on your CV if you were trying to make a name for yourself. Several chefs – Gordon Ramsay and Heston Blumenthal, for example – launched their own careers by working with Marco.

Marco's first restaurant, after completing his training, had been Harvey's, in Wandsworth, South London. It was there that he won his first Michelin star, almost immediately after opening, and it was awarded a second in 1988. Harvey's ballooned into something huge. Pretty much from day one it had diners talking. In one of the biggest culinary cities in the world, it quickly became the place to go, and people were booking weeks in advance to get in the door.

Now, Jean told me, Marco was relocating from Harvey's to the Hyde Park Hotel – and there was the possibility of a front-of-house position there for me. Stay in County Kildare or head back to the bright lights of London? There was no contest. I knew that Marco might well turn out be a nightmare to work with and that I might be shouted at constantly. However, the fact was that I needed a change, and I mentally gave my notice in at the K Club when I got that call.

I picked up the phone and rang Marco. Considering his ferocious reputation, I was quite nervous contacting him. What's more, it was a hugely important phone call for me: I wanted this job. The conversation was very brief, but I was surprised – Marco sounded like quite a luvvie and spoke in an accent not unlike Mick Jagger's. He was concise and to the point – he always is on the phone, I was to learn.

'Come and meet me,' he said.

The job interview was a disaster, and, in hindsight, I think it was a little test for Marco's amusement to find out what kind of character I had. I went to the restaurant, as arranged, and was left sitting there for two and a half hours. It was during lunchtime service. I arrived on time, was seated in the reception area and was just left there. I think Marco left me in situ to see how much self-discipline I had. I have no doubt that it was all orchestrated and that my reaction was being observed. It was my first, though certainly not my last, experience of his somewhat evil sense of humour. It was an intimidating couple of hours because I had a lot riding on getting this job and had absolutely no idea what to expect. But I kept my cool. It could have been very annoying, but the feeling I had as I waited there was, *this is the Premier Division, and I want to play*. The K Club was like Arsenal at that time – achieving a huge amount, but just a little bit boring and safe in its game style. I'm kidding of course, but there is a grain of truth in that, if you think about it. Restaurant managers are like football managers – they're brought into a team in a blaze of glory, but their shelf life is very short. You're only as good as the last meal you've served, or the last match you've played. So, although he may have already been playing mind games, I wanted to work for Marco because his was the best club in England at that time.

The upside to all this waiting was that I had plenty of time to size up the place. I could see how popular the restaurant had already become. I was also really impressed with the room and with

its atmosphere. It was a big, beautiful room decorated in creams and golds, with lots of light – elegant, but modern. A very pretty room. It was quite luscious, and my first thought when I sized it up was, *I've come home.*

After my long wait, Marco came out for literally five minutes and said, 'Hello, when can you start?' In this business, job interviews tend to be brief, but this was my shortest yet. In the restaurant trade your CV counts in terms of where you've trained and who you've worked with, but you don't often get asked about it in an interview situation, not in the way you would in other careers. It's more about what type of person you are. Marco didn't ask me questions about my CV – he's not that sort. He took me at face value and decided to try me out.

I didn't know what to expect before I met him, but Marco's certainly an imposing presence. This big man – he's six feet, five inches tall – comes out wearing his Reeboks and tracksuit bottoms, with loads of kitchen cloths around his waist. Big flopping hair, very intimidating. I knew I wanted the job, and, believe it or not, I was very happy to just have a five-minute conversation with him.

When he said, 'Can you start in a week?' I immediately said, 'Yes.'

Then it dawned on me. I thought, *How am I going to work this out? I've got nowhere to live. I don't have much money.* I knew I was going to have to get cracking, fast. But I was really pleased as well.

It's good to start getting to a position in your career where opportunities are opening up for you. I first went to Ireland thinking it was going to be the best place to work in at that time, but it didn't turn out to be necessarily good for me on a personal or professional level. I wanted to get back into the heart of things, back to the top of my game, and that's where working with Marco slotted into place for me. I would have been stupid not to take that job. Small things like moving countries and having nowhere to stay weren't going to stand in my way.

It's no exaggeration to say that at that moment in time Marco Pierre White was becoming the king of the restaurant trade. He was the man to work for. If I was looking for change, discipline and chaos in the kitchen, I was certainly about to get all three.

Marco lives up to his reputation. He is fearsome-looking, demanding and extremely temperamental. But some of his traits suited my personality down to a tee. He's very funny, with a black sense of humour that made me laugh – when I wasn't on the receiving end of it. Extremely disciplined and hard-working too, which was exactly the sort of focus I was looking for at that point in my life.

During the years that followed, I learned to live with the colourful language, to duck the flying plates and to fall in with the unpredictable personality that was Marco. We became close friends and colleagues who complemented each other. I have no regrets about returning to London and working with him. Why would I? He was one of the hottest chefs around.

People are always asking me what it was like to work for Marco Pierre White. Where do you start? I liken him to a Mafia don. If you're part of the Family, you can be very close to him. But if you want to tread your own path, as I was to discover later when I opened my own restaurant, you can very quickly find yourself out in the cold. That's his modus operandi. Initially we had a good working relationship, and there was a great deal of mutual respect. Marco commands hard work and conscientiousness, which are values I share. He tends to like the old-school way of doing things, and I think that my background with the Roux brothers helped me get the job. Marco started his training with them so we had that in common. I am a very hard worker and knew the hours involved would be demanding, but that didn't spook me. It was a journey I was ready to take.

My time at the K Club had been a quite unsettled period in my life, so going back to work in London was like finding Mecca. I was in my mid-twenties, it was 1994, and the boom times were starting for London's economy and, consequently, the restaurant industry. Up until that moment I had been one of those people who was never really happy. I couldn't settle down in one place for very long. I don't know whether that's me or if that's the way events had happened, but I always felt that I was looking for something else. That was until I started working at the Restaurant at the Hyde Park Hotel.

For the next few years, my life became work, sleep, work, sleep. I was working most days and nights in a two-Michelin-star restaurant, so normal life went out the window. Eleven shifts a week. Six days a week. I could kiss goodbye to anything else in my life. It's no contradiction to say that while I was settling down, it was only in terms of my work life as opposed to my personal one. The restaurant trade – particularly at that high level – is not good for your personal life. You don't get to socialise like a normal person because you're working when other people are socialising. It's not great when it comes to friendships or relationships with people who are not in the trade. I think that's why people in the restaurant industry often hang out with and date people in the same business.

You don't always get to eat well either, which is something that really surprises people. Most chefs want to impress customers with fantastic meals, but they don't put so much thought into feeding their staff. Marco's staff food in the Hyde Park was pretty good, but I would get really tired of it because we got bloody

chicken every bloody day. They used to have all of these chickens that they roasted off to make stocks for various sauces. Then all of the cooked, dried-out chicken would be used to feed the staff. So I had chicken nearly every day for five years: roast chicken with mash, chicken curry and so on. Saturday was the best day because we got a roast pork dish,

and I'd be sitting there thinking, *I can't believe it's not chicken.*

Customers would come in and say, 'Have you tried the food?'

'Oh yes, I have sir, it's wonderful.'

'What's the steamed sea bass with caviar like?'

'Oh, it's lovely sir, especially with the champagne sauce.'

Then I would serve it up, go on my break and eat chicken curry with rice. That's restaurants for you.

But this was the place I wanted to be and the kind of service I wanted to do. It was refined, and it was luxurious, yet it was quite a relaxed sort of service in many ways. That sounds odd given that we were working a two-Michelin-star restaurant, which became three-star during my time there.

People's expectations certainly changed when *that* happened, but our style of service never really did. It was a friendly style and not at all as formal as you might expect. As I've said, Marco has a great sense of humour, and, while there was an element of strictness, you didn't always have to follow the rules to the letter. For example, you could clear glasses with your hands and without using

The elegant Hyde Park dining room.

a tray, which is regarded as a strict no-no in Michelin-starred restaurants. There wasn't that formality that I've always regarded as a right pain in the arse.

The Hyde Park was one of the finest dining rooms in London. Expensive, luxurious, not unlike a private dining club – a bit intimidating if you weren't used to fine dining. Not the kind of place to pull a scam you'd think, right? Wrong. One day, a mother and daughter came for dinner, ordered a meal, ate it and refused to pay. They didn't complain that something was wrong or say that they weren't satisfied – they just said they had no money. They weren't embarrassed, they didn't try to do a runner. They just sat there and said they had no money. It was a really awkward one for us. What do you do?

I moved them from the table to the bar area, and I went to see Marco. I said, 'Marco, I have customers who can't pay the bill,' and Marco said, 'Well, call the police.' The receptionist, Hayley Edwards, had gone to speak to them in the bar, and an argument erupted. One of the women took hold of Hayley's blouse and ripped it. The whole restaurant fell silent as people realised something was going on. I managed to take them to Marco's office, and, when they came out, they were all the best of friends. They left quietly and happily, without paying the bill.

Over the years I got used to people complaining about things, but you'd be surprised, especially in upmarket restaurants, how often customers complain about other customers. In upmarket restaurants, posh people like others to be posh too. One night, we had a group of toffs and a group of Essex people sitting near each other. The Essex people were having the most fun, laughing and joking and being perhaps a little loud, but certainly not rude or nasty.

The toffs were going, 'Oh gosh, so obnoxious – the noise is just terrible.' One of the guys at the Essex table heard them and went, 'Are you talking about my girlfriend – is there a problem with you mate?'

He grabbed the man by the neck and said, 'If you've got a problem with me I'm going to sort you out.' There was a marble side shelf on a nice plinth where we used to keep bottles, and he whacked the guy's head against that. 'You're laughing at my girlfriend. I saw you mate. How dare you ruin my evening, you fucking toff.'

Again, the restaurant went very quiet. The only way we could sort it out was to get each group outside to talk to Marco, who handled it very well indeed. He said to the Essex guy, 'I do apologise but we don't normally allow this type of person into the restaurant.' Then he said pretty much the same thing to the other group. It was a bit Machiavellian but it was the best way to handle a manic situation because their personalities were poles apart. I believe that the Essex people were enjoying themselves more because they understood their environment. Yes, the Hyde Park was a three-Michelin-star restaurant, but the atmosphere there was always relaxed – it was a case of anything goes.

Some customers actually complained to me about what other customers were wearing. We never imposed a dress code. Some people would come in dolled up to the nines and think everyone else should be too. But then we had the likes of Bjork's manager coming in every week with a group of friends, wearing a T-shirt, shorts and flip-flops. He was eccentric, a devout vegetarian, but a really lovely man. It's not about how you look, it's about who you are and if you enjoy having a good time. Sitting next to him one night was a table for four – Swiss people, very glammed up, and they called me over: 'How can you allow someone to come in and eat at a three-Michelin-star restaurant wearing shorts and flip-flops?' I didn't indulge them. I said, 'To be honest with you, we don't have a policy of how you should look. You can turn up in whatever you want. You can wear a diving suit for all we care.' But look at who the owner was – this big, hairy-headed man who ran around in Reebok trainers and baggy tracksuit bottoms causing havoc and playing jokes on people. There was a manic atmosphere to the place that I have to say I kind of fell in love with. It broke down all those social barriers that you get in some restaurants and got back to being what I adore most – a place where you enjoy yourself.

Still, there are certain expectations of a restaurant of this calibre. There are many boxes that have to be ticked in terms of service and utilities. For example, you have to have really good quality glassware. I mean, you just can't have cheap glasses. Riedel, an Austrian brand, is regarded as the Michelin-star glassware. Yet the glasses are easy to break because they are quite fragile, and they are expensive as well. But you have to have them. That goes right across the board. The silver cutlery, the tablecloths and napkins all have to be top quality. It sometimes surprises people, but getting Michelin stars isn't just about the food. The first star tends to be about the food and is defined as 'a very good restaurant in its category'. The second star is defined as 'excellent cooking, worth a detour', and the third, which is extremely rare, is defined as 'exceptional cooking, worth a special journey'. There

are currently just eighty-one three-star restaurants in the world. The food has to be exceptional, but, believe me, in my experience it's about a lot more: the third star in particular is all about the chef or the patron.

While there are certain expectations of the quality of cutlery, napkins and decor, and while everything obviously has to be clean and sparkling, it's also about the vibe of a place – that something special you can't buy from a supplier. It's like a marriage: everything has to work together and be greater than the sum of its parts. It's down to consistency and detail, which is quite a challenge because it's a constant thing that you have to maintain. And 'maintain' really is the key word because once a restaurant starts to get certain accolades, expectations shoot up. Michelin stars do tend to attract foodie customers with lots of money to spend. Patrons become quite demanding, and, let's face it, they're paying a lot of money to eat at your establishment.

A couple of months into the job I had what I would describe as my baptism of fire with Marco. The stories of his temper in the kitchen are all true, and, no matter how long I worked with him, I just never knew when the switch was going to flip. This incident involved a picky customer, an enraged Marco and me avoiding a flying plate of food.

It was partly my own fault. As is common in high-end restaurants, we used to serve *amuses bouche* before the starter – essentially free samples of dishes from the kitchen. One evening I brought an *amuse bouche* of red mullet to a table, and one of the customers complained that he didn't like this dish and asked for something else. Perhaps naively, I brought the dish back to the kitchen and told Marco what the customer had said. Big mistake. I can still hear him roaring as he threw the food at me (and thankfully missed). 'What the *fuck*! It's a fucking freebie! Who the fuck does he think he is?' This was followed by the far-from-*amusing bouche*, directed, along with the food, at me: 'Go away, you stupid boy!'

I was shaken, of course, but also annoyed with myself for letting this incident happen. Needless to say, it was not the last time I would avoid a flying plate, and over the years I became quite adept at ducking Marco's missiles.

Jean Cottard and I used to take it in turns to take orders, and it was always a balancing act because we averaged eighty covers a night. Before service, we'd organise a list of all the food items that we had available, which was limited because everything was fresh and cooked to order. We would have a list on our pads of available numbers of dishes and would tick them off as they were ordered.

One night, Jean had taken an order: two scallops, one halibut and one turbot. One of the customers had actually ordered foie gras, but there was none left. After initially trying, 'No, you ordered scallops' – which the customer was having none of – the scallops went back into the kitchen. All hell broke loose. Rather than talk to Jean, Marco bellowed, 'Get me Nicholas!'

I thought, *Here we go, here we go.* I knew what was coming.

'Who the fuck fucked up?' – and he ripped up the docket into tiny pieces and threw them at me. They descended on my head like confetti. Marco roared, 'Now fuck off and get fucking order in that restaurant. What do I have to do? Do I have to close this restaurant to get proper managers?' Blah, blah. I didn't talk to Jean for the rest of the night.

There was another occasion where a customer had, again, ordered foie gras. But there were two different dishes: a foie-gras terrine and a pan-fried foie gras. Jean put through an order of terrine, but the customer had ordered it pan-fried. When the dish came out, the customer said, 'Sorry, I ordered pan-fried,' and Jean said, 'No, no, no, you ordered terrine. I'm sorry, I'm not changing it – it's your fault.' Don't get me wrong, Jean always remained

The master and apprentice. My mentor and friend Jean Coffard.

calm and said it with a sense of humour. The customer ate the terrine. Jean would rather have a face-off with a customer than bring something back to the kitchen and risk the wrath of Marco.

Another night, it was very busy, and we were all under pressure. The starter kitchen was downstairs in the base-ment, and Marco had to send through orders via a tannoy system. He'd call out, say, 'Two ter-rines, two crabs,' and then the food would be brought upstairs when it was ready. One night, the kitchen downstairs brought up the wrong starter. It was supposed to be crab but the terrine of langoustines was sent up instead. As it was sitting on the tray ready to go, and Marco, in usual scary mode, just said 'Crab! Go, go, go!' I served the langoustines to the customer. Eating it, the customer said, 'There isn't much crab,' and I said, 'It's inside the terrine,' and he said 'OK, thanks very much,' and that was it. I got away with it.

I'm forever championing my role as the person who bridges the relationship between diner and chef, but if a customer complained in a Marco Pierre White restaurant it generally ended in tears – for the customer. He used to love kicking people out, and the more notorious he became for it in dining circles and the media, the more he would do it. In the end, it almost became a badge of honour to have a showdown with Marco.

Some poor customers would complain, not knowing what they were letting themselves in for. I remember one guy in the Hyde Park who was having a good old moan about his *ménage* of seafood – a fish and vegetable dish with deep-fried squid on top. The guy started to get cranky, saying the squid was chewy, horrible and not worth the price tag. Complaints like this would infuriate Marco because he was obsessed with timing everything, which created consistency. So if you didn't like the way a dish was cooked, it wasn't the restaurant's fault, it was yours. This man insisted that I send back this dish, and as I approached the pass I took a deep breath.

Marco's first question, as it often was, was, 'Is he German?'

'No boss, he's not German.'

'Basically, he has two options. He stays or he leaves. He has ruined his own evening.'

That last sentence was always my cue – my green light – to start clearing the customer's table, to tell them we wouldn't be serving them any more that night, and to ask them to leave. (Of course the bill was not an issue.)

Was it a tactic to increase Marco's notoriety? I actually don't think so. His philosophy was that they had come into his house and were eating at his table, even though they were paying top dollar to do so. Every single dish that was produced in that kitchen was of a high quality. OK, we didn't always get it perfectly right, but it had nothing to do with the quality of the ingredients. Everything was Class A produce, cooked to perfection. There were four or five sous-chefs working with Marco every night – these guys were trained chefs, not young commis. Everything was timed. There was no allowance for error. Most chefs don't use timers, but Marco was completely fixated by them. That was how you cooked in his kitchen, and that was how he knew there was nothing wrong with that guy's squid.

×

Those days at the Hyde Park Hotel were glamorous times. Because it was a high-end restaurant, a three-course dinner would cost £85, and this was fourteen, fifteen years ago. Coffee and petits fours would set you back another £6 or £7. But in the heyday people were queuing up to eat there and pay those prices. People wanted the experience, and their enjoyment of that experience was usually helped by the fact that a lot of them were on expense accounts. I would estimate that during my time there 40 to 50 per cent of the tables were corporate, and it wouldn't have been unusual for people to order bottles of wine at £600 a pop. They were perhaps closing a multimillion-pound business deal, and spending that sort of money made them look good. I mean, it's just ludicrous when you think about it, but it wasn't unusual at that time. They could spend that kind of money at lunch or at dinner. That's just the way it was in those days – there was a 'club' feel to the place, and everyone wanted to go there and to be seen socialising and doing business there. Remember, the food was damned good. What you got was consistently good, and the chefs were working their asses off behind the scenes.

Even with all that cash flying around, there were still some occasions when people spent money in a way that astounded me. The most memorable was when we had a Malaysian prince booked in for dinner with his entourage. The bill came to around £2,000 for six people, but what was really amazing was that, when it came to paying, one of the group came up to me carrying a briefcase full of cash. It was like something out of a Bond movie. He came up to the desk, opened the briefcase and said, 'Can I have a look at the bill? £2,000? OK, that's fine.' As he was counting out the cash, he asked, 'Is service included?' When I said it wasn't, he handed me another £500 for service for the staff. I thanked him, and, as they were leaving, I went to open the door and held it open for the Prince and his group. One of the entourage, the Prince's butler I assume, thanked me and handed me £100. But there were two doorways, and when I went to open the second door, they thanked me and handed me another £100. I could have happily opened doors for them all night!

In many cases, the huge bills would be down to the wine. We did have one £30,000 bottle of vintage wine, which was never sold during my time there, but it wouldn't have been unusual for people to spend several hundred pounds on a bottle. Our wine list started at £40 and soared upwards in price groups of £500, £600, £2,000.

There is a strict protocol involved if a customer wants to order a very expensive bottle of wine. If it is opened and the customer decides they don't like it or that it's corked, that would be disastrous for business. So there was an insurance policy, mentioned at the bottom of the wine list, that if you didn't like the wine, or even if it was corked, you would still have to pay for it. A restaurant buys the wine in good faith from a wine merchant, and you have to indemnify yourself against any problems. It was great for the restaurant but not necessarily good for the customer, because the onus was on them, even if the wine was corked. Naturally we took serious measures to prevent that from happening and ensured that the bottles were laid and stored correctly. That was our responsibility.

People always assume when you have very high-profile guests that there is loads of security and protocol involved. Phone calls in advance, lists of demands, that sort of thing. The truth is that most of them are very nice and are not seeking attention at all. One evening, Tom Cruise arrived in with a group of people. A booking had been made, but not in his name.

We had no advance notice that one of the world's most successful movie stars would be dining with us until he showed up at the door, and with none other than Dustin Hoffman as well. They had worked together on *Rain Man* and were taking the opportunity to meet up for dinner when they were both in town. Tom's then wife, the beautiful actress Nicole Kidman, also joined the group for dinner that night. Tom was just a nice man, not looking for any special treatment – a bit shy even. And I remember he was tiny.

Word was out that the Hyde Park was the place to be, and many celebrities passed through the doors. Bear in mind that we were part of the hotel too, so many people would be staying there. We had Paul Gascoigne in one evening, wearing a pink suit and licking his knife as he ate his dinner. Gary Barlow was in another night. Jon Bon Jovi arrived in for dinner with friends on a night off when he was making a movie in London.

Another time we had to turn away Mick Jagger because we were absolutely fully booked. You'll remember that I had to turn Mick away from the K Club the year before because he refused to wear a tie. I mean, not serving a Rolling Stone rocker because he won't wear a tie just beggars belief. I fear that Mick may have thought I was out to get him because on the night his party arrived at the Hyde Park we couldn't accommodate them.

To put it into context, we only had seventeen tables in the restaurant. It's always nice to think that you can magic a table out of nowhere when somebody important turns up, but when you're running a restaurant with just seventeen tables, holding back tables 'just in case' is simply not an option.

Mick arrived, with company, looking for a table for four. He was wearing a very smart navy-blue suit and a nice overcoat. A great presence of a man and quite distinguished, even though he was very thin. We gave them the option to wait for a table in our only spare space, which was a very tiny coffee area, but they chose not to wait. It would have been nice to have been able to take them – I'm guessing it would have been fun. Needless to say, I didn't rub it in by telling him that I'd turned him away from the K Club on a previous occasion. It's awful – I mean, I love Mick Jagger, but I've found myself turning him down on the two occasions he wanted to come to the restaurant I was working in. I felt really sorry that I wasn't able to host him and hoped he didn't think I had it in for him. If he's ever in Dublin I hope he comes to Pichet – and he wouldn't have to wear a suit and tie.

The Hyde Park was a great place to be, and, to this day, I believe it was one of the best restaurants Marco Pierre White ever had. It only lasted five years, but I really did enjoy working there over that time. I have some great memories of the place. Even though it was the place to be seen, I still like to think that people came for the food. There were some wonderful star dishes on the menu. A very popular dish was a *tian* of crab and tomato, with a vinaigrette of tomato. It was a lovely dish of beef tomatoes, crabmeat and apple, which was layered and formed into a very attractive diamond shape. It was set into a tomato coulis with dots of basil puree around the plate. A wonderful dish and a big seller, because crabmeat is popular and will always sell. Another favourite was *chaud froid* of chicken oysters with celery cream, remoulade of celeriac and truffle. The oysters are two small, round pieces of dark meat on the back of the chicken, underneath the belly. Some regard this as the most tender and flavourful part of the chicken. It's a piece of meat that can divide people, but those who love it really love it. Marco would buy in these special chickens just for that part, which was quite remarkable. There were only two per bird, but each dish would have six or seven chicken oysters. If you are spending €8 to €12 per chicken, say, this becomes very costly. Most restaurants won't put it on the menu for that reason. Other restaurants would buy in chickens and not use the oysters – some chefs wouldn't even know what they were. Like the crab, the dish was not particularly complicated, but there was a certain amount of manpower involved. You need a lot of chefs to do that type of work. Marco would then use the carcass of the chicken for stock – and the staff food of course.

We also had a very nice rabbit dish: vinaigrette of rabbit *printanière* with herbs and creamed truffle. And there was a sea bass which was extremely popular. I've already mentioned the cost of the menu – £85 – but the sea bass is worth noting. It was a poached fillet with a champagne sauce and a leek garnish, but because there was a layer of caviar on top of the fish there used to be a supplement of £20. People had already paid £85 for three courses and were then asked to pay a further £20 for a slither of caviar. But they loved it. They used to lap it up, although I would think to myself, *I know it's caviar but that's not even a very big portion.*

What made it special was that Marco was in the kitchen cooking all of this himself. That's what made that place great. There are so many chefs who are rarely in the kitchen because they're lending their names to cooking utensils or trying to land a television series. But during

that time Marco was always in the kitchen. Of course, he was later to famously hand back his Michelin stars and to pursue wider-ranging ambitions as a restaurateur rather than a chef, but when people went to the Hyde Park in the belief that Marco was at the stove, that was very much the case.

Marco used to live down the road from the restaurant and would be there from about 8 a.m. until late at night, up to midnight. It's like everyone who works for himself. He was striving for a third Michelin star, and he was very, very disciplined. We were all on a journey to achieve that. When you see the boss come in and work so hard it does make you give 110 per cent of yourself as well.

Marco even did an awful lot of the physical cooking during that period. If you ordered a lobster salad, for instance, he would stop what he was doing, crack the lobsters open and cook them *à la minute*, which means the dish is prepared when you order it. That only lasted for a while, because it's impossible for one chef to sustain that level of work no matter how energetic they are. Eventually the other chefs were allowed to prep the lobster.

In those early days Marco wouldn't even allow us to cut the cheese in the dining room. We had a cheeseboard basket which we would present to the customer to make their selection. We then had to take it back to Marco who would cut the cheese himself. You'd have to wait until he was finished whatever he was doing and then be ready to let him know what the guest wanted. If you weren't, he'd get huffy and tell you to go away and come back, which could cause service problems as the customer would have to wait.

One evening, our French head waiter Mathieu took an order and presented the board to Marco, who was in an impatient mood. He called out a large order, and Marco started to cut the cheese into big chunky doorstoppers, as was his style, but, as he was cutting, Mathieu realised he'd made a mistake with the order selection.

The volcano erupted. Marco exploded and started shouting, 'Get me Nicholas, now!' Knowing what was coming, I composed myself and headed for the kitchen. Marco was in a rage, telling me to sack the waiter on the spot, to get some order out there. Bizarrely, he then proceeded to throw a huge soft cheese at the wall. He told us to leave it there, not to touch it, as it would serve as a reminder to us not to make silly mistakes in service.

Incidentally, I did not sack Mathieu, but he did leave of his own accord some time later, and the cheeseboard was eventually left for us to do in the dining room.

At that time Marco was living and breathing solely for his restaurant and his food, and he was a bit like a mad scientist. His manner was such that he demanded everything from his staff. He kept us on our toes, and it was easy to get on the wrong side of him. What made him scary was this Jekyll and Hyde element to his character. As I said, he's a very intelligent man, but he expected everyone to be on the same wavelength as him. You could get yourself into trouble very easily by simply not being in tune, which can easily happen when you're working long shifts in a busy restaurant day in, day out. People are only human: they lose their focus if they're tired or having a bad day, or are having issues at home with family – normal things.

I've grown used to working with temperamental chefs over the years, and some of them were so badly behaved that I would just shrug off their hissy fits. But Marco was a different animal, and many of the staff – myself included – were a little afraid of him. He knew that and worked the tension he created to his advantage. Personally I would say that I often worked on fear, even though I have quite a relaxed personality. It was draining, but, on the plus side, it got my adrenalin going and helped me stay motivated.

There was one other characteristic of Marco's that really impressed me. He had a serious bullshit radar. The man could spot a liar from about a hundred paces. In the restaurant business, a lot of fibs are told to cover up mistakes that are made, but if you lied to Marco there was little chance you would get away with it. Mind you, that didn't stop me from trying. I endeavoured on numerous occasions to get myself out of the shit. Sometimes I managed to get away with it, sometimes I didn't. One night I accidentally forgot to store away a very expensive cheeseboard. Roger Pizey snitched on me. I love Roger; he's a very good friend of mine and one of the funniest people I know. He was one of the sous-chefs on the *Hell's Kitchen* television series and has worked with Marco for years. But the man snitched on me, and the cheese had to be thrown out. I tried to bullshit my way out of it by saying I had given responsibility to one of the commis, but, even as I was saying it, I could tell that Marco could see through me. Not only was he right to be pissed off about the cheese, but also it didn't put me in very high regard with him because anyone would rather have an honest person working for them. Sometimes, though, in that pressured environment, when your back was against the wall, lying did seem the easier option.

Marco would also make things difficult if he felt waiters weren't being honest about calling tables away. This is common lingo with restaurant folk to describe how they time the cooking and presentation of courses. Put simply: I've served you your starter, and you've eaten it. I clear your plates, go to the kitchen and call your main courses away. Waiting staff are constantly playing a timing game with a busy kitchen, trying to work the balance between giving chefs enough time to prepare dishes and giving customers enough time between courses. And, to be frank, sometimes you would bluff the kitchen and time things to make your life easier. Marco was obsessed with timing and would never let us play it our way. He would think to himself, *OK, it's going to take Table 2 five to seven minutes to eat their starter. I'm not going to wait for the waiter to call this away. I'm just going to do it automatically.* Sometimes we would be completely caught out, and, as far as Marco was concerned, it was our fault if the customers didn't eat the food quickly enough.

Timing, lateness … Marco was absolutely obsessed with them. Sometimes, it used to really piss me off. I was often the last person in the restaurant at night but had to be in at 10 a.m. every morning. One morning I was late for work, and Marco was there, cutting the meat, and he said, 'Can you make sure you come to work on time?'

I said, 'Marco, I left here at 3 a.m. this morning.'

But he didn't care. He just didn't see it that way. There were occasions when he would be there until 4 a.m., entertaining guests, and I would be asleep at the reception desk, waiting to close. He would wake me up and say, 'Why didn't you give me the keys? I would have closed up for you.'

I'd say, 'You're having a laugh, aren't you?'

Being Machiavellian, he wouldn't have locked up. You were always better off waiting for him to finish chatting to friends and then locking up the restaurant yourself.

He did that quite a bit, and he also did it because he could. I think a lot of owners are like that. They have the power because ultimately they know that you are their employee and that you have to work there. They do it because they can. So there is that element of control. It's frustrating, and the Hyde Park is not the only place where I have experienced it.

When you're Restaurant Manager, and you're working late, you start to develop the Cinderella mindset, thinking you've got to get home by a certain time. You're thinking, *What time will I get out of here tonight? I've still got four, five shifts to do this week.* If your mind is set to finish at a certain time, and it doesn't happen that way, it can be tough mentally, especially if it happens on a regular basis. The hours are already gruelling and make it tricky to hold down a relationship or to stay in touch with friends. If you've planned to meet up with a girlfriend or to celebrate a friend's birthday, and it doesn't work out that way, it can play havoc with your mind.

Physically you can handle the tiredness, especially when you're younger. It's a case of *get through it, have some coffee.* Mentally, it's more difficult to get through, and I think that's why an awful lot of people think to themselves, *This career is crap. This is not for me.* You have to be able to absorb its punches, and, more importantly, you really, really have to love it.

I worked at the Hyde Park for five years, and for most of the time I was extremely happy there. The reason I lasted for so long was that I was in love with my job. I had a real sense of purpose. I was being well paid, and I wanted to save as much money as I could for my future. That helped me cope with the pace, although a lot of guys moved on after a year. Towards the end, the hours really started to get to me, and I started thinking about an easier life. I never felt that I wanted to get out of the trade, but the eleven shifts a week were starting to feel overwhelming. When you're continually working from 10 a.m. up until as late as 2 a.m., six nights a week, you can become quite removed from the rest of the world. I've long been used to working when other people were socialising, but the hours were getting to be too much. I couldn't see past the Groundhog Day atmosphere of being in the same premises, doing the same thing day in, day out. I was a mouse going around on a wheel. I didn't read papers. I didn't watch television, except for omnibus editions of *EastEnders* or *Coronation Street* at bizarre hours of the day. I'd play with my PlayStation to try and wind down after a shift.

Sunday used to be my only day off, and, for some reason, I fell into the pattern of

going to the furniture store Habitat every week. I lived in a very nice loft apartment, and I thought that if I filled it with nice things, material things, that this would make me feel better. Also, I was determined to do something with my day off, and, in my mind, relaxation was about going and buying things in Habitat. Maybe it's a phase that everyone goes through in their twenties.

It really was an odd way to live. I could feel myself hitting a wall, but I didn't have the will or the energy to do anything about it. With the benefit of hindsight I can see that I was completely burnt out. In my head I was going, *I can't do this anymore.* My brain felt like it was turning into a sponge.

I started suffering from that recurring condition – I call it 'grass is greener somewhere else' syndrome. I needed another life: to see something else, to do something else. And I am just one of those characters who, once I get something into my head, will not let it go.

I can remember when it hit me. I was in a relationship with the most understanding girl around that time. Tellingly, she was in the trade as well. Many girls I have dated have been in the trade (as is Denise, the woman I ended up marrying, who works in Pichet with me now). That's the case with many restaurant staff: we date people in the same business. If you are going out with someone who works in a restaurant and you have a nine-to-five job, there is no way you will be able to understand those long hours or their working weekends. I don't think our profession is alone in that regard. Doctors and nurses tend to have relationships with people they work with, and it's the same with many people in catering. They tend to stick to people in the same job because the relationship has a better chance of lasting. Of course there's a negative side to that as well, because it's harder to get away from talking about work. Anyway, one day I was shopping in the Elephant and Castle in South London with my girlfriend. I turned around to her and said, 'What am I doing?'

She said, 'What do you mean?'

I said, 'I want to change my life. I can't cope with this anymore.'

She said she was happy, but I knew I wasn't. I suddenly realised that I wanted not only to get out of the relationship but also to get out of the Hyde Park.

Funnily enough, it was around this time that I met a young chef named Conrad Gallagher, and he started courting me to come and work with him in Dublin.

Main Courses

Loin of spring lamb with peppered cous cous, simple ratatouille and red bell pepper jus (served pink)	£17.95
A supreme of guinea fowl with organic greens, parsnip risotto, roasted parsnips, pumpkin seed pesto and harissa paste	£14.95
Fillet of beef with spaghetti of vegetables, shallot puree, roasted shallots in red wine and parmesan tuille	£18.95
Pan seared monkfish with autumn cabbage, squash puree, roasted salsify, pearl onions, truffle and balsamic vinaigrette.	£16.95
Fillet of salmon with a skin of cous cous, fricassee of fava beans, spiced cabbage and creamed polenta	£12.95
Roast breast of duckling with sweet potato gnocchi, sweet potato fries, red onion marmalade and salad of tarragon	£16.95
Daube of beef with pumpkin mashed potato, autumn squash and roast spring onions in a madeira cream	£14.95
Roasted Sea Bass with confit of fennel, fennel puree, spiced lentil and sauce bouillabaisse.	£17.95

Side Orders

Creamy rosemary polenta £2.95   Boiled new potatoes £2.95
Whipped basil mashed potatoes £2.95   Green salad £3.95
Orzo in soya £3.95
Vegetarian dishes available upon request
Tasting Menu available upon request
Separate menu for desserts

Peacock Alley

CREATIVE CUISINE

47 SOUTH WILLIAM STREET, DUBLIN 2. TEL: 662 0776–677 0708. FAX: 671 8854

ILLUSTRATION COURTESY OF BRIAN KENNEDY

Conrad Gallagher's true talent came out in his menu.

COURTED BY CONRAD

PEACOCK ALLEY, PART I

Everyone always wants to know what Conrad Gallagher is like. He's one of those big personas that everyone has an opinion of – especially the people who've had dealings with him. Most of the impressions people have of Conrad are true. He is gifted with food, that's pretty indisputable. He's a terrible businessman, as numerous episodes with creditors have shown. And he is a complete charmer. Seriously, this guy could give charm seminars. I've always joked that Conrad would be a fantastic fruit-and-veg salesman on the market – he just has that way with words.

I was feeling bored and looking for a change, and perhaps Conrad picked up that vibe from me because he started asking me about moving to Dublin to work for him. He said, 'Come to Dublin, I'm looking for a restaurant manager.' I just thought he was a decent, engaging restaurateur-entrepreneur who wanted to make it big, and I was looking for a rabbit hole to fall down. We exchanged numbers.

I had spent five years with Marco Pierre White at the Hyde Park, and to this day that remains a highlight of my professional life. I loved it there, but change was definitely coming. The Hyde Park was about to close, and Marco was moving over to the Oak

101

Room in another hotel, Le Méridien Piccadilly. When he asked me to go over to the Oak Room with him I said yes and shook his hand, but I felt bad because in my head I was thinking, *Actually, I want to leave because I need to do something else.*

Even though Conrad Gallagher was already a bit of a star in Dublin, I didn't know much about him at all. At one point he came to do a *stage* in the Hyde Park. A *stage* is when a chef comes to do a period of work in another restaurant – it's sort of like a training period. Conrad came to work in the basement kitchen, and I remember finding it interesting that Marco didn't speak to him once. (There were two kitchens in the restaurant: a basement kitchen, where starters were prepared and preparation work was carried out, and the upstairs main kitchen, where the majority of the cooking took place.)

One day, we were sitting on the staircase that linked the basement kitchen to the main one, having something to eat during a break, and Conrad kept asking me about Dublin. I committed, rather stupidly I think now, to the move. I didn't do my homework about it, made no enquiries at all, I just said OK and gave my notice in.

Some people say Conrad has a physical similarity to Marco Pierre White – you know, the big man with the unruly hair – and I always find it really funny when they do. You see, I think Conrad thought he *was* Marco and would have loved that comparison. And I think he wanted me to work for him because of the Marco association.

Years later we met in London, and I took Conrad out for dinner knowing Marco was going to be there, because I knew that Conrad wanted to meet him. What Marco did that night was typical of him: he invited me to his table and left Conrad sitting on his own. It was awkward, because he was facing Marco's table but couldn't move because he hadn't been invited, and wasn't confident enough to come over and say hello. That was Marco being controlling, just the way he likes it. Eventually, he went over to Conrad's table and said, 'I suppose you want to poach my Nick again, do you?' Then he just walked off.

Conrad had been very charming coming up to the move. It was all, 'Tell me what you want. You are the greatest. You are my best friend,' and, let's face it, it's very flattering to hear that, especially when you feel you're in a bit of a rut. I wanted to be hugged, professionally speaking, and suddenly there was this big, charismatic Donegal man, with his arms outstretched, charming the socks off me.

I committed myself to working with him because I was bored in London. I lasted two weeks.

I hated it. I mean, working there was horrific for me. When I first walked in the doors, I thought, *What have I let myself in for?* It was a long, narrow room, and, frankly, I thought it was a bit grotty. I think it seated around seventy people. There was this lounge on the left-hand side, a poky area with cheap-looking sofas. In the middle of the room on the right-hand side there was a staircase going down to the basement kitchen. It reminded me of a longboat, with seating on either side: nasty-looking chairs around small rickety tables. I will always remember the tables, which were very small and cheap-looking. They had metal legs that were always wobbling, and they were set quite close together. I just thought it was an uncomfortable space. Are these things that only a *maître d'* would notice? I don't think so.

For some people, I am sure, it's all about the food, and Conrad was producing some magnificent cooking there. He had some great staff working for him in those days. But at a certain price range customers are not just paying for the food. They are paying for where they are sitting. I am not saying it has to be posh – I've worked in places where we had the poshest cutlery and zero atmosphere – but the room should be comfortable, and I didn't think this one was. It was a hard room to do anything with during the day – but, in any case, it wasn't busy during the day: it was always a night-time haunt. It looked much better in the evening when it was lit with candles and soft lighting.

Peacock Alley marked the beginning of a new period in Ireland's restaurant culture. It was the mid-1990s, and people were starting to have a few bob in their pockets after years of recession. It was a hugely popular restaurant with media and advertising types who often had expense accounts – the type of customers restaurateurs love. It was located on South William Street, where the Barclay lap-dancing club is now. It's a very fashionable area in Dublin's south city and a popular street for restaurants to this day. Everyone wanted to eat and be seen there, and it was usually booked out well in advance.

Marco Pierre White's food, although it was brilliant, tended to be quite simple in many ways. But Conrad had a much more gimmicky, American approach: lots of height and lots of flavours going on. The presentation was very stacked-up in style – not the sort of plates an accident-prone guy like myself would like to be running around with! Luckily, I only took orders. Because the kitchen was in the basement the waiters used to have to run up the stairs with these mile-high dishes. There was a lot of falling over and a hell of a lot of swearing. So what I used to do was send the stuff up the stairs and then reconstruct the dishes.

Over the course of that fortnight, Derek Bulmer, then head of *The Michelin Guide*, came in for dinner. Derek was re-inspecting the restaurant. He always works under a pseudonym and even avoids allowing his photograph to be used in interviews. Very unusually, he was booked in under his own name. When he came in, I said, 'Hello Derek, nice to see you going by your real name tonight,' which made him laugh.

There were a number of policies at Peacock Alley I didn't like. For example, the existing manager (more on that later) wanted us to clear everything with a tray, which I've always found quite stuffy. It's an approach that a customer is not going to get offended by or even notice, so what's the point? Just clear the table.

Another thing that really pissed me off was that Conrad never fed his staff. This is something I feel very strongly about. Restaurant staff work hard and long hours, and restaurateurs who value their staff should feed them. The general policy is, if you are doing an eight-hour shift you are entitled to a half-hour break with a meal. I think it is up to employers to feed their staff. Some do it, some don't. Conrad didn't. So on our lunch breaks we would have to go out and get a sandwich.

If you work in a hotel you tend to be treated much better as far as food is concerned because you're usually working very long or split shifts and you will get to eat in the staff canteen. A restaurateur, on the other hand, will often try to pawn you off by saying they are just too busy to cook staff food. They want to impress paying customers – they're not interested in feeding staff, and they don't want to cook for them.

When we set up Pichet, Stephen and I agreed that we must make staff food. They work between eight and ten hours a day, and they're entitled to be fed. Maybe the fact that I am so firm on this is down to my French heritage. In France, working in a restaurant is regarded as a career far more than in Ireland or in the UK. People are respected, and they're certainly fed. It's like Napoleon said: an army marches on its stomach.

I've always maintained that it's a bad policy not to feed people because then they start stealing from you. They will sneak over to the fridge. They will take some cheese, and the cheeseboard will be cut down to nothing. They will create false orders then take turns to sneak around the back and eat them. People start to pick chunks off the bread, eat leftovers from guests' plates or go down to the fridge and make themselves a sandwich. It's very demeaning for staff to have to do that. People get tired during an eight-hour shift without food. Their brain starts to wander, and orders get messed up.

If you do not provide a professional environment for the people who work for you, the people you rely on, there will be mutiny – it's just a matter of time. That's what happened to Conrad. There was stealing going on under his nose. He didn't have a clue what was happening because he didn't have the structures or the disciplines in place that would allow his staff, and therefore his business, to thrive.

Sometimes if it was quiet at Peacock Alley, we would find zany ways of entertaining ourselves. One day a colleague and I thought it would be really funny to stick a £1 coin to the pavement outside and watch how people would react when they saw it.

We glued the coin to the ground, hid behind the doorway and took turns at peeking through the letterbox to watch if people would try to pick it up and what their response would be when they realised it wouldn't budge.

Over and over again, people would try to pick up the coin while we surreptitiously watched them, laughing our heads off. Some would try to take it, see that it wasn't moving, look around nervously and carry on. Others were more determined and would try and kick the coin to loosen it. Fortunately everyone was more focused on the coin than the letterbox – if they had looked up they would have spotted a pair of eyes, watery from laughter, watching their efforts. Childish? Absolutely. But hilarious – at least, we thought it was!

There was another difficulty for me at Peacock Alley, which was to prove insurmountable. When I arrived to take up the position of Restaurant Manager I realised that Conrad already had a manager in place, Sharon Hollywood. Sharon and I have met many times since then (and have become good friends); she now works as General Manager at Fire Restaurant on Dawson Street in Dublin. We had different personalities and didn't really click at the time. To be fair, the position we were both in wouldn't have helped anyone get off to the best of starts. We didn't really understand why the other was there and how that affected our own roles. It was a silent stand-off. I think it was wrong of Conrad not to mention it to her, or me, and it certainly doesn't give a good impression when you begin a job to find the position has already been filled.

I arrived three days before I was officially due to start because Conrad had some big party on and said he needed me to start straight away. It was very stressful because I was obviously packing up in London at the same time and had lots of loose ends to tie up. I just didn't feel ready. But, being polite, I arrived three days early and was very pissed off to find that his manager was still in place. I thought, *What is going on here, who's in charge here?* It really rang alarm bells for me. I decided to try to make a go of it – I didn't really feel I had any other choice. There was a touch of animosity because this other person was in charge, and I thought, *I just can't be dealing with this nonsense*, but I didn't want to be causing conflict either because that wouldn't be right. However, after a fortnight, I said to Conrad, 'Look, I'm sorry mate, I'm going to have to leave. I don't feel I can make the changes I want to with the restaurant. You've already got Sharon working here. You told me the wrong thing.'

There wasn't really a confrontation, as I had made up my mind. Conrad did try to stop me from going but I just apologised and told him it wasn't for me.

Despite everything, something very special came out of that horrible fortnight: I fell in love. A young woman named Denise McBrien was working as a receptionist at Peacock Alley, and we just hit it off from day one. Even before I developed feelings for her she always kind of impressed me. I remember being struck by how clued in she was at service. She had a great feel for what a customer needed and didn't need. I remember one day the businessman Ben Dunne gave her a £100 tip for looking after him so well – a huge tip in those days. I thought, *This girl has got a smart head on her shoulders.* She sort of became my comfort blanket over that two-week period.

But it was complicated. I realised that I really liked her, but she was due to get married in a matter of days. When we got talking about her wedding, I discovered she was very unsure about taking this huge step in her life. She and her fiancé had a twelve-month-old son, Conan, and were planning to tie the knot, but Denise wasn't certain if she was in love with him. I think she wanted to do the right thing, to marry her little boy's father. She would tell you now that she was thinking to herself, *Is this really the right thing to do, and, if not, how do I get out of it?* She didn't want to upset her family, and, of course, everything was booked.

On the day I left Peacock Alley, Denise gave me a kiss on the cheek. Neither of us was sure what to do, but it was becoming apparent that there was something more there than friendship. I decided that even though I'd left the job, I'd stay in Dublin for another three weeks. Naturally, I did what any bloke in this tricky situation would do: I tried to ignore the enormity of what was happening and went on the piss for two weeks. I hit the Dublin pub scene, and, after being like a caged animal working those lengthy shifts for five years, I hit it with some aplomb.

It was an emotionally draining time because neither Denise nor I was sure what the next step would be. In terms of my career I had just walked away from a job that had seemed to offer so much, and I was feeling quite lost. I didn't know what to do, so I went into party mode. It was a good old classic case of male denial.

The night I was leaving Dublin to return to London, Denise came to see me in Break for the Border. She told me later that she had a lift to go home to Maynooth (where she lived) and stood outside trying to decide whether to go in or not. Finally she decided to come in for drinks and came back to my apartment with all the gang for a party. We sat and talked all night until we realised it was 10 a.m. There was a search party out for Denise as she was very sensible and would never not come home without getting in touch.

I was aware that there were feelings there, but I didn't know whether or not Denise would go ahead with the wedding, and I certainly didn't want to be the one who would stand in her way. I told her there was going to be no pressure from me, that she had to do what she wanted to do. I mean, who wants to be the bloke who causes someone to call off their wedding? I thought, *This is big stuff here*. And it was very, very early days – what couple knows within days of meeting whether the relationship is going to develop into something stronger? It's funny: you go somewhere to work, and something else happens that changes everything completely and informs whatever you do after that. It was as if it was meant to be. I do think that it was fate that I met somebody and that everything fell into place, despite my life being pretty chaotic.

Denise made her decision to not go ahead with the wedding, and we've been together ever since. Conan is now thirteen, and he has two brothers, Luc (aged five) and Alex (three). Denise would say that it was the right call and that I was just the trigger that encouraged her to make a very difficult decision. I went back to London after those rocky few weeks, and Denise followed me over a few weeks later.

THE OAK ROOM
MARCO PIERRE WHITE

AT SIX I WANTED TO BE A CHEF, AT SEVEN,
NAPOLEON, AND MY AMBITIONS
HAVE BEEN GROWING EVER SINCE

SALVADOR DALI

THIS MENU IS INTENDED AS AN INDICATION OF
TYPICAL DISHES AND PRICES AT THE OAKROOM.
THE MENU IS SUBJECT TO REGULAR CHANGE

PRICES INCLUDE VAT

THE OAK ROOM
MARCO PIERRE WHITE

21 Piccadilly London W1V 0BH
Telephone: 020 7437 0202   Fax: 020 7437 3574

PICCADILLY CIRCUS

MARCO AND THE OAK ROOM

I was on the move again, but this time I didn't have just myself to think about. Things had moved very quickly with Denise. We didn't really know what we were doing – we just took a chance. We'd only known each other a few weeks. We hadn't even gone on a date. But when I moved back to London, Denise decided to follow me, and to bring her little boy Conan.

This brought responsibilities. I had to try and get my job back with Marco, which was nerve-wracking because I had committed to working on his new project, the Oak Room, before changing my mind and leaving for Ireland. Not that I was afraid – the devil you know and all that. At that time, calling Marco was the safest and best option for me. Though I'd left him in the lurch, we didn't leave on bad terms, and there was still a mutual friendship and respect there. I liked the way Marco worked. He knew the way I worked. But I still knew he would have a certain amount of control over me.

With my tail between my legs, I rang Marco, grovelled and asked him for my old job back. I knew I was going to have to face the consequences for doing that because essentially I was showing him my weakness. You should never do that with Marco Pierre White because he will enjoy nothing more than manipulating it.

111

Making the phone call was hard enough on the ego, but I was actually shitting myself the day I went back to the Oak Room, and, just like the first time I met him for my job interview, Marco left me sitting there for an hour. I was very respectful and very nervous because I simply wanted my old job back and didn't know if I'd blown it. I felt that he was toying with me and that he'd known all along I'd come back. When that was what happened, when he was proven right, he loved it. There was no animosity there, but he did enjoy having the upper hand. I got my job title and similar responsibilities back, but I didn't get the same pay. Fair enough: beggars can't be choosers, I was just happy to get back into the mix. I knew in my own mind that I would have to work much harder because I was now trying to get back into the circle and to regain the respect I had before I walked away. Still, I was very happy to be employed and decided to keep my head down and get on with the work.

To be fair to Marco, he took me back straight away without making any nasty remarks. But he had little ways of letting me know that I was no longer flavour of the month. I wouldn't be invited to the post-work drink. I'd be left to close up and made to do little jobs that I didn't have to do before. Honestly? I could cope fine with that. I just got on with things and was thankful that I was back in the fold. I tried to look at it like I was starting afresh, and, in a way, that did help me to adjust and to focus mentally.

Even though it was embarrassing asking for my job back, I never considered going to anyone other than Marco. I still felt a certain loyalty towards him, and he was still by far the best restaurateur in London. It would have felt wrong, if I was going back to the UK, to work for anybody else. That's what Marco's like. Even though he was annoyed with me for leaving for Dublin, he would have been furious if I then returned and worked for someone else. It would have been like setting up a crime syndicate in the same territory as the Mafia, with Marco as the Don and London as his patch.

Denise got a job at the Oak Room too and worked as Head Receptionist there for five shifts a week – mostly during the day. We used babysitters from an agency on the occasional night that we were both on and had a local woman mind Conan during the day when Denise was at work.

There had been a very quick turnaround on Marco's new project because by the time I came back, after about six weeks away, the restaurant was up and running. The Oak Room was fabulous. It was located in Le Méridien in Piccadilly Circus. You entered through a huge and very beautiful mirrored door to find a large room with a line of striking cut-crystal chandeliers overhead, oak-panelled walls and twenty-foot-high ceilings. There was an olive-green carpet, cream velvet banquettes down both sides and radiators covered with white oak. Did I mention the Bugatti bronzes behind each chair? Or the fantastic, opulent tables, each one with a big lamp on it? Or the elegant, comfortable chairs with arm rests? There was also a lounge area that could take 100 people. It was easily one of the finest three-Michelin-star restaurants in Europe at that time.

It was perfectly symmetrical. Everything had to be in line. We used to take a ball of string and make sure every little detail was perfectly lined up, from the glassware to the cruets to the lamps. It was very, very old school. A room like that commands a different attitude, a different mentality, even a different atmosphere. If the Hyde Park was elegant but relaxed and informal, like a young uncle who's a bit rock 'n' roll, the Oak Room was a great-aunt: perfectly groomed, very mature, very serious, almost stern. It's amazing, even though the restaurant itself had the same chef, a similar menu ethos and many of the same members of staff as its predecessor, the sheer grandeur of the room alone changed the vibe completely.

The age of opulence. I loved the old-school elegance of the Oak Room.

A room like that can be a challenge to work. There's less buzz, it was a hard room to fill, and if it wasn't busy it lacked atmosphere. Unless it was full, it would lose its soul. We used to feed about seventy people a night. It may not sound like a lot of people but at that level it is. We needed more staff for such an enormous space and had more head waiters positioned around the room. A lot more to control and a lot more players. We all had to be more alert. But it was a stunning place to work as a front-of-house person, a great room to glide around in.

Jean Cottard was there, and we all brought our own personalities into the service, but nevertheless it was service at a much higher level. The waiters wore traditional white jackets. We used more trolley service as part of the performance and were allowed to be a bit more extravagant and formal in our dealings, compared to the Hyde Park, where everything was plated up in the kitchen. For example, there were a few carvings that were done at the table, including a fantastic flaming leg of lamb. The dish was dressed with thyme, which was then lit so that its powerful aroma wafted through the restaurant as it was brought to the table. We would present the dish to the customer, then it went back to the trolley on a chopping board and we sliced the leg of lamb in front of the customer.

We brought over a lot of the clientele from the Hyde Park and attracted new customers as well. Certain restaurants are designed to attract certain types of people. The Hyde Park, for example, had the feel of a gentlemen's club, whereas the Oak Room was very much a couples' restaurant. It drew an older clientele – quieter people. There was a new *table d'hôte* menu – essentially an *à la carte* menu for a set-menu price – that we never had at the Hyde Park, and that proved to be a hit with customers. There was a choice of five starters, five main courses and five desserts for a set price, which in those days was £55. There was a full *à la carte* menu as well.

We still got it wrong sometimes. One night, when Robert Reid was the Head Chef there, Jean took an order for lamb for a party of eight people, but with the wrong cooking instructions. The food had to go back, and Robert started pelting us with the lamb – throwing it at us – because we had the order wrong. Another time, I took main-course orders for Table 5 and Table 3, and the tables got mixed up. Table 5 had ordered pig's trotter but they were served rabbit, and vice versa. Remember, this was a Michelin-starred restaurant, a foodie paradise. So the funniest, most amazing thing was that nobody was any the wiser. By the time I realised the mistake, they were all happily tucking in – too late to do anything.

When I went to clear the table, one person who had

I don't feel like chicken tonight ... no fine dining for the staff.

ordered the pig's trotter but who had in fact been eating rabbit, said, 'That was the best pig's trotter I have ever tasted.' That's the wonderful thing about fussy food – people don't expect it to look like itself.

Sometimes customers are memorable for all the wrong reasons. While I was Manager at the Oak Room, Andrew Lloyd Webber used to do restaurant reviews for one of the UK newspapers, something he only did for a very short period of time. A customer had written to him to say that they had had a bad experience in the Oak Room. They had written a letter of complaint to us, but got nowhere, so they then wrote to Andrew to see whether he could help with their enquiry. Andrew wrote to Marco, and Marco, being Marco, either didn't reply at all, or sent his stock answer: 'Thank you for your comments. I read them with interest.'

Some time later Andrew came in for lunch with two other guests and asked me whether Marco had received his letter, which I knew nothing about. I had to go back to Marco and say, 'Marco, Andrew Lloyd Webber is in the restaurant. He would like to find out whether you received his letter and do you have any reply for him.'

Marco just put his hands flat on the pass, and he said, 'I'll tell you what. Here's my reply: you go back and tell Andrew Lloyd Webber he is a pathetic little man.'

I said there was no way I could do that. But Marco was only getting warmed up. He said, 'Yes, I want you to go and tell him that he is a pathetic little man.'

I had to go out there, thinking, *Is this for real?* I went over and said, 'Marco has got a reply for you, Andrew. Yes, he has called you a pathetic little man.'

Andrew's reply was 'What, what, what?!'

That was the only answer I got. He never did review the restaurant. Actually, he never came back after that.

When some people go to eat at an award-winning restaurant they decide they want to be critics too. One night, we had a table for four in, who called me over to complain that one of the bulbs in the chandeliers wasn't working. There must have been about fifty bulbs in each of the chandeliers that ran down the centre of the room.

'We can't believe a restaurant of this stature has a light bulb missing. We are refusing to eat here.'

I said 'Really? Do you know how long it takes to change a light bulb?'

There wasn't even a punchline. I said, 'It takes a twelve-foot ladder and four guys to change one of those light bulbs. We can't do that during service and interrupt the entire room.'

They said, 'Well it's just not acceptable. We are not paying top dollar to sit here and see a light bulb missing from a chandelier.'

They actually walked out. I couldn't believe it. At first I thought they were joking. I was expecting Jeremy Beadle to pop out from under the table. I've heard many complaints in my time – some justified, some not – but that has to rank as the most extraordinary I've ever experienced.

When you're operating a restaurant that's part of a hotel, there are often little power plays going on. There was a fire door in the lounge area of the Oak Room where Marco liked to hang all these opulent paintings. One of them was actually hung on the fire door. The hotel fire officer used to complain but Marco never moved it. Because we operated separately to the hotel, none of the hotel staff were allowed to come into the restaurant without prior permission. The restaurant was Marco's, and people had to knock to come in. That worked both ways. We stayed within our own domain too and weren't allowed anywhere else in the hotel.

Marco had been coaxed there after doing a deal with the Granada TV group, who owned Le Méridien. But he's not a corporate-type person, and it wasn't the ideal marriage. There was a lot of red tape and paperwork and rosters which we weren't used to. There was a very corporate weekly meeting, which of course Marco rarely attended because he wasn't interested in the facts and figures. So that relationship drained itself.

Unfortunately, Marco was starting to spread himself thinly. Over that period of about two years, he opened the Mirabelle in Curzon Street, and he was spending more time there and in his other restaurant, the Criterion, over the road. We had a very good head chef in Robert Reid, and the same team was working with him, front of house and in the kitchen, so it didn't really matter too much. But when the press got word that Marco was running from one restaurant to another, our customer base dwindled.

Early in his career, Marco was always in the kitchen. And when he opened a couple of other places, all of which were run by him, that didn't bother me. They still had his cooking, his ideas and his personality, even if he wasn't always physically at the pass. But it did bother the customers. If a customer is paying to eat in an award-winning restaurant bearing a chef's name, their perception is that the chef is in the kitchen. And when that one person – in the Oak Room's case, Marco – is no longer guaranteed to be there, it stops people coming. It really mattered to customers, and I can't blame them.

I know that in-demand chefs who run various establishments like to say things like, 'If you buy an Yves Saint Laurent suit, do you expect Yves Saint Laurent to have stitched it?' But some people feel that there is Yves Saint Laurent prêt-à-porter and then there is Yves Saint Laurent couture. And if the chef isn't actually cooking there, then what are they paying for? You do still have a team of highly trained professionals doing the same job as the main person, but you've got to weigh up whether you think it's good value or not.

I think it's gone too far. Now when you say 'Gordon Ramsay at Powerscourt', for example, it's boring, because no matter how good a restaurant it might be he is never there. You are just paying for his name and his input into the menu. Or you can flick through your Argos catalogue and see all these chefs' names on gadgets, but how do you know if they've ever even tested them? There is a difference between juggling a few different restaurants and merely putting your name to endorsements without any further input.

What happened at the Oak Room was that once Marco had left everyone just sort of lost interest because there was nobody to give out to them. People started to take short cuts – it's just human nature. There was nobody actually in charge apart from Marco, because he was such a control freak, so everyone just sort of mucked about when he wasn't there.

One day, a tabloid newspaper photographer came in and coaxed all the staff into posing for a picture with this big busty model. We shouldn't have, of course, but there was nobody there to say no. I was trying to duck out of the photo so I wouldn't be seen in it, but everyone was in the same boat. There was an air of chaos about the place. When the picture was published, all hell should have broken loose, but it didn't. Cracks were starting to appear.

Eventually, Marco fell out with the management company, and the Oak Room closed. Marco became more focused on the Mirabelle, where he was enjoying a certain amount of success and good reviews. It was around this time, in 1999, that Marco made the dramatic decision to hand back his three Michelin stars. He had been the youngest chef ever to be awarded three Michelin stars, during his time at the Hyde Park, and he had kept them when he moved to the Oak Room. It drew a huge amount of fuss and media attention at the time – a stroke of genius on Marco's part because it allowed him to continue working as a restaurateur, even though he would no longer be in the kitchen. Marco explained how he felt he had three options: to continue to be a prisoner at the stove, working six days a week to keep up what he had achieved; to live a lie and continue to charge high prices based on his name, even though he wasn't always cooking, or to hand back the stars, spend more time with his family and reinvent himself.

I had been aware that Marco was toying with the idea of giving the stars back. He had said that he didn't want to be one of those chefs who tried to sustain standards without being in the kitchen, that he could only do so by constantly being there. I do think his motivation was genuine because I had seen at close quarters for many years how hard he worked. He simply wanted to spend more time with his family. Very honourable and honest, but it came as quite a bombshell to the rest of the team. He hadn't taken the other people who worked with him into account. We had all worked our asses off to get the three stars. What I didn't like was the air of *OK, the Marco Pierre White train has stopped. You can all get off now.*

STRUTTING WITH THE PEACOCK

PEACOCK ALLEY, PART II

I started thinking about coming back to Ireland. I had never truly wanted to leave, and I think the move back to London came about because I felt there was nowhere in Dublin where I really wanted to work. Peacock Alley hadn't been an option as I'd felt the whole place was falling apart. But I'd always been happy in Dublin; actually, I'd felt at home in Ireland since the first time I walked up the driveway of the K Club many years earlier.

I had a real sense of déjà vu: I seemed to keep going back and forth between the two countries, not knowing what I was looking for. I started thinking to myself, *When am I going to settle down?* I was in my thirties, that time in life when people question where is their base, their home. I had a loft apartment by the river that I adored, and I loved the whole London way of life and its hectic ways, but Denise and I had a young child, we were hoping to have more children, and I just didn't feel settled there. I knew that Denise would have liked to move back.

One day, out of the blue, I was at reception in the Oak Room when Conrad rang. 'Nick, I am moving Peacock Alley to the Fitzwilliam Hotel. I want it to be a two-Michelin-star restaurant, and you're the man to help me achieve that. Will you come and work

121

for me again?' What is it about me and flattery? I've often wondered if I'm particularly susceptible to it or if it's human nature to be more attracted to a job, a position in life, when somebody really wants you to join them.

Denise didn't push me because that's not her style, but we talked about it and thought it might be worth a try. I had the same old dilemmas: am I moving just because the grass seems greener? Will I be able to settle in Dublin? I love to tie myself up in knots analysing things, but sometimes I just need to take the plunge.

The big pull was that it was a return to Dublin. I had fallen in love with an Irish person and had an underlying love affair with the city. It was always somewhere I thought I would like to return and even retire. Another part of the appeal was that it was a new set-up. There would be some creativity involved. I have always liked the idea of starting in a new room, a new space, from scratch. We would be bringing the good name and reputation that Peacock Alley had for its food to a better environment. So Denise, Conan and I went back to Ireland, and I went back to Conrad Gallagher. Yes, despite legging it out of Peacock Alley after a fortnight, I ended up going to work for Conrad again. What's more, there were times when I quite enjoyed it.

Coming back meant getting used to change in so many ways. It might seem that, after working the front line with Marco, returning to Dublin, which was really only emerging as a restaurant city, would mean a welcome change of pace. But it wasn't like that at all. When you've worked at the same place for a long time, everything is mapped out, and you don't have to worry about having the basics in place – you know which nights will be busier than others and how many staff you need to have on. I knew what was expected of me. Then I came back to Dublin and had to set things up from scratch again. While it was hard work, it was exciting too.

Conrad was a revolutionary character in Dublin social circles around this time, and the buzz was justified. I mean, he'd seen the opportunity to take cooking in the city to a whole new level. He had built up his persona through the media. I guess he was Ireland's first celebrity chef, and he was very successfully tapping into that whole thing when it was still quite novel. He was there at the right time in the right place, and I always thought that if he had kept cooking – kept to the kitchen, where he was absolutely gifted – that he would be a very wealthy man today. He would have been a very popular and well-known chef, instead of being known for the wrong reasons, for his poor business dealings.

The Fitzwilliam Hotel was newly built, and the restaurant was on the top floor. It was a great location, overlooking St Stephen's Green, right across from where the Luas stop is now. Designed by Terence Conran's team, it had glass, wood and lots of white and was clean and understated, all trademark elements of a Conran design. It was modern, with a runway of lights on the ceiling and banquette seats. Walking across the room was a little like walking along a catwalk at a fashion show. It was a place to see and be seen.

Proud as a peacock. Conrad in the Peacock Alley dining room

Conrad actually ran two restaurants there for a time: he brought the Peacock Alley name to the upstairs restaurant, where I worked, and then there was a more casual restaurant called Citron, where they also served breakfasts for hotel guests. This was also called Toast for a brief period.

My job was to manage Peacock Alley, which was to be Conrad's flagship. I was responsible for the normal front-of-house elements: the wine lists, the set-ups, the organisation, staffing and service requirements. That was my domain, my baby, and I really enjoyed it. We pulled it off, too. In the early months, we were flying. Dublin was booming and so were we. On average, I'd say we were doing fifty for lunch and up to 110 covers for dinner every night for the first six months. We were generating good chatter, getting great reviews, and everybody loved the room. The price for a set meal was £45 – still Irish pounds in those days – and we had a great wine list and cheeseboard, so people were prepared to come in and spend money on luxurious extras. We had quite a mixed clientele but they tended to be big spenders. It was a very grand place, and people were happy to splash out, whether they were treating themselves or maxing out the expense account.

We often got people behaving wildly. One night this well-to-do man came in with his girlfriend. There was a lot of toing and froing to the toilets, and I became suspicious that they were taking cocaine. I became even more suspicious when they asked me to get a plastic straw and cut it for them, then went back to the bathroom with that. Then they finished their dinner, packed up for the evening and left – or so I thought. There is a back staircase in the Fitzwilliam, near a lift that leads out to a rear car park, that only staff used. As I was walking down there with one of the other waiters, I heard a woman's voice moaning away. The shock I got when I saw the man lying on the floor, naked, and her, on top, with her back to me. Let's just say she was making him a very happy man. She couldn't see us, but he could, and I remember his head popping up, looking at me. I couldn't believe what I was seeing. I very briefly thought about saying something, but what can you do? Tap them on the shoulder and ask them to desist? I left them to it. They thought they were being discreet, I guess, because the hotel was quiet that night too. Extraordinary.

Conrad used to have lots of little business tricks. He used to have one set of prices outside on the street, and higher prices on the menus inside. His belief was that if you went in, sat down and noticed the difference, you weren't going to embarrass yourself by getting up and leaving, especially if you were trying to impress whoever was in your company. In any case, most people would have booked their table and would not have read the menu outside before coming in. His idea was to give the impression that it was less expensive than it was to people who walked by and had a peek at the menu. Most people didn't care as they were on expense accounts anyway, but what a chancer.

I was quite happy there. Well, content. I had a secure job in a good restaurant and was getting well paid, but, as time went on, I developed a growing unease with how other staff were being treated. Conrad was still in his old habit of not feeding staff, and one night there was a little revolution. The staff would have been aware that other restaurants fed their workers so while they knew they wouldn't be fed, they grew to resent it. They decided to take matters into their own hands. Tired of working long shifts without getting a proper meal, one busy Saturday night the staff decided

they'd had enough. Mutiny kicked in. Quite spontaneously, everyone stopped working and said, 'We are not getting back to work
until we are fed.' There were 120 people booked in that night – the
place was packed – and if the staff weren't willing to work, things
weren't going to end prettily. So I had to go and get some money
out of the till, run up to Burger King and get everyone some food so
that they would continue with evening service. Atrocious.

People often ask me if I got paid by Conrad, and I have to say
I always did. There was never a week where he didn't pay me. But
it became apparent over time that others weren't getting paid, and
they worked very long hours. He was shrewd enough to look after
the right people. It was the poor waiters and kitchen staff down the
pecking order who got messed around. In those days you had people desperate to get work in a high-end restaurant, keen to say they
had worked somewhere like Peacock Alley, and Conrad could have
changed his staff overnight. We went through a lot of people. As
the months went on, things started to snowball. Some waiting staff
wouldn't be paid one week and would have to wait until the following week to get their wages. Then a member of staff would leave,
and they wouldn't get their holiday pay, or their back week – those
important bits and pieces that they were entitled to. Someone else
would come to work with us then leave after a couple of weeks
because they weren't getting paid. Eventually, some members of
staff tried to talk to Conrad about it, and things became quite con-
frontational. There was shouting and promises and the occasional
'fuck off, then', but things didn't change.

It was ludicrous and a real shame, because Conrad was fortunate at that time to have some very good staff working for him.
He may have been a great chef, but his staff were also key to
the restaurant's success. He had the likes of Martin Clegg (a very
good front-of-house manager), Simon Keegan (an excellent sommelier who now works at the Four Seasons), myself … Denise

was working there too. A good team of experienced people, ready and willing to work.

When people don't get treated fairly, an air of distrust quickly builds. One staff member even resorted to taking some bottles of wine home with them because they knew they wouldn't get paid. Items would be voided off the computer register and the cash taken. Tips became a contentious issue. The practice was that they were pooled, but sometimes staff would take them off the table and keep them for themselves, because they knew what was coming down the line and they wanted to make sure they had some money. It was a terrible shame the way things started to turn.

Because I was always paid, and because I like Conrad Gallagher very much, it's actually very difficult for me to tell it as it was. Even recalling it now is terribly frustrating because we had a great room, a terrific location, one of the best chefs – in his prime – and everyone wanted to go there, yet this horrible rot was setting in, and it was completely unnecessary. The thing is, Conrad Gallagher has an endearing personality. I mean, if you spent any time in his company he would come across as a very nice guy. He's very likeable, and I think that's how guys like him are able to survive and to come back again and again – it's the gift of charisma. For all of his dodgy dealings, I have seen him be a good friend to people. He was extremely loyal to Denise when she was pregnant with Conan and working for him. When she took maternity leave, Conrad rang her up every Friday to see how she was. He offered to pay her when she was on maternity leave. He was really, really decent to her. To this day she remembers it.

Even when he was wrecking my head and I knew what he was saying to me was a load of guff, I always had a certain regard for the guy. He's a rogue, and everyone loves a rogue. And I love being flattered! Despite the way that Conrad's business career has unravelled in recent years, people are often still impressed and interested when I say that I worked for him. I always got on well with him, but I didn't like the way he operated with other people. I've thought about this, and I think he actually doesn't understand the difference between reality and storytelling. The guy would tell you anything to get out of the shit. He was fixated with his own image, obsessed with celebrity. He loved going to nightclubs and having all of these women fawning over him. Where he fell down was that while he projected this celebrity-chef persona, there wasn't enough substance behind it.

I suppose the best comparison I can draw is Marco. He loved, absolutely loved, being seen as this rebellious culinary genius, but the truth is that before he handed back his Michelin stars and turned to television and endorsements, he lived and breathed for the kitchen: he worked his arse off morning, noon and night. Conrad wanted that image, that lifestyle, without putting in the level of work that you need to be celebrated for the right reasons. He wanted to be a celebrity chef and was very keen on getting television deals. It's reached saturation point now, but at the time the celebrity-chef thing was still a novelty and there weren't many in Ireland who had as high a profile as Conrad. But it seemed to me like he just wanted to be celebrated and to be seen driving around in the Porsche, wearing the sharp suits.

I will never really understand why Conrad let it all go to pot, because he really was at the forefront of Irish cooking in those days. I think that while he's a terrific chef, he was just playing at being a restaurateur. Lots of people do: they think it's glamorous and easy, but the truth is it's one of the toughest jobs out there, especially if you want to enjoy any sort of longevity. I've always maintained that if Conrad passed the business end of things over to his businesspeople and stayed in the kitchen doing what he did best, he would be a massive success by now. He might even have been a millionaire, fêted in food circles here and quite possibly further afield. He was that good.

The most important person in Conrad's life in those days, who in my opinion was the brains behind that business, was Domini Kemp. I've got huge respect for Domini. She was born in the Bahamas and moved to Ireland with her family in the 1980s. She had also trained as a chef in London before getting involved with Conrad. They were engaged and she was pregnant with his child at that time and was looking after the business as well. I really liked her – she's a pretty amazing woman. She and Conrad parted ways years later, and she went on to set up the itsabagel chain with her sister, Peaches, as well as opening their restaurant in Sandymount and becoming an excellent food writer. I honestly believe that Conrad would have been in a much better place if they had continued to work together.

I could see even then how Conrad was too laissez-faire about the business side of running a restaurant. There was very little cost awareness, not enough stocktaking. Payments would be made *ad hoc* out of the till, which made budget planning impossible. The extent of some of it was quite mental. I mean, Conrad would come up and ask, 'How much have we taken tonight?'

'Eight grand, boss.'

'OK, give me the cash out of the till.'

I'd never see it again. Where did the money go? Damned if I know. All I do know is that this sort of thing certainly wasn't common practice in any restaurant I'd ever worked in, and it destroyed any possibility of balancing the books or doing any financial planning.

Say Conrad was closing up and heading for a night on the town. He would just take wads of cash out of the till and say, 'I'll take that home with me.' It wasn't his to take home. I mean, that's the money you need to run the business. It's basic accountancy. I should clarify that they were his business takings, not the hotel's

– he had a lease arrangement with the hotel to run his own shop – but it certainly wasn't a normal system of business.

Some of the bookkeeping practices were, quite frankly, bizarre. Sometimes after cashing up Conrad would tell me to put the cash in an envelope and to leave it under his office door. The next day he would come in and say, 'Where is the money?'

'What do you mean, "Where is the money?" I left it under the door.'

'No, it's not there. The money has been nicked. It'll have to come out of tips.'

Things like that used to really alarm and perturb me. And they would happen a couple of times a month. The saddest part is that Conrad had the potential to be great, but his head had been turned. He was more interested in playing up his media image and flashing his cash – which wasn't actually his cash at all – in nightclubs. Around this time he opened a brasserie, Lloyd's, on Upper Merrion Street, and more often than not he would be working down there, when he wasn't out partying. I was aware that he'd be drinking there until the early hours and then hitting the clubs. He seemed to be out of control, and he certainly wasn't at the Fitzwilliam as much as he should have been.

Such a mess, because Peacock Alley would be a very successful restaurant to this day, if only Conrad had stayed in the kitchen. Instead, staff suffered and suppliers suffered, and while Conrad may turn around and say, 'The rent was too high,' or whatever, you can't avoid the facts. A business takes time to nurture and to grow, and you are very lucky to make any profit in the first year. So if you are taking money from the company and not paying your VAT and not paying your staff you are going to smash into a brick wall.

Towards the end of my time there, we were always fielding calls from irate suppliers, people looking for their money. There were occasions where stock wouldn't be delivered except on a cash-on-delivery basis. Wine suppliers were taking their stock from the shelves so we needed to sell the wine we had left in order to buy more. We'd be typing up a 'revised' wine list the next day with whatever stock we had. Ridiculous.

I remember the night before we opened the doors to the public for the first time: it was all spanking new with a fully stocked bar, and it was wonderful. There was an air of anticipation and excitement. Great fanfare, great reviews – but look at how it all went. I lasted as long as I did partly because of Conrad's endearing personality and partly because he managed to convince me that everything was fine. Maybe I wanted to be convinced. He had the gift of the gab, and I was always paid on time, so what could I say? I did try a couple of times to talk to him about the management issues, but probably not as often as I should have. It was difficult, because he would always appear unconcerned, always on top of his game. Wearing a smart new suit, as if there was nothing going on, rearranging the deckchairs on the *Titanic*. Because I was front of house, the business side of things wasn't my domain. But you notice. It was quite sad to see everything go to pot, and eventually I had to say to him, 'I can't wait any longer, I have to leave. I have to go and do something.' It was just getting depressing, and a bit scary.

I decided after ten months that I had enough of my time with Conrad and Peacock Alley. It was just soul-destroying to see a restaurant with such enormous potential falling apart, and I felt it was time to get out. I was increasingly dismayed not only about how other staff were being treated but also because Conrad was no longer in the kitchen in any meaningful way. He would show up in his chef's whites, but he wouldn't do any cooking. He would be in his office, on the phone, at the pass doing a couple of bits and pieces, having a couple of meetings, and that was it. By the time I left, he wasn't cooking at the Fitzwilliam at all. I think he worked very hard there for the first four months and then got bored with being so busy. When the chef is not in the kitchen and word gets out, the punters don't come back. Regardless of his business dealings, or lack thereof, I have always felt that this was the biggest reason for his downfall. By the time I left, the custom had already dropped off drastically.

I don't know whether Conrad thought everything would smooth itself out, or if he believed he was untouchable, but I wasn't hanging around to find out. He did try to persuade me to stay but I hadn't a notion of it – there was too much going on that I didn't like. It felt like Peacock Alley had a massive crack down the middle and it was only a matter of time before it fell apart. It simply wasn't going to last.

Not for the first time in my life, I found myself in the mind-set of 'What the fuck am I doing?' I had to decide what was best to do, and, at that time, the best idea seemed to be to leg it back to London. I have to say, I really was missing London. I was also thinking of my career, so the obvious person to speak to was Marco.

There may have been other options in Dublin but I didn't really explore them at that time. My instinct was telling me that I had made a huge mistake professionally and the most secure and preferable option was to go back to where I was most com-fortable, working with Marco. I was feeling a bit punch-drunk from my experience at Peacock Alley and Marco was the devil I knew.

After talking, he invited me back to come and work in one of his restaurants in London, the Criterion. It wouldn't be the same position I had before; in fact I felt a bit like I would be starting all over again. I was initially relieved to know there was a job avail-able for me in London, but that was quickly replaced by a feeling of 'Here we go again – back to Marco.' He must have felt like he had me by the short and curlies.

I have to admit, returning to be part of Marco's entourage was a bit of a blow to my ego. So it was a really difficult decision. Denise and I had just bought an apartment in Dublin, but we managed to rent it out, and our family once again made the move over to London.

Shortly after I left, that whole ugly scenario with the paintings happened, which remains one of the dramas most people remember about Conrad Gallagher.

He was arrested and accused of stealing three Felim Egan paintings from the walls of the restaurant, though he was later cleared of those charges in court. They were beautiful, abstract paintings, on massive canvasses. I think there were seventeen of them in all, owned by the hotel. I reckon the most expensive ones were valued at about €4,000 or €5,000 at the time, substantial money. Conrad assumed they were his, because they were hanging on his four walls. There is no logic in that, of course, but I do think he genuinely believed they were his. The hotel would have counted the paintings and catalogued them, and Conrad would have been given a piece of paper to sign to acknowledge the fact that there were X number of paintings hanging in his restaurant. In his logic he would have been saying to himself, *I'm signing that piece of paper to say that they are my paintings – they are in my restaurant. Therefore they are my paintings.* Bizarre as that may sound, if you knew Conrad you

Clipped wings. Conrad was charged with stealing paintings from the Fitzwilliam but was later found not guilty.

133

would know that this is how he thinks. When he had a falling out with the hotel, he took some of them down and kept them. He put them in storage in his house. The General Manager of the hotel, John Kavanagh, a very nice man, went through so much stress over that whole episode. They had to go to court to get them back.

Conrad really does have the gift of the gab though. I still don't know to this day if it is complete and utter manipulation or if he believes all the bullshit at the time. Some years ago, when I was leaving Restaurant Patrick Guilbaud to go and work in the Clarence, Conrad got in touch with another job offer for me, to work at the Fitzwilliam Hotel, which was on its knees at the time. He was going, 'I'll pay you €450 a week, there'll be big tips, it'll be great. I'm going back into the kitchen and we can turn this place around.' I was almost tempted by all this stuff that was coming out of his mouth. I was happy to have the discipline in my head to hear my sensible voice going, 'No. He is full of shit.' I stuck with my number-one choice and went to work in the Clarence. I'm relieved I listened to myself!

Conrad Gallagher has a great eye for restaurants. He loves restaurants, and he was quite ahead of his time in Ireland in his international cooking style and outlook. I don't think he has used his talents to their full potential yet. He has the ability to bounce back, as he's already shown to some extent, like a cat with nine lives. I have to admire his gumption in coming back to Dublin, the city where he experienced the height of his success and the most dramatic elements of his downfall.

Marco's legendary dry wit even came through in his menus.

STRIPPED BARE

THE CRITERION AND THE BELVEDERE

I had to prove myself again with Marco when I went back to work with him after all the toing and froing. When I returned to London, he put me in the Criterion. I was happy there, but I wanted to go back to my comfort zone in the Oak Room. The Criterion was a big Byzantine, opulent room with gold ceilings, lots of marble and mosaics. Many people regard it as one of the most spectacular dining rooms in London. Because it was such an enormous room, it was also popular for special events and launches. It's been in business for over 135 years and is very much part of the history of London. The famous adjoining bar was a very popular spot for cocktails and people-watching. I was content there, for sure, but restless too. Having spent some of the happiest years of my career at the Oak Room, it felt strange to be back in London and not working there.

Still, it was good to return to the city. I was looking forward to getting back to working in one of the great food capitals, and, this time, I was keen to enjoy myself and not spend every minute at work. It was one evening during this period that I innocently went into town to collect Denise from a night out with her friends – and ended up becoming the star attraction of what turned out to be

136

a very wild hen party. It marked the beginning of my new party piece – stripping. I know this doesn't fit the image of the sophisticated *maître d'*, but in my defence I didn't have much choice.

Marco's then wife Mati's sister Annabel was having her pre-wedding girls' night out at a very cool club called the Red Cube in Leicester Square. Set over three floors with private rooms and a great top-floor restaurant, at that time it was a collaboration between Marco, the music manager Simon Fuller and the well-known and successful London-based restaurateur Jimmy Lahoud. It was very much a place to be seen at that time – on the night they were there, members of the England soccer team were partying in another private room.

Denise was invited to the party as she's a good friend of Annabel's and had asked me to collect her at about 2 a.m. when I finished my shift. When I got to the club there was a massive queue: it seemed as though the entire city wanted to get into the Red Cube that night. After trying, and failing, to get through to Denise on her phone, I went up to the bouncer to explain I was only there to collect my girlfriend, but he was having none of it.

Time for Plan B: the strip-o-gram story. The bouncers changed shifts so I went back and told the new doorman that I was hired as a strip-o-gram for the hen party, and, as I had the name under which the girls were booked, he let me in and got somebody to show me up to the room. The guy asked for Mati and introduced me as their stripper for the evening, much to the delight of the girls who all started shrieking.

There was no way I was getting out of there with all of my clothes on. I was pushed into the middle of the room by all the women, much to the surprise of Denise, who quickly decided to egg me on too. As I twirled, bumped and grinded my way in time to the music blaring from the speakers, the girls got louder and I got braver. Off went the jacket as I swung it around my head. Off came the shirt after I slowly unbuttoned it. *Nick, this is complete madness*, I thought to myself as I seductively (I hope) unfastened my belt and let my trousers slide down to my ankles. More screams as the girls all tried to grab my legs and my boxers. Fortunately, at the crucial moment, the music stopped, and I got out of there with my dignity just about intact, as everyone cheered, whistled and laughed. I made it home alive with Denise, and the strip-o-gram act has become my party piece ever since.

Marco and I had some great laughs over the years, and he frequently got me into trouble. One night, when I was working as Manager at the Criterion, we'd had an exceptionally busy lunch-through-dinner service and I hadn't had a chance to eat. At about 10 p.m., Marco came in with a group of three people. He would always sit at Table 53, the round table at the back of the restaurant, and he invited me to join them. I decided to serve them, rather than sit, as I still had a lot of work to do. On this night he was in party mode, and bums were barely on seats before he asked for four champagne flutes, four straws and a bottle of sambuca. I knew this meant he was going to do his sambuca party trick. That involved filling the flutes with sambuca, lighting the top to get a good flame, slapping the palm of his hand over the glass, then removing it and breathing in the fumes before sinking the whole glass, in one go, using the straw. No easy feat.

Marco was in his element watching his friends become increasingly incoherent as they sank one sambuca, then two, then three, then four. While I was enjoying watching them, I was fretting that it was going to be a late night for me because there would be no moving them. Marco called me over to try one but I was having none of it. I wasn't in the mood – I was feeling quite tired and just wanted to go home and eat something. The group was having a right old time, and Marco suggested that they go on to Titanic – his new place nearby – and that I join them. Realising I'd no choice in the matter I asked the head waiter to lock up.

Titanic was in its heyday, and it was jumping. Girls were dancing on tables, and the centre of the room was ten deep. We took a table for ten, and I sat between Marco and his pal, a Welsh gangster (who was subsequently shot dead), who was accompanied by his busty blonde moll. Out came the flutes, the straws and the sambuca again. Worn down by persuasion, I not only joined in, I tried to play catch-up. I got six of them into my system and waited for the room to start spinning.

One contradiction about Marco is that while he has an excellent memory and is obsessed about things like timekeeping and getting cooking times absolutely right, he has a huge tendency to repeat himself. Whenever he told a joke it was a complete head wreck because I would have heard it a million times before, but Marco would be telling it like it was his first time, so I would be there, feigning surprise and getting ready to laugh at the punchline – again. He could tell a joke really well in fact. But over and over I'd find myself with him in different company, listening to the same joke. It wasn't like a normal conversation you would have with a friend, where you'd politely interject and say, 'Remember you told me that joke on a night out' or whatever. Marco was the landowner, the Don, and he would keep that little bit of distance between you. The result? You laugh at the joke. He was telling all of his favourites that night.

In the haze that followed the sambucas, I vaguely remember the blonde hitting her man with a glass which shattered all over his head, sending blood spurting everywhere. That sobered everyone up for a time. Marco brought him to the toilets to help him, but I wasn't going anywhere because I was unable to pronounce my words let alone move. I remember Robert Reid – the Head Chef from the Oak Room – arriving and wanting to know what on earth was happening. It was around then that I realised it was 3 a.m. and decided to leg it for the night bus home.

The fresh air hit me like a champion boxer, and when I got on the bus it was packed with people coming from nightclubs – none of them as drunk as me. To my utter shame, I got sick on top of a poor young girl, and, as she screamed, the bus shud-dered to a halt, and I was thrown off in disgust. I had no idea where I was and tried to walk, with the help of the wall, in the direction I thought was home. A cab driver picked me up and somehow got me home at 5 a.m., where, on autopilot, I managed to open the security gate, crawl up two flights of stairs and stagger into my apartment. As I rushed to the toilet to be sick again, I saw Conan was in the middle of the lounge floor casually eating from a packet of Rice Krispies. Denise woke up due to all the noise I was making and was screaming at me and threatening to pack her bags.

I eventually fell into bed. Fortunately I wasn't working the next day. Marco rang at noon, fresh as a daisy, sounding like he'd spent the previous evening at a Buddhist retreat. He thought the whole night had been hilarious. My glasses were coated in sambuca, and my suit had actually hardened from the amount of dried-in sugar and alcohol that had been poured all over it. Thankfully Denise didn't pack her bags, and I have not touched a drop of sambuca since. I never will.

Lots of times you get customer complaints that are absolutely justified, and you would always try to rectify them on the night. Sometimes, though, you get complaints that border on the completely barmy. We once got a letter from a woman to the Criterion actually complaining that the lighting in the bathrooms made her look ugly. The lighting was quite old-fashioned, with bulbs around the mirrors like you'd see in a 1940s movie star's dressing room. She wrote in her letter that because the lights were so bright she realised that she was uglier than her friends, and it had ruined her whole evening. She wanted to know what we were going to do about it. We just thought it was hilarious. How could we reply to that? 'We will endeavour to make sure the lights give you a beautiful glow'?

After a year at the Criterion I was transferred to another restaurant Marco was running, the Belvedere. The Belvedere was a nice enough place, which Marco had taken on and renovated. It was in the middle of Holland Park, and it was really awkward to get to, which was not only a pain for me personally but also made it very difficult to get and keep good staff. Staff were always coming and going, and I was always having to provide cover at the last minute. It was very, very stressful, and I only lasted about six months there.

The Belvedere was a beast of a restaurant, which had been reconfigured to Marco's taste so that he could stamp his personality on it as opposed to just reopening and sticking his name over the door. He must have spent a fortune on it. Italian marble was imported and fitted to the stairs. It was very plush and one of the more flamboyant rooms I've worked, created by the very well-regarded restaurant designer, David Collins.

David Collins is best known for creating the look of some of London's hottest restaurants. His most high-profile clients have included celebrity hang-outs such as Nobu, Claridge's Bar, the

Connaught Bar and Restaurant Gordon Ramsay. His style is luxurious and modern, with clean lines. He was actually born in Ireland, but most of his work is in the UK, where he is in huge demand in the hospitality industry. He was also involved in the redesign of Langton's Hotel in Kilkenny.

Jean Cottard and I were transferred to the Belvedere to provide the service in this outpost of Marco's growing empire, and it was hard work. For long periods of time, I used to arrive at 10 a.m. and would still be there at 2 o'clock in the morning. Jean was approaching retirement at this stage so we employed another head waiter to help, but it didn't work out. There was one period where I worked sixteen days in a row and thought I was starting to lose the plot.

The Belvedere didn't suit Jean at all. We had a computer booking system, and poor Jean, being old school, couldn't cope with it. He loved handwritten dockets and a handwritten bill. I felt sorry for Jean, and even though I tried to train him he just couldn't get his head around the system. It used to upset him, so I just let it go because I love the man. Unfortunately it added to my workload because I would have to do the bills and close up every night. More pressure. It got inside my head after a while.

One lunchtime, while Marco was in the restaurant, the alarm – which always had a mind of its own and would go off whenever it pleased – started to shriek again. I couldn't turn the thing off so I found myself tearing it off the wall in my little office. That seemed like a great idea for the following days – no more fitful alarm incidents. Unfortunately, the restaurant was broken into about a week later. A cigarette machine was torn off the wall, and whoever decided to pay us a visit that night left the taps on and flooded the restaurant. More bad karma. I felt awful about it because I hadn't done what I should have done, which was get the alarm repaired. After all, I was the General Manager, and that was my job. It was a pretty bad time.

The Belvedere became quite the party restaurant and was very popular for large special-occasion gatherings and even weddings, all of which involve a huge amount of work because you have to clear the room each time to prepare for the next bash. There was a ground-floor restaurant and a mezzanine, and each level could sit about sixty people. Sunday was the worst day to work because it was so busy, and you would still be tired after a hectic service on Saturday night. We would regularly do 200 covers because all of the families in the surrounding area used to come in for Sunday lunch throughout the afternoon. It was exceptional value, £15 for three courses. But it was a nightmare, an absolute nightmare. We got lots of people just showing up without a reservation, then complaining if we couldn't take them because we were already stuffed.

Because the Belvedere was a stone's throw away from Marco's house, Marco would be there constantly, and Mati, his feisty Spanish wife, used to come in sporadically and work in reception, which only added to the stress. She would come in maybe three days a week to work on the desk, have her little criticisms and go back to Marco with her take on what she had seen. On one occasion I arrived half an hour late – rare for me – and she made a meal of it, spending the day complaining about dust on the stairs and whatever else she could find.

Michael Winner, the film-maker and restaurant columnist, used to eat from the Belvedere every day. We used to bring his lunch to his house at 1 o'clock. I rarely served him but had to deal with him a few times. He was … what is the word? … obnoxious. If you were five minutes late bringing up his lunch, he would refuse to take it. I remember once when he dined at the Hyde Park he kept dropping his napkin so he would get more attentive service than anybody else. He must have dropped it ten times, and we had to change it each time.

On another occasion, in the Belvedere, I needed a relay on Michael Winner's table, because we were overbooked that night. A relay is when you need a table back to resell it. I very kindly asked him if he would like to move to the lounge area, but before he could go in somebody else had sat down there. There followed a huge scene where Winner huffed and puffed and got very cross. Fortunately Michael Caine saved the day when he called Winner over to join him at his table. Michael Caine is a very nice man. Michael Winner, in my opinion, is a nasty rude little man. Not very nice at all, especially not to waiters or managers. He would have an issue with a good service because the orange juice wasn't sourced from wherever he thought was the right orange farm. He was actually all right with me in the Belvedere, but it was still a pain in the arse whenever he came in. You'd be stressed and busy enough without having to deal with the quirks and demands of Michael Winner. You couldn't relax into service when he was there.

Another person who used to come to the Belvedere was the then-young music executive Simon Cowell. He dropped by one day to have lunch with Marco. While he wasn't the superstar he is nowadays, he was still a big noise. Even then he used to wear the high-waisted trousers, and he had the same haircut as today. Marco called me over and said, 'This is Simon, would you mind parking his car?'

I didn't ask how to drive it or open it because I just thought it would be a normal car to drive. It was a Maserati Quattroporte, a big kahuna of a sports car, worth nearly £100,000, so you kind of needed to know what you were doing. I'm not really a car man and didn't know the ins and outs of the model. I was standing outside the car for at least ten minutes, too embarrassed to go back in and ask how I was meant to open it. The key was like a credit card, and you open the car (I now know), by brushing along the car with the

keycard and activat-
ing a sensor. I even-
tually figured that
out and managed
to get into the car,
only to wonder
how on earth I was supposed
to start the engine. I thought the only thing to do
was to take off the handbrake. Luckily we were on a bit of a slope,
so I glided it along, and, as soon as I was out of sight of Simon and
Marco, I jumped out and pushed the car into a parking space.

Simon and Marco share the same macabre sense of humour,
and when I went back into the restaurant after parking the car as
only I could, Marco encouraged me to touch this metal wall light,
which promptly gave me an electric shock. They thought it was
hilarious that I was so gullible and tried to get me to do it again,
which wasn't going to happen. Fool me once, shame on you. Fool
me twice, shame on me and all that. In some ways, that incident
sums up Marco's sense of humour. He has that schoolboy sense of
comic mischief that delights in trying to make other people look
stupid. For all I know, Marco knew that I didn't know how to drive
the car and they were laughing as they watched me through the
window. It wouldn't surprise me.

Years later I had the opportunity to park Bono's Maserati. I
knew by that stage how to start the car – you actually put your left
foot onto the brake, *Knight Rider* style, and swipe the card against
a light, and that ignites the engine. I drove it round St Stephen's
Green while listening to U2's new album *How to Dismantle an
Atomic Bomb*, which was on the CD player. It wasn't even out in
the shops yet. That was pretty cool.

Marco loved to have people at his beck and call. He especially
liked having people drive him around, something I tried to avoid

for years. But one August while I was working at the Hyde Park it was particularly quiet, and I found myself becoming Marco's driver, ready to jump whenever he took the whim to go fishing or hunting. I knew he would wreck my head, and that's exactly what he did.

I never felt comfortable behind the wheel of Marco's Land Rover. One night I was driving it very late, and I felt myself falling asleep, which really alarmed me. It was the early mornings and late nights that were a problem because Marco never seems to sleep and he expects you to be able to do the same, even though I'm an eight-hours-a-night guy. It was not uncommon to get up early in the morning, drive somewhere for two hours to go fishing, get out of the car, set everything up, only for him to say, 'Actually I don't want to go fishing today. Let's go back to London.' I'd pack everything up, get back to the city and the office, and he'd say, 'Actually, yeah, let's go fishing.' You could be restless, have a girl-friend at home waiting to go out, other things to do, but your time was Marco's. Marco could never understand that because he was his own boss and never had to answer to anyone else. Business was good. He did what he wanted, and he just didn't care about anything else.

One day, after being summoned on one of his whims to go on a fishing trip, we were involved in a car accident. It was 5 a.m., and I was at the wheel. We were driving from London towards the south coast when our car collided with a van driven by a woman. Thankfully none of us were seriously hurt, but it gave me a nasty fright. I had never wanted to be Marco's driver, and here I was behind the wheel at the scene of an accident. Marco being Marco thought the whole thing was a great adventure. And nothing was keeping him from his 'fishies'. He insisted that we were all fine and should carry on our fishing trip, though I was certainly not in the mood at that stage. We continued, and a few miles down the road we were stopped by police who were very unimpressed that we had left the scene of an accident. There were at least five police cars, and they initially believed that Marco had been driving – which was not the case – and referred to him as 'mop head'. That didn't faze Marco in the slightest, because he had found something much more interesting than what the policeman was saying to him. He had noticed a man standing at his bedroom window, watching the proceedings with a pair of binoculars. The man was completely naked (apart from the binoculars), standing there in all his unclothed glory. He was having fun watching us, but he didn't realise that we could also see him. Marco thought it a good idea to tell the by-now-very-irritated policeman about the naked guy. We all turned to look at the naked man, who quickly stepped away from his window.

Even after this Marco *still* insisted on going fishing. I was shitting myself about what had just happened. We stayed at our destination for about an hour while Marco teased me that I could actually go to prison for leaving the scene of an accident. Very helpful. Before we went back to the restaurant, I pleaded with him not to tell the other staff. Of course, the minute he stepped into the restaurant, he bellowed, 'Guess what happened to Nick!'

As it turned out, I did end up in court and got ten points on my licence for five years and a £2,000 fine.

Marco wasn't cooking in the Belvedere, but we did have a great chef in Matt Brown, one of Marco's longest-serving members of staff and a talent in the kitchen in his own right. He went on to work as part of the *Hell's Kitchen* team. A nice man, who doesn't suffer fools. Matt had an incident with Marco at the Hyde Park, when he complained about not getting the correct wages and walked out. He took two bottles of water and threw them into the windows of the restaurant, smashing the windows just before service. Marco sorted things out with Matt, and he is still working with him. Marco likes to have this element of control over people but if they stand up to him, he does respect that.

Marco's policy of turfing out badly behaved customers, which had become such a talking point in the days of the Hyde Park, continued in the Belvedere. I was always at peace with that policy, much as it may infuriate some restaurant-goers to hear. I know some people will be outraged at the idea that the customer is not always right but that is my firm view. The problem is that often people assume that they own the restaurant when they come out for dinner. Some people even take it to the extreme and think they can abuse the staff. But just because they are spending money in a place for, say, an hour or two, doesn't allow them to behave in a rude way.

After six months of those insane hours at the Belvedere, of continually trying to sort out the understaffing issue, and of liaising with the builders who seemed to be constantly working in the place as though it was La Sagrada Família, that cathedral in Barcelona they've been working on for 130 years, I went into meltdown. Mati was niggling at me, I was tired of the building work and the long hours, and I felt that I couldn't stick it anymore. I never had the same affection for the place as I did for, say, Le Poulbot or the Hyde Park, and it makes it much harder to cope with the stress and fatigue of the job if you're not enamoured with your surroundings. Marco understood my decision, and we remained in contact, but it was time for me to get out of there.

The sense of achievement I found in working for Marco Pierre White is immense because I got to be part of his great success story. I always reminisce about the Hyde Park in particular, because it's one of those phases in my life that I will always miss. It was a different era in restaurants. The place was held in such high regard and was a temple to food, but without any of the stuffiness that goes with most restaurants of that calibre. It was very rock 'n' roll, impossible to recreate.

That was the end of the road for me and Marco. I couldn't stay in London because I couldn't work for anyone else there. If, for example, I went to a Gordon Ramsay restaurant, that would have been regarded as switching sides, and the Don would have lost the plot. Dublin was beckoning once more.

A little bit of France in Georgian Dublin.

THE FRENCH CONNECTION

RESTAURANT PATRICK GUILBAUD

Denise and I had already started to build our lives together, and now we were trying to bring our relationship to the next stage, thinking about where to settle down. We decided to move back to Dublin. This time the move felt much more organic and natural. The only thing I would really miss was our apartment in Bermondsey, in South-East London. It was on the river and was part of an old eighteenth-century theatre. The floors sloped down the lounge, and our television set, which was on wheels, used to roll around the place as a result. But it was a lovely old apartment – high ceilings, beams, brick walls and a balcony overlooking the river, where we could watch the ships and river taxis pass. It was near a very well-known London pub, the Mayflower, and was a little oasis in South-East London that still had a village feel to it. It was just beautiful. Unfortunately Dublin doesn't have many of these types of buildings, and those it did have either been demolished, which is a great shame, or cost €3 million.

I had been offered a job as Floor Manager at Restaurant Patrick Guilbaud on Merrion Street. The place has a fantastic reputation in Irish foodie circles and has held two Michelin stars since 1996. They've been going for almost thirty years now so what they do works very well for them. When you see the restaurant name you might assume Patrick Guilbaud is the Head Chef, but his role was more restaurateur during my time there. I didn't get to know him very well but he's a flamboyant character who's often credited with bringing fine dining to Dublin, and I think that's certainly justified. His consistency is very impressive – I mean, to get two stars and to keep them for as long as he has is just amazing.

I had an interview with Stephane Robin, a Frenchman who is very much part of the Guilbaud set-up and has been there since the early days. Then I met with Patrick Guilbaud himself and Fred Cordonnier, the Head Chef. I'd worked with Fred briefly, years earlier in the K Club, so we had a connection. He is the nicest man, and our paths have crossed many times over the years. We would also work together in the Clarence for a time, as well as at the Village at Lyons. I've got a real affection for him – he's one of those great characters in Irish restaurant circles. A good man, and a great cook, who works hard – he's very passionate about his work. Guillaume Lebrun was Executive Head Chef and partner, another serious talent and a very nice Frenchman to boot. I have huge respect for him and we got along very well as he respected passionate people. They had a great sommelier there called Charles Derain, who now runs his own wine company, Nomad, which we use in Pichet. I like Charles. He has a quirky personality and is a touch defiant of the Establishment, but because he had such great knowledge and passion and such a love affair with wines he gets away with it. The restaurant had all the right people and was a great place to work – and work I did.

It was very intense. They were looking for someone who could do ten shifts a week, and, still feeling exhausted after my time at the Belvedere, it was tough going. When we came back to Ireland I was feeling physically tireder than I'd ever done in my life. But I needed the job. Unfortunately, that meant it didn't matter how burnt-out I was feeling: I had to keep working my butt off. Split shifts were the worst. I'd arrive in at ten in the morning for lunch service, finish up at around four, have an hour and a half break, then I'd be back on until, perhaps, two in the morning. There was no time for any other form of release – it was just front of house, sleep, front of house.

When you work in the restaurant world you learn to be able to grab a catnap whenever you can. I'm a great believer in fifteen-minute snoozes – they make me feel much more refreshed. So that's what I used to do, especially in the wintertime when it was dusk by the time I took my break and when there was nothing else to do except go for a cup of coffee for an hour. There was a pillar in the restaurant against which I used to prop a chair during the breaks between lunch and dinner service and just fall asleep.

There was a taxi famine in Dublin in those days – difficult as that may be to believe, post-deregulation – and I can remember standing at St Stephen's Green in the early hours, absolutely knackered, trying to get a cab home to Neilstown, where we were living with Denise's father, Gerry. Home to sleep and then back the next morning on a bus into town.

The hierarchy was that Stephane was Head of the Restaurant, as he had been there for so long, and I was Floor Manager. That involved making sure the roster was done, keeping everything clean and polished and silverware gleaming, making sure staff arrived on time and doing staff training. Guilbaud's employed almost exclusively French staff – at least that was the case in my time – young French men and women who would come over for the piece of paper to say that they had worked in a two-Michelin-star restaurant. Actually, there were so many French staff that we used to call the place 'the French village'. Some of them would not have spoken great English. In fact, they all spoke French to each other, which made it hard for the ones who wanted to learn

English, and some of them lived together in staff housing as well. I would speak French to them because that was the normal thing to do. If you are coming to Ireland to learn English, don't work in a French restaurant!

By the time I worked there Guilbaud's had moved from its original Baggot Street premises to the five-star Merrion Hotel. It was a very wise attachment because the Merrion is a very beautiful hotel – the best in Ireland in my opinion. Understated, it has an elegance about it and an amazing array of artwork. Crucially, Guilbaud's has its own entrance and is set in a lovely Georgian townhouse. The reception area is at the front, and then you walk into the opulent lounge area. When I first worked there, there was a big photograph of Patrick on the wall, with a spoon and an egg. (I found this picture bizarre, even though years later I would have a photo of myself balancing teacups on my head hanging on the wall at Pichet!) Then you go down the steps to this massive square room with fantastically impressive high ceilings. The ceilings are almost too high, and, while the acoustics are great, you can lose a bit of atmosphere and intimacy. The actual layout of the restaurant is very traditional: tables down one side, more down the middle and a massive fireplace at the end. A well-designed restaurant, with good kitchen space.

My first job would be ironing the tablecloths. I was a real stickler about having them pristine, but the laundry press was always breaking down and would never get the creases out. We used to do our own laundry in-house, and there was a little poky room downstairs with three domestic washing machines and a laundry press, which always acted up. We wouldn't have enough napkins and would be ironing the damp ones

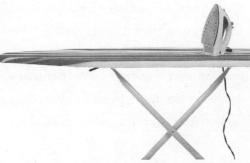

trying to get them dry in time for service. We would really be up against it because we were doing between eighty and ninety for lunch and 100-odd for dinner. Then I'd get the tables ready, grab a bite to eat, and off we'd go again with dinner service.

Guilbaud's used to go the whole nine yards with presentation, bringing dishes out to the customers on plates covered with silver domes and lifting off the domes on cue. They were famous for their *canard à l'orange*, which would be carved at the table on a big silver-domed trolley and presented to the customer with a flourish. It was a particular type of French duck, Challan, which is quite expensive. At the end of the day, it was just breast of duck with orange sauce, so there was a bit of smoke and mirrors going on, but what made it special was the quality of the ingredients and the sense of theatre.

Some people are intimidated by that style of fine-dining service, but they shouldn't be. It's just a bit of ceremony, and you're paying premium prices for it. If you embrace it, it can be a bit of fun. The food at Patrick Guilbaud's is expensive – though they do a good-value lunch menu – but the wines are pretty reasonably priced. Mind you, people didn't seem concerned with what they were paying when I was working there. Bills of 500 or 600 quid were quite normal.

Although Guilbaud's was not cheap – not by anyone's standards – it was always packed, every single day. I mean we were relentlessly busy. These were boom times in Dublin, and the restaurant already had a long-earned good reputation. Some people went there because they loved the food. Some people went there to be seen, to keep up with the right people. There was loads of corporate entertaining.

Things have changed so much now, and a lot of high-end restaurants are suffering. As well as simply not having the money, I
think people have moved away somewhat from that very formal
style of dining. But I believe that Guilbaud's will continue to thrive
because it has such a loyal clientele. People who love it really love
it, and, of course, they love to see who else is sitting in the room.

The businessman Tony Ryan used to go there a lot, as did Bono.
The Irish rugby team, including Brian O'Driscoll, used to come in
when they were in town. They were enthusiastic foodies, knew how
to look after themselves and never messed about. Very respectful
customers. John Rocha used to entertain a lot there too. A good,
decent man, and his wife Odette is lovely. A lot of judges used to
come, and we got an awful lot of corporate people entertaining clients – heads of banks, business executives and media moguls. What
was nice was that we also got ordinary punters who would come
for a one-off experience, a treat – people would have saved up for
that experience. And it was an experience. Everything was orchestrated, done to a tee. And it was a beautiful service.

I did enjoy my time in Guilbaud's, even if I didn't feel that I
completely fitted in. It was good for my employment record and
for my reputation within the Irish restaurant industry. There are
certain places where you need, and want, to work, to benefit your
career, and the best of them was Restaurant Patrick Guilbaud.

Patrick and I got along OK. I didn't quite get him, nor he me, I
expect. He didn't always go along with the service formulas you'd
expect in a two-Michelin-star restaurant. On a busy Saturday night
we'd be trying to do relays – changing over tables for another sitting – and he would busy himself by putting his fingers into the
dirty glasses to carry them rather than gathering them on a tray,
which quite surprised me for the kind of restaurant it was.

During my time there, Derek Bulmer, then head of Michelin
Guides for the UK and Ireland, came in. It didn't really cause

any panic or paranoia, because Guilbaud's was a very well-oiled machine, very consistent, which is what it's all about. I think the only time that a restaurant like that would fall down would be if it didn't have the right number of staff. They had a good system in place. Stephane would take the orders so there were no mess-ups, and then everything that followed was an organised system of service.

Guilbaud's was a very strict and formal restaurant, even for a two-Michelin-star. While the places I had worked in London were a bit more flamboyant and extravagant, this was very old school – and not in a relaxed sort of way like, say, Le Poulbot. You couldn't talk on the floor. Having a joke was a major no-no, and I did feel from early on that it didn't really suit my personality. Me being me, I tried to get to know the staff and to have a bit of fun with them, but it just didn't work that way. It was a serious place, and everyone worked long hours.

To be fair, while it didn't set my world on fire, Guilbaud's did me no harm at all. It is one of the best places in Ireland in terms of reputation, if not the best, and it hasn't done my CV any harm at all to say I worked there. But I think maybe they were looking for someone who they could groom into their way of thinking, their ethos, and I wasn't that type of person. I had just come back from London, and my style of service is efficient but relaxed. That's what I do.

I stuck it out for seven months until I got another job interview and then an offer from the Clarence. Over that time, I got to know some of the regular customers and to immerse myself a bit more in Dublin restaurant life. It's important as a *maître d'*, because people just love when you can acknowledge and greet them by name, even when you're working elsewhere. You get to know their tastes and habits, when to be discreet and when to have a bit of fun with them.

I do get a real buzz from remembering the various quirks of customers. It helps keep service lively if you can anticipate people's needs. It may not sound like much fun, but it can be. For me, it's a bit of a game. I've got the worst memory in the business. I've forgotten how you want your coffee by the time I leave your table. So it's important for me to keep my mind focused on service rather than let my head drift out of the room. I do remember certain things – I'm pretty good at remembering where people sat on their last visit, and I try to give them the same table. Like the journalist, Emer O'Kelly: when she comes to Pichet she likes to sit at Table 15. I also like second-guessing a customer by knowing their quirks. The politician Mary Harney has a thing about toothpicks. The first time she came to Pichet I didn't know her that well but I noticed she was fiddling with the sugar as though she was looking for something. I realised she needed a toothpick, and now any time I see Mary

Harney a little flag in my head waves, 'Toothpicks!' I love if I can spot from someone's body language what they're looking for, because I like to be one step ahead. I think it comes from my dad's advice when I was younger. He used to liken service to snooker – if you want to win the game, think six shots ahead.

By now, you'll have noticed that I've moved around a lot in this business. Six months here, three weeks there, over and back between Ireland and the UK. Do I get bored easily? Yes and no. I would say that for many years I've been looking for the right home, and if I don't think it's where I'm at, I get very unsettled. Restless, I look over the hill and start searching for other things.

I think even from a young age I was very restless, a bit of a daydreamer. Then I'd wonder what was happening somewhere else and think, *Am I wasting my time here?* I moved around a lot because I got frustrated with restaurants, owners, the way they were performing. I wanted to take my job seriously and not be stuck in a rut. Looking back now, I don't regret that because I wasn't institutionalised by being stuck in one place.

It's easy to say, now I've got my own place, but I don't feel much regret that I spent so much time searching, even though it probably brought a lot more upheaval into my life. My sporadic movements helped me gain a huge wealth of experience of different people in different situations. And it's only been by taking risks that I've been able to move higher up the ladder.

A lot of people who get restaurant work are not inclined to take it too seriously. Even the word 'waiter' has derogatory connotations. It's a word I hate, to be honest. My dad always says, 'Do not call yourself a waiter. Call yourself a *chef de rang*', which essentially means 'station waiter' but just sounds a bit more elegant. While that's a bit of a mouthful, the whole job-description thing is interesting because it defines what you do. When I was younger, I used to catch myself saying, 'I'm just a waiter', which I shouldn't have been doing because I was buying into that derogatory element.

John Healey, to me, is one of the best head waiters in Ireland. He worked at the Four Seasons in Ballsbridge, and I did a bit of consultancy with him when I worked for Conor Kenny & Associates, a hospitality consultancy based in Dublin. He also does front of house on the RTÉ show, *The Restaurant*. John's favourite line is, 'Service is an attitude,' and that sums it up for me. Having the right attitude is what makes a good waiter. What else? Somebody who's comfortable enough in their own skin to be servile, who is polite and can treat others how they would like to be treated. You need to be well groomed, to be knowledgeable. There are too many waiters who know nothing about wine, or who are vegetarians so can't describe a rib-eye steak. You've got to be a bit of a foodie – a character who loves food, wine, service, the

My well-thumbed copy of the French classic.

smell, the atmosphere, the cabaret. You've got to live it and like it, because it's hard work, and if you're not into it it's going to feel harder.

I know there are certain waiters who are grumpy. Don't get me wrong. There are certain waiters who don't give a damn, or who are having a bad day, or who can't sustain the energy to work long hours. There are certain staff who know they are on a split shift the following day but will still go drinking till 6 or 7 o'clock in the morning and cannot perform. A good waiter is somebody who performs 100 per cent every day and is proud of what he or she is doing – but there are not many people like that. That's where this trade falls down, and that's why people get disgruntled when service is not up to scratch. We all make mistakes, that's fine, we're not computers. But the right attitude will bring you a long way.

A lot of people who work as waiters literally *are* waiting – for something better to happen. Even now I get people dropping into Pichet looking for work, and when I ask them what kind of job they're looking for, they'll say in a voice of desperation, 'I'll do anything – waiting, anything.' That annoys me, because they think waitering is easy. I find it irritating that so many people see what I do as a stepping stone to something better. If someone is going to work with me I want them to be if not passionate about it then at least serious about it.

Lots of people think they should skip all that hard work and go straight into being a restaurant manager, but they haven't got a clue. They want to be in the suit, giving orders and making more money, but they have no idea what they are doing. That infuriates me because in this business you really do have to start at the bottom. Just make sure you're doing so in a good establishment where you will be looked after, trained and respected.

The beautiful art-deco entrance to
U2's hotel, the Clarence.

ROCK 'N' ROLL NIGHTS

THE CLARENCE HOTEL

I was approached to work in the Clarence by Anthony Ely, who was the Head Chef at that time and who I knew from Restaurant Patrick Guilbaud. I had huge respect for Anthony, so I thought why not go along for the chat. They were looking for a restaurant manager for the Tea Rooms. I had always been interested in working at the Clarence, mainly because I adored their restaurant space. Even way back when I was at the K Club I went to have a look at the Tea Rooms, and I fell in love with it. It had a magnificent twenty-foot-high ceiling – there was a church-like feel to it.

Funnily enough, in between leaving Guilbaud's and starting at the Clarence I had an offer of a job as restaurant manager from the Commons, a restaurant on St Stephen's Green. There was a good chef there, an English guy called Aiden Byrne. He has since gone on to work at the Dorchester and then opened his own gastropub, the Church Green, at Lymm in Cheshire. I went to meet Aiden and had dinner at the restaurant, but the menu just didn't appeal to me. Aiden was doing lots of offal dishes, and I didn't think these would be that popular with the Irish palate. I mean, who wants to eat kidneys? The room was beautiful, a Michelin-star room if ever I saw one. I felt you could really revive a golden era there,

163

that old-fashioned way of fine dining. At that time, a lot of government ministers and high-end businessmen were going there, as
were the corporates. It would have been a great place to serve,
but it didn't last, so it was fortunate for me that I didn't take up
that option, tempted as I was. I think the Commons struggled
because the chef was just cooking what he wanted to cook, which
is a great idea in theory, but you really do need to think of your
customers. Then, of course, I got that call from Conrad Gallagher
about going back to the Fitzwilliam Hotel. So it was a very flattering time, but confusing too.

I remember making my decision after having a few pints
with Denise's father, Gerry, in Coman's Pub in Rathgar. I was still
wondering where to go and what path to take next in my career,
although I think my gut was telling me to go to the Clarence.
Knowing I was a big fan both of jazz music and fine dining, Gerry
told me that jazz was fine dining but that the Clarence was rock
'n' roll. He said I had played enough jazz and that maybe now it
was time to play some rock 'n' roll. It was a reference that made
perfect sense to me, and soon afterwards I went to the Clarence.

I worked as Restaurant Manager in the Clarence for four and
a half years, from 2001. They were good times. God, I loved the
place. I felt really at home there. The Clarence is a small, bou-
tique hotel. I could get my own staff, which I did. We had a full
team of fifteen, with staff who specialised in room service for the
hotel, so we managed to do a good service, a good product.

The housekeeping at the Clarence was always top notch, one
of the best things about the place. There was a great woman, Kate
Kavanagh, in charge of housekeeping, and she used to run the
place like a military operation. She was very passionate about what
she did, and even when the cost-cutting took effect, she always
made sure that everyone performed and used to keep the rooms
immaculate and beautifully done. Hats off to the woman because

it wasn't an easy feat to achieve, but the housekeeping in the Clarence was always amazing.

Anthony Ely was the main man, the Executive Head Chef. We got on extremely well and are firm friends to this day, even though he went back to England to work in the Bibury Court Hotel in Cirencester. We used to go out for a pint after work and talk about the day's service. Anthony was very ahead of his time. He did his training at the Square, a very highly regarded two-Michelin-star restaurant in London owned by Philip Howard, for five and a half years. His food was exceptional.

The exclusive private dining room in the Clarence.

I would say the Tea Rooms was a very confused sort of place that suffered something of an identity crisis. To me, the room was ideal for a brasserie, but Anthony was going for Michelin-star fine-dining standard.

It's always more difficult running a restaurant that's attached to a hotel, no matter how great the food or the atmosphere. There is always a bit more red tape, you're stuck with paperwork, budget constraints and bureaucracy. It can have an influence on whatever vibe you're trying to create. In the early days that wasn't an issue. We were very busy. We improved the service. We had a very good team. The food was amazing.

There were just a couple of problems. First was the location. I hate to say it, but many Irish people don't like to go to Temple Bar,

especially at the weekends when there are lots of stag and hen parties. Car parking is expensive. It gets quite wild during the night – we often used to have guys pissing near the staff entrance. Temple Bar is a fantastic location for a party night out, but for customers looking for a civilised meal the location worked against the Tea Rooms.

The second problem was the Kitchen – not the chef's domain, but the nightclub of that name, which was right under the restaurant. The club was thriving in those days and used to kick off towards the end of every service. Every night at around 11 o'clock the floor would start vibrating from the dance music. It was the hottest club in town at the time, and people used to come to dinner thinking that they would then be able to get into the nightclub automatically. It didn't work that way because the club was a separate entity to the rest of the hotel. It was hugely popular but then it got into difficulty with letting too many people in. I think that was one of the key reasons why they couldn't really allow it to stay open, because it was a bad reflection on the hotel. It didn't sit well because I think it was completely and utterly a different vibe. You have a four-star hotel with a five-star service, then you've got this crazy, rave nightclub pulsating up through the floors.

I think it could have been a great club – it had a lounge bar and VIP area, and there were a lot of catacombs and tunnels. But it was quite grotty inside once you turned the lights up. They completely gutted it once the club closed and were going to turn it into a spa and gym, but that never happened, and the space ended up being neglected. The empty bottles from the bar and restaurant were sent into the basement, where the club used to be, via a chute. But many of them would miss the bottle bins and smash on the ground. Because the basement area was neglected after the nightclub closed, maintenance problems such as floods and leaks were also an issue.

The Clarence was a very fashionable place to be at that time. You'd get tourists coming in hoping to meet Bono, because he and the Edge owned the hotel. Masses of Spanish students would come in hoping to get a glimpse of the boys from U2, and we used to get a lot of celebrities through the doors as well because of that connection.

Much as I would love to tell you stories of people being obnoxious or demanding, it's been my experience that most celebs are very well behaved. The cooler ones, anyway. We got judges. We got film stars. We got pop stars. We got actors. Ray Winstone used to come in a lot when he was in town. He is such a nice man. I remember he once held a party in the downstairs study and he invited us in to have drinks. We were there until about 4.30 in the morning talking about football and about his life and drinking whiskey. He was in town with his family and friends and wanted us to join in the fun. Jonathan Rhys Meyers would stay often. We had Ricky Gervais. Naomi Campbell was a regular.

The boys from U2 were regulars, of course. Thursday night was their night out, and they would always come in and have dinner. They were fairly plain eaters and would generally go with what was on the menu. No caviar or anything like that. They would often have the fish and chips, or sometimes they would just ask for baked beans on toast. They liked good wine and usually ordered Stag's Leap, a very nice Californian wine.

I found them to be very personable – they always asked about our families and were just very down-to-earth people. But it was madness on busy nights when they came in. There were always fans lurking outside, trying to get past the doormen in the hope of meeting the band.

I remember one day Bono came in for lunch, shortly after he had been honoured by the French Government with the Legion of Honour. He brought the letter from the French President with him, and he was so chuffed. It was a big accolade to get, and it was lovely to see him so pleased.

Another night Bono brought in Robert De Niro and the McNally brothers from the famous New York restaurant, Balthazar. We hosted a lot of parties with Bono and his friends, people like Guggi and Gavin Friday. It was always quite a relaxed experience because they were pleasant to their staff – there were no starry egos to contend with. The Clarence was a home for them. It was their baby, and I think they just really loved the place.

Gavin Friday came in one night, table for four, wearing these big black sunglasses. I gave him the menu, and he said, 'It's very

dark in here. I can't even read the menu.'

I said, 'Gavin, sunglasses.'

'Oh, yeah, yeah, yeah.'

He'd actually forgotten he was wearing them. I don't think he was messing with me – if he was fooling me, he managed to do so with a very straight face. A very funny and eccentric man.

We had a lot of musicians coming through the doors because for a good few years virtually every act that was playing the Point venue would stay there. It meant we often accommodated working bands by feeding them before or, more often, after a gig. One night Rod Stewart was playing in the Point, and we had his entire entourage for dinner after the concert. We were expecting Rod to arrive, but he never turned up. Anyway, we fed the entourage. There were about twenty-three of them, and we took the order at about 10.30 or 11 o'clock at night. Then, suddenly, disaster: a piece of glass appeared in one of the fish courses. A nightmare scenario for a restaurant. We were racking our brains as to where it could have come from, but it didn't matter. We had to comp the whole meal, because otherwise that could be very detrimental to business.

Musicians wouldn't always eat in the Tea Rooms as many of them would rent out the famous penthouse on the top floor and do their entertaining and dining there. The penthouse was this fantastic, massive suite on two floors, with two bedrooms downstairs and a glorious big lounge upstairs, with a massive television and an amazing view of the city. There was a baby grand piano and the *pièce de la resistance*, a balcony with an outdoor hot tub. The colour scheme was bright, and there were cream rugs on the floor. It was an amazing place to have a party. Many of the wealthy or famous would have parties there, and we would serve them canapés, sandwiches or late-night snacks, before and after the concert if they were performing.

Sometimes if the parties got really wild residents would be asked to pay for any damage caused. There were always parties going on in the penthouse, sometimes involving up to thirty people. Only two people could actually stay, but you could host groups until about five in the morning, and you would be able to hire staff until 2 a.m. One night I was working the penthouse for a large group of girls who were having a hen party and having great fun. They were a good bunch of girls, but when I went up they were all wearing next to nothing because they were dipping in and out of the hot tub. And, of course, when they saw a man coming in, they all went bonkers. I managed to get out of there in one piece.

I had been working at the hotel for about two years when Denise and I got married, in 2003. We had hoped to get married in 2002. The church had been booked, and we even looked at l'Ecrivain as a reception venue – my best man Kevin was the manager there at the time. However, I had a meltdown, and we broke up for a short period. I moved out of the house. But I knew that I couldn't let Denise go, and for her birthday that year, even though we were apart, I bought her two tickets to New York as we had both always wanted to go. We stayed in the Mercer Hotel. To start with it wasn't a very romantic trip as Nicole Kidman was staying in our hotel. Denise was fascinated and was more interested in Nicole than me. Unknown to Denise I had an engagement ring in my pocket. Eventually, on the third night, I plucked up the courage to propose. Luckily, Denise said, 'Yes.'

We went home and set the wedding date for 16 August 2003. Madonna's birthday, no less. Denise, a huge Madonna fan, swears this is a coincidence. It was an amazingly hot summer, and the weeks leading up to the wedding were great. And then the day itself was amazing. We had the church ceremony in Terenure and then travelled in a big old-fashioned car to the Clarence. We had photographs taken overlooking the river on the balcony of the penthouse. Denise and I took the whole wedding party up to the penthouse for drinks before dinner, and we had some job getting them out.

Then we had dinner and a party for sixty family and friends in a room on the first floor. (I always thought that first-floor room

On top of the world. Denise and me outside the penthouse suite of the Clarence Hotel, on our wedding day.

The dreaded best man's speech. luckily Denise wasn't having second thoughts!

would make a great restaurant, but it was always used as a function room.) The Clarence helped to make sure the room was 100 per cent spot on. The flowers were amazing, there were scented candles everywhere. We got the best of everything. The Clarence gave us our wedding at a massive reduction – I think it was about €5,000 – if we allowed our photographs to be used for the hotel's wedding brochure. They even gave us the food at cost price. As well as being a beautiful experience for us, we got to see the hotel as guests who were staying there saw it.

Conan stayed in the hotel with his nana that night. He ordered breakfast in bed and then went down for more. It was great as he joined us the next day and the next part of our lives started.

I had a lot of funny experiences during my five years at the Clarence. There was one customer who used to come in who suffered from narcolepsy, that condition where you fall asleep suddenly. A terrible condition to have to live with, I'd imagine, but really strange to deal with when you're working in a restaurant. He was a big stocky man, who used to drink a bit, but a very nice man who loved to have a chat. I would be talking to him, then suddenly he would hold me by the arm and he would fall asleep.

When it happened I wouldn't like to disturb him so I'd be kind of stuck there, with everyone laughing at me. He'd wake up and resume the conversation, then fall back asleep again.

Nothing in my career to date had prepared me for one early-morning encounter with two frisky lesbians. I'd better explain myself! I was on breakfast duty, and, because room service was quite busy, I offered to bring up one of the breakfast orders myself. A polite knock is always a good idea when you're bringing breakfast into a hotel bedroom, and, when I rapped on the door, two female voices chorused, 'Come in.' When I opened the door, there were two young ladies in bed together with their heads above the sheets. I was a little bit taken aback – not really embarrassed, just caught off guard. It was only as I put the tray on the side table and went to leave that I realised I'd forgotten the jam and would have to come back with it. 'I've forgotten the jam, I'll be back with the jam,' I stuttered. When I went back to the kitchen, all of the guys were suddenly very helpful, offering, 'Oh, let me take the jam up.' I thought I should be professional and take the jam up myself. By the time I went back into the room it was clear that the girls were very much enjoying themselves. They were frolicking naked on the bed, shall we say. I put down the jam and left them to it, but it was certainly a talking point amongst the staff for the rest of the day.

Sometimes, when service was slow, and when we were in a zany mood, we would have a bit of fun. I had a very good friend in the Clarence's sommelier, Sheerin Wilde, who has gone on to be a very successful restaurant manager. Sheerin and I were a good team but sometimes we brought out the worst in each other. We both had a wacky sense of humour and were big Tommy Cooper fans. I remember one lunchtime when just the two of us were on for lunch and it was quiet – just a couple of tables booked. After I took one of the orders, we were joking and having a bit of banter with the table. Very nice people. It turned out they liked Tommy Cooper too, so I started doing jokes and impressions.

I had been out shopping that day and had bought a Tommy Cooper joke kit, which I was very eager to try out. My kit included fake thumbs and a handkerchief. You take out the hanky, hide it under the fake thumb, then it disappears and reappears from your pocket. Just like that! I did the routine, and they were in stitches.

About forty minutes later, I thought to myself, *That food is taking a long time to come out*. The customers were enjoying themselves so hadn't said anything, but I thought I should go to the kitchen and investigate. So I went into the kitchen and said, 'What's the story with the food, is it coming out?'

They said, 'We haven't had a docket.'

I said, 'What do you mean you haven't had a docket? I put the docket in about half an hour ago – what's the story?' I looked in my pocket, and there was the order: the docket was still in my pocket. We had been so busy having the craic that I completely forgot to put it through. I remember begging the chef to fast-track the order. Sheerin and I thought this was hilarious, but then we had to go to the customers.

I was so embarrassed about the whole thing that we had to tell the customers that the gas stove had gone down, or that we had just woken up the chef, and, 'Guess what, he has decided to cook for you today.' I stayed in Tommy Cooper mode and said, 'Sorry for the delay, we've given the chef some coffee and he's sitting up now.'

Sheerin and I just couldn't stop laughing about it, which was really bad of us, but it was just one of those funny moments in time where two guys on the floor had nothing better to do than look after two tables and ended up fucking it up. We got away with it because the customers were really easy-going and hadn't even really noticed the delay. The docket in the

pocket has happened to me a few times; I think it's because I'm a bit of a daydreamer.

Sometimes if I am in a zany mood and a customer is rude to me I can be very mischievous. One night this large party came in, very well-to-do, with an extremely posh woman in the group. Let's call her Hyacinth Bucket. I greeted them, wished them a good evening and offered to take their coats. Hyacinth was incredibly rude: she took off her very expensive-looking fur coat and handed it to me as if I was one of her minions. Basically, she didn't even say hello, just barked, 'Take my coat.' I was boiling. At that time the coats were hung behind a curtain area, and I threw her mink on the ground and left it there.

Then she suddenly said, 'Oh, I need to get something from my coat.' I froze, then leapt for the curtain, but she got there before me, in time to see her beloved mink lying on the ground. Without thinking, I turned to Sheerin and said, 'For Christ's sake! The coat hanger is still broken! I told you to fix it!' Not knowing what was happening, he had to apologise profusely. She was very upset, and we had to grovel. It was a nice mink, too.

Sometimes if I'm not in the mood for a very rude customer, I can be irate back to them, which is usually more trouble than it's worth. One day a lady rang the Clarence looking for a table at the Tea Rooms, and there wasn't one available. I didn't realise that she'd already made a booking with somebody else. She became very cross and said, 'Do you know who I am?' I replied tersely, 'No, I don't know who you are, but quite frankly it doesn't matter who you are, because we don't have a table.'

She got very angry and decided to come down to the hotel in person to complain. She arrived at the reception desk and said, 'I was on the phone to a very rude Englishman, and I am utterly upset. He was extremely rude to me on the phone and I demand to speak to somebody.'

The Deputy General Manager happened to be an Englishman named Michael Conrad-Pickles, and he was called to speak with her. He came down and said, 'Can I help you Madam?'

She said, 'Was I speaking to you on the phone? You were extremely rude!'

Michael replied, 'Calm down, Madam. I don't remember any conversation with you.'

She said, 'I was speaking to an English person.'

He said, 'Well there is more than one English person in this hotel.'

Right on cue, I came down the stairs. Michael said, 'Maybe it was this gentleman?' gesturing to me. 'Nick, did you have a conversation with this lady earlier today?'

Sensing trouble, I shrugged my shoulders, adopted my very best French accent and replied, 'Non,' before getting out of there very quickly.

There's a certain class of restaurant-goer who loves complaining just for the sake of it, and they are the bane of my life. Don't get me wrong. I don't think you deserve to be asked to leave if your steak's been overdone. That would be a bit evil. But if a customer is determined not to enjoy themselves and seems set on causing strife, it can be a great relief to ask them to leave.

Basically the method we use is that we refuse to serve them any more. We say, 'You have upset your own evening and we will no longer be serving you food this evening. We think it's best that you leave now,' and then start to clear away the table. More than nine times out of ten, it works. Customers who experience this feel intimidated and embarrassed. Why would you sit there at an empty table in front of other diners? There's no point.

Most people leave quietly, but there has been the odd occasion when they didn't. If someone is very angry and has already taken it too far, they might want to shout and rant and cause as much of a scene as possible, which puts you in a much more vulnerable position and you will need to get help to remove them.

On one occasion at the Clarence, we had a guy who refused to budge. He'd ordered four glasses of good wine which cost €12 each. After his three courses and four glasses, he started shouting to the people at another table what a rip-off the place was.

'Sorry Sir, please calm down. The prices here are good value for Dublin. What is your argument?'

He said, 'I'm disgusted with this place.'

I said to him, 'What are you actually doing here? Why did you come here tonight?' Did he not read the wine list? Did I force him to choose the more expensive wine? No, he saw the prices, and he chose that wine. Why was he now abusing me in front of all these people?

On he goes, 'You're a rip-off, rant rant.'

I said, 'You are getting out of order. I want you to leave.'

And he said, 'No, I'm not leaving.'

I said to him, 'What do you mean, "not leaving"?' Did I have to stand there and take abuse? Could he not just moan to somebody else outside? I took a breath and tried again, 'Sir, I think you should leave now.'

He said, 'No, I'm not leaving.'

I had to call Security to get him out.

When that sort of thing happens, it upsets your entire evening's service and can also play on your mind and make you question the whole philosophy of your job and why you're doing it.

From a front-of-house point of view, why should we have to put up with obnoxious behaviour? It's nice to react to rudeness instead of having to go, 'I'm terribly sorry, I'll find out what's wrong,' when there is patently nothing wrong. You don't want to come off as aloof or, worse, arrogant. I don't want to be that person. But sometimes, you have to politely explain to a customer that they are actually talking out of their arse.

You do not charge a customer if you are ejecting them. That would just be wrong. They may have had copious amounts of wine and food before they started being horrible, but you'd still rather take the hit just to get them out.

One night, in the Clarence, a woman came to dine alone. After she ordered her food she started to complain about the music. Like most hotels we had piped music playing from a random playlist. I remember what was playing when she complained: 'Every Breath You Take' by The Police. A good song, right? I mean, in the context of background music, it's hardly pan pipes. On and on she went about the music saying it was like being in an elevator. I explained that the music was chosen for the establishment and that we couldn't accommodate individual tastes. She started swearing at me – I mean, profusely swearing at me. She would not stop. So I thought, *I've had enough of you*, and removed her from the restaurant. I did my table-clearing thing and asked her to leave. Eventually, I had to get one of the doormen to help her on her way. It was only later that I discovered she'd been barred from the bar in the Clarence for causing a scene two years before.

Sometimes you can land in trouble when a genuine mistake makes a customer suspicious. Another night, two very well-to-do customers wanted a cognac and ordered a Hennessy XO, which is a very fine, and very expensive, blend of the drink. It was a busy night, and, through some confusion (not having realised what they'd ordered), I grabbed the VS – a less expensive blend – and brought two glasses to their table.

But one of the customers had seen me pouring the VS and was absolutely convinced we were trying to rip them off. Sheerin went over and had to apologise to them profusely, explaining to them that there was a mistake in communication and offering a cognac on the house. But they were ready to kill him.

Another time, Sheerin told me the story of what happened in one of Dublin's most popular and best-loved restaurants, the Trocadero, a great old-school place that is very popular with actors and theatregoers. Sheerin had been working as a commis under the head waiter, Pat Hennessy – a brilliant guy to work for. On this night it was very, very busy, as it always is there, and Pat was running around looking after everyone. He was serving a large party and came shooting out of the kitchen with main courses, but on the way the lip of the sole of his shoe got caught on the edge of a step. Pat went flying. Nobody knows to this day how he saved himself from falling and even managed to hold onto all three plates. However, a chicken Kiev had other ideas and went flying through the air, bouncing underneath a table where two ladies were dining. Incredibly, neither they nor the other customers noticed this had happened, so the waiting staff set about rectifying everything. A replacement Kiev was quickly put on order while Sheerin set about finding the rogue chicken. He made some excuse that people who had previously been sitting at the table had lost their house keys and that they might be under the table, and, with the ladies' blessing, looked frantically under the table with his lighter to try and locate the errant Kiev. There was no sign of it. The staff decided to forget about it until clean-up later that night.

Unfortunately, about an hour later, Robert Doggett, the *maître d'*, came out looking very concerned. Robert works in the Troc to this day and is one of the best front-of-house people you'll find anywhere. He said, 'Do you know anything about what happened on Table 2?'

The waiters said, 'In what respect? Everything seemed to go very well on the table.'

Robert said, 'I just took a phone call from a customer who asked, "Why is there a chicken Kiev in my handbag?!"'

The lady had reported that when she got home she put her hand into her handbag to get the keys to the house and took out a chicken Kiev instead. The garlic butter in the centre had spilt all over the bag. I've heard of bringing a doggie bag home with you, but I'm not sure that was what she expected!

On another night in the Clarence, I was working with the then head waiter, a man named Mark Noonan. There was a big group of ladies in that night: young, well-to-do, very well dressed, and Mark was very keen on serving them. They were having an aperitif at the bar, and the barman, Conor, was taking care of them.

Mark said to Conor, 'I'll do this. I'll look after this.'

Conor refused, saying, 'That's what I'm here for: I'm the barman.'

Mark said, 'It doesn't matter. Get out of the bar.'

So Conor turned to Sheerin and said, 'He is throwing me out of the bar.' Sheerin and Conor then locked the door of the bar from the outside so that Mark couldn't get out, even though his tables in the restaurant were waiting to be served. Sheerin then came down and told me, 'Nick, I have to inform you that Conor has locked your head waiter in the bar because he was very rude so we are going to let him sweat.'

It eventually dawned on Mark to ring from the bar phone down to me in the restaurant reception to ask to be freed. I knew what was coming and picked up the phone when it rang, saying, 'Hello, locksmiths?'

Mark knew full well that there was no help coming for another little while and put the phone back down.

Celebrity customers tend to be gracious, undemanding and well behaved. However, one night we had Shane MacGowan, Kate Moss and Pete Doherty stay with us in the Clarence. They came in for dinner, and they were off their faces. I remember that Shane had a broken ankle. He was in a wheelchair and just looked grey. Pete Doherty, looking scruffy and dishevelled, wheeled him in. I can't, in fairness, say that they were rude or obnoxious, just erratic, sloppy and all over the place. It was like trying to contain a group of crazy teenagers on spring break. At one stage Kate went missing, and one of the staff had to go after her to make sure she was OK. It was just mad stuff.

We had this fricassee on the menu, which Shane ordered. We gave him a knife, a fork and a spoon, and he threw the spoon and the fork away, flung them across the room, and proceeded to spend an hour and a half eating this liquid dish with a knife. I kept handing him a spoon, and he kept throwing the spoon away. They were just so out of order. Pete was falling over onto the banquette, incoherent.

They kept ordering more booze, and Shane couldn't talk, what with being drunk and having no teeth. He was going, '*Shhh shhhh shhhh shshh.*'

I said, 'Will you point to what wine you want?'

And he answered, '*Shhh sheehhh.*'

It was a surreal experience. They eventually left to go upstairs and continue their party in the penthouse suite. Shane could drink until whatever time. It's very funny to recall now but it was actually a nightmare situation. You could see that there were some hard things going on there. It wasn't like recreational drug use, it was more than that – full blown.

I wasn't impressed with Pete Doherty. He was awful, dirty – that's the only way you could describe him. Actually, I quite like his music and it's a shame because he should be great. You just feel sorry for him. It's a sad existence in a sense because he *has* talent but substance abuse has taken over his life. I don't really get the whole Kate Moss thing, either, though she does have an attitude. It was sad that night to see her in such a state.

Staffing became a big problem in the Clarence as the years went on. In the early days there was loads of staff. It was good, fun and very manageable. Then one day the accountants stepped in, and we basically had to cut the budget by €30,000. This all happened at a time when they were thinking of closing the hotel, and they were going to revamp it into something wonderful – a Sir Norman Foster-designed hotel. Instead, it all went downhill. It became much more difficult for the staff.

Losing teaspoons is the restaurant equivalent of losing socks in the wash: they always disappear into some invisible void and constantly need replacing. But budgetary constraints meant that cutlery wasn't replaced, and we used to have to fight for teaspoons. I had to fill in about three purchase orders just to get something new in the place, and it felt that the business was led by budgets and meetings and became less and less about customer service.

When I first arrived we had wine glasses shaped like chalices, beautiful crystal-cut glasses, but gradually they started to break, and we just couldn't replace them. The uniforms started to get shabby, and the whole feel sort of disintegrated a bit. I was still trying to produce a good service and keep everything going because I really loved the place. So that was very frustrating for me and the Head Chef and for the staff.

We had signed a document saying that we knew the hotel would be closing and that we were very happy to stay on during renovations. They spent about €5,000 on these designs, and we all went to the meeting where Sir Norman Foster explained to us about the whole new look of the hotel – it was to be amazing. Wow. We were all so excited and thought, *We want to stay for this; this will be something exceptional.* It would really bring the Clarence up to the twenty-first century. There was talk about a sky bar and a swimming pool on the top floor. There was going to be something like 1,000 bedrooms.

PR is a massive thing for any customer-orientated establishment. You have to let people know you're there and what you're doing. I felt that the Clarence, during my time there, didn't get that extra push it needed to be as successful as it deserved. I always thought that what they should do with the Tea Rooms was turn it into an all-day diner. But it just didn't happen. There were many influences. Many of the people who ran it wanted it to be a fine dining place. I think not marketing it was a real failing.

Our service suffered because this cost-cutting exercise meant that we had to get rid of staff. Yet it was still €27 for breakfast, and that's seven or eight years ago. If you're paying that price for breakfast, it should be special, but staff shortages meant we simply couldn't always deliver. It became a bit of a nightmare, and quite stressful. We didn't do a breakfast buffet because it was not what the General Manager wanted. We still had to do table service, taking orders. You can't do that when you have about 100 people coming down for breakfast and only have a shoestring staff. Look at it from the customers' point of view. They were paying €230 a night to stay there.

I got disillusioned with the whole cost-cutting thing. It was hard sometimes. I guess it was because the hotel was losing money. I was trying to serve people with a severely limited amount of stock and I'd think, *Something is wrong here.*

We used to do a lot of functions at that time. One night we catered for seventy people, and there were only four members of staff serving, which was a complete and utter nightmare before we even started. We were just running like idiots trying to get the job done. I tried to address it a couple of times but never really got anywhere. At one stage I complained, and they promoted me to Food and Beverage Manager on extra money. That was a good vote of confidence, but I was still working with limited resources. I gladly took the position and was supposed to be taught about the figures and all that, but then in July 2005 the General Manager left, and I felt like I was managing a sinking ship. We were starting to get complaints and – something that is far more serious for a restaurant – people were getting fed up, leaving without making a complaint but just not coming back. I would be thinking, *What am I supposed to do? How can I rectify this?* The obvious thing was to get more staff in, to train them up and to give them the tools to do their job properly. But that wasn't going to happen.

A real low point for me was what I now refer to as the Saint Valentine's Night Massacre. I hate Valentine's night. Everyone who's ever worked in a restaurant on Valentine's night hates it. It should be crossed off the calendar as far as I'm concerned. It can be a busy night for a restaurant that might be hoping to get a good night's takings to make up for that post-Christmas slump. But it's a notoriously difficult event. First, it's all tables of two. Restaurants hold out for fours or tables for sixes. They want groups because there's a bigger spend, but on that night the tables go as twos, like Noah's Ark. It's not like you can cut the tables in half. This means that it's a lot more work for restaurant staff, but the spend is not necessarily higher. People will only have one bottle of wine, or maybe no drinks at all.

Then you've got the restaurant staff, who are under pressure because they are trying to pack the place for two sittings to make up for a quiet period. If there's a special Valentine's menu on, the customers feel like they're being ripped off – and often they are. A restaurant might abuse the customer by saying, 'Tonight, especially for Valentine's, we are doing a special with a wonderful free glass of prosecco on arrival. Just €75 per person.' All nonsense, pure milking it, and people are gullible and want to make a good impression on their partner, so they buy into it.

The worst places are the restaurants that want to decorate the room with helium balloons or put rose petals on the tables, trying to contrive the vibe of lurve. I've been down that road where the manager goes, 'Oh, wouldn't it be a great idea to scatter rose petals on the tables, to put love hearts in the food. Let's have a special passion-fruit mousse with love hearts. It'll be great.' No it bloody won't. Don't assume I'm not a romantic. It's just that I hate organised romance, especially in a restaurant. It's kitsch and not really romantic at all.

Why couples go out on Valentine's is beyond me. I mean, I just don't understand why they put themselves through it. It can be such pressure for all but the most secure of couples, who tend to stay at home with a pizza and a DVD in any case. Couples don't necessarily enjoy themselves. They have to make an effort on that particular night, just because it's Valentine's. That can become an issue for a restaurant because the atmosphere, I have to say, is never electric. The man obviously wants to have sex but maybe the wife doesn't, but he is taking her out for dinner and he has maybe bought her roses, but it's the middle of the week, and neither of them want to be there anyway because they're tired.

So, one year's Valentine's Night at the Clarence Hotel was easily the worst night of service of my entire career. There were dark forces conspiring against us, and no love in the air for either me or the staff. Everything that could go wrong did. First of all, one of the main lights wouldn't work, so it was a really weird atmosphere: one side of the restaurant was dark and the other bright.

When I counted the table plan I thought, *How the hell are we going to do this?* The most people we had served in the Tea Rooms was maybe 135 but that would have been spread out over five or six hours. That night we had 120 people booked, all wanting to be fed within two hours. It was completely our fault that we had taken too many people, and that all came down to the sporadic type of service that we were doing.

Everyone always wants to eat at 8 o'clock. In restaurants we try to do two sittings, but that doesn't happen. People are notorious for arriving late, they're always chatting at the bar and then forget the time. I accept all that. I would be the same if I was going out because I'd never think of the restaurant, I'd just think of myself and my evening. I would always advise people to arrive on time on busy nights for a restaurant.

Restaurants rely on the queuing system. If you want a service to run smoothly, you allocate five tables every half an hour. The idea is that the orders trickle into the kitchen in a steady flow. If one person is taking orders, that's fine. If you are in a busy restaurant you might have three or four waiters taking orders. Things go wrong if there is a flood of orders into the kitchen. A restaurant that cooks food to order simply cannot cope.

That night, we knew we were going to suffer. I put on my juggling hat and went to the front line. As orders flooded into the kitchen the chef slowly started to go berserk. Then one of the guys cut his finger, so off he went. One guy was hungover, so he couldn't perform. We were overwhelmed. The chef couldn't pump out the food any quicker, the staff were at their utmost limits, and I was apologising to quite a few tables at this stage to say that it's going to be a longer wait than normal.

I can still hear people shouting at me: 'Where is our food?! Where is our food?!' I was giving them bottles of wine on the house but the situation became really unmanageable.

Eventually the chef said to stop the service: stop taking orders. It's all very well him saying that from the safety of the kitchen, but what were we going to say to the customers? I really, really wanted to go and hide somewhere, but I had to go out and face the music. The house of cards had collapsed. I remember thinking to myself, *Will the ground please open?* I might have a few tricks up my sleeve but there are some times when I just have to admit defeat. People will always see through you, so you are better off being honest about it and admitting when something is your fault. Some people will accept it – some people won't. It's terrible when service falls apart, because our customers are there to be fed by us, and if we fail at that then we are at fault.

Everyone got fed – eventually – but it was awful. We got a lot of complaints and gave out complimentary meals and free stays in the hotel. It's hard not to take a night like that home with you.

If business is free-flowing, and you do a steady fifty every night, thirty for lunch, you know exactly how many staff you need. In the Clarence,

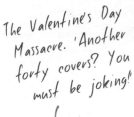

The Valentine's Day Massacre. 'Another forty covers? You must be joking!'

because business was so up and down, we would try and pack everyone in on a busy night. Eventually the bubble burst, and people said, 'I'm not accepting this type of service.' And, as a restaurant manager who gets to know his customers, I started to notice that they were not coming back.

I have to say I really did enjoy my time at the Clarence until I got disillusioned with cutbacks, red tape and paperwork. When I realised change wasn't going to happen, I felt stuck in a bit of a rut. The fact that I stayed there for so long is an indication of my affection for the place. I really got my teeth into it and thought that in the grand scheme of things it was going to be developed and revamped into an amazing hotel. To be fair, that this didn't happen wasn't the fault of the management or the staff. There were issues with planning, and then the recession kicked in. They bought offices next door and were planning to expand – they had a great vision for the place. But it just didn't happen quickly enough. It was very unfortunate.

By the end of my time at the Clarence I was ready to leave. Actually, I didn't really *want* to leave but because of the way things were going I felt I needed to. The General Manager left. Then Anthony Ely left to go back to England. You know that feeling you get when people you've teamed up with are moving on, and you feel you want to do the same thing? The Clarence had lost its sparkle.

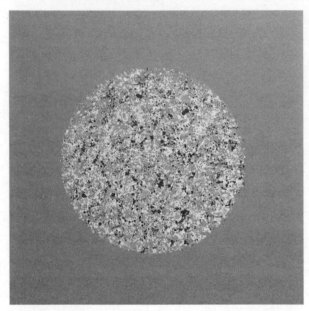

Planet Munier.

PORTRAIT OF THE ARTIST

DISCOVERING A NEW TALENT

Some years ago, while I was working at the Clarence, I decided to try therapy. It was Denise who suggested that it would be a good idea to go and talk to someone because she felt that I was getting ... not quite angry with myself, but more and more frustrated. It's not that I'm a workaholic – I can quite happily take time out and do nothing for weeks on end. But this career can encourage an obsessive nature if you're not careful, and frustrations can manifest themselves and then take over your entire life.

I was getting increasingly disappointed and disillusioned with where my career was going. I had been moving from restaurant to restaurant for years, bouncing back and forth between London and Dublin, and just didn't know what I was looking for. While I still loved what I did, the service elements had become monotonous, and I had no creative outlet, no escape from the long hours and late nights that are all a part of the restaurant industry.

For me, service is all about the anticipation, about looking at the person sitting at the table, about thinking what they want before they even ask you for it. It's like a sixth sense to me. There are only a small number of people who are into that. I was in danger of losing that passion, and then, one day, while I was talking to Denise about it, she dropped a little bombshell of a suggestion: 'Maybe you should go and talk to somebody.'

My reaction was, 'What are you talking about?'

She said that she thought I might be too fixated on working, on earning money, and that there could be an issue there. She arranged for me to go and meet this therapist in Clontarf. I was expecting the therapy to be straightforward. I would tell the therapist a bunch of things, and he would figure out what was wrong with me and give me a solution. What actually happened was that I was supposed to just sit there and talk about myself for hours and hours. Weird. I used to just waffle and make things up, all the time waiting for the therapist to tell me what was wrong with me. Denise was right about my fixation with money. Therapy taught me that for sure: I'd hand over €50 at the end of the hourly sessions and think to myself, *What a waste! I could have been saving that!*

I have always had a thing about money. When I was starting off in the trade, Jean Cottard used to advise me to save as much as I could and to work as hard as I could. These were principles I carried throughout my life, and they have served me well, but sometimes they have caused problems.

Unfortunately it became a preoccupation, wondering how much I could save. I think where I was coming from was that I always wanted to have something to show for my hard work, so I became obsessed with how much money I had in the bank. Over time, I got a reputation for being Mr Tight, and it caused a lot of rows in my life. It's not that I am not a generous person. The money thing for me was more about security. For example, the idea of debt is alien to me. I just can't understand it. I have never had a credit card in my life and have always believed in the idea that if you can't afford it then don't buy it.

But when it started to cause conflict with those closest to me, I knew I had to address it. The money thing definitely became an issue coming up to the wedding. Denise wanted to spend €16,000, and I said, 'You are completely mad – I am not going to spend €16,000 on a wedding. That's a down payment for an apartment or a house!' Immediately afterwards, I thought, *Oh my God, have I just said that?*

I think also it was the idea of a big wedding that scared me. Originally, there were about 150 people on the guest list. It has always spooked me when people say, 'I'm having 150 people to my wedding,' and I think, *Who are these people that you are inviting? Do you know them?* The reasoning is usually along the lines of 'No, I don't know them, but I can't offend him, and I can't leave out Bob who has the allotment down from my mother.' It becomes a monster. Knowing how hotels rip people off when they are having a wedding, it just didn't sit well with me.

So that was sort of a rift that we went through, and it didn't do our relationship any good. I realised that my reaction to the cost of the wedding was very strange, and it got me thinking, *I'd better go and get some help here.*

Have I mellowed on the money issue? It's funny, it doesn't really go away. It's like anything you get obsessed about. It's always there. You just have to be aware of it and not let it take over your enjoyment of life.

The Who.

I stuck with the therapy, because Denise was intrigued by the process and was hoping that it would help me. She wanted to know if I was enjoying it, if I felt better about myself because of it. Over time I got into it, and it became part of my routine. Eventually, I had a eureka moment and realised that I needed another outlet, rather than being focused on 'money, work, money, work'.

The therapist said to me, 'Well, what do you enjoy?'

I have always been very passionate about art. It was what I wanted to do at a young age. I always had this desire to splash colour everywhere and remembered that I even used to dream about making my own clothes. In therapy, all of these things came back and started to pour out of me.

I fell into catering because it was the easy option, because it was the world I knew best and because I was good at it. I never really had to think about whether or not it was what I wanted to do. I had the personality for it, it was a family trade, and, because of that, it was relatively easy for me to make the connections I needed to get started. But maybe, just maybe, I was no longer happy doing that and that alone.

I had always dabbled in art, but not to the extent that I wanted because I never made the time. During one of the therapy sessions, I took a piece of wood and painted it blue with a white line on it. I called it *The Letterbox*. The therapist said, 'That's obviously signifying that you are feeling trapped or you are feeling inhibited. Next week, you can spend an hour drawing.' I thought, *That sounds like fun, doesn't it? 50 quid to draw for an hour. I could draw at home for nothing.*

But I went along with it. I got these pastels, and, during the session, I started creating aggressive, manic images. The therapist asked, 'Do you feel better?'

I said, 'No, because I felt anxiety about putting the colour to the page, and I don't know whether that's helping me or not.'

He said, 'Well that's what you need: an outlet to do something completely different.' Then he says to me, 'You will never make any money out of it.'

'Why do you say that?'

'Because you are not an artist.'

That really annoyed me, and proved to be something of a catalyst. I thought to myself, *Blow you, mate. I'll prove to you that I can do it.* I came out of that session thinking, *Why am I still coming here to be put down?* But maybe that was the point. Maybe I learned something that I always knew subconsciously. And maybe therapy helped me push open that door. Did it calm me down? I don't know. But art has calmed me down. It has proved to be the complete release that I needed.

I turned the box room at home into my studio, and painting became my new obsession. For a while I didn't want to go back to work at all. I just wanted to paint. The extremes to my personality were kicking in again, and all I could think about when I woke up in the morning and when going to bed were colours and painting.

Organised Chaos.

I felt at one point that I didn't want to work, just paint and become a painter, but obviously it's not as easy as that. I've always been a dreamer, and maybe it was the Frenchman in me too. I'd always shown my practical side in the world of restaurants, and now I was getting to be expressive at last. It was the sense of creating and the feeling of achievement that it gave me that were so satisfying.

Originally, I watered down acrylics and played around with them, but I started to work more in oils because of the intensity of texture and colour that they gave me. What I do is very abstract, very modern, mostly on canvas, but when I'm on a roll I will work with anything: newspaper, card, wood, whatever I can get my hands on.

The best thing for me is that these paintings seem to come out of nowhere. I used to try and plan ahead, to have an idea of what I wanted to do, but that never worked at all. The less I think about the end result, the better it seems to work for me. Sometimes a mistake turns into something beautiful. Because I'm quite messy

Rainy Daze.

and chaotic, I might drop the can of paint onto a canvas, and it might fall in such a way as to be really beautiful (or sometimes not!). Then I work with that, and it turns itself into something magical. That's why I get such a kick out of it. Recently, I finished a painting and I had no idea what I was doing. I thought I'd lost it, then it became something amazing. I hadn't had a drop to drink, may I add, but it gave me that sense of … wow, that warmth, that goose-pimply feeling of achievement. You do need to know when to stop, and that's often the hardest thing about doing abstract – knowing when something is complete, when to leave it alone. You have to put the brush down and say, 'That's it, it's finished, enough.' If you touch it again you might ruin it.

I tend to work on several canvasses at once because I get very bored – I start something else while the paint is drying on another canvas. I used to paint to music, but it's just pure silence for me now, just me and the paint and my surroundings.

I think painting is such a lovely medium because anyone can do it. It's just a question of having the patience, the time and some-where to go and do it. And having the confidence to go ahead and get started. I've never been to art college; everything I've learned has come from DVDs, or books, or just following my instincts. I can't draw to save my life. I love doodling, and doodling grows and grows into something else.

Even though my paintings can look chaotic, they have brought real structure into my life. My goal now is to retire at fifty and go and paint for the rest of my days. That would be really, really cool.

I used to be afraid that people would think I was an idiot or that I was up myself. You know when you go to a gallery or an exhi-bition, especially for modern or abstract art? You read the artist's mission statement and think, *What is this guy on?* I used to worry that people would think that of me. A lot of people can be quite cynical because there is a lot of pretentiousness in the art world. I

Picket, london.

think that attitude is changing, especially with contemporary Irish artists, like the late Tony O'Malley, who just did it for the love of it. His paintings are huge canvasses with amazing colour and structure. They're all about textures and are extraordinary to see. Or Sean Scully, who is deservedly celebrated. He's best known for his rectangles, oblongs and squares, but it's the sheer scale of them and the confidence that he had to go and do that – to stick to what he knows – that are the achievement, in my view.

There was another reason to keep painting. I found, over time, that it made me far more relaxed in my working life. I mean, it made me such a different person. I was no longer looking for something elusive and feeling frustrated in my day job. It definitely helped me find balance. It's a wonderful experience when you get to have a creative outlet in your life. Painting has changed me and has made me happier as a front-of-house person.

It was a great relief to have left the Clarence because it was just becoming a complete and utter rut for me. I almost got depressed about it because they weren't putting the love into the hotel. They had all these core people who had been there for years, who loved the place, but they weren't being taken care of. I'd think to myself, *Just pump in a couple of million quid and make it fantastic again while waiting for it to be revamped.* But it wasn't to be.

After the Clarence, I didn't really know where I wanted to go. At that time Marco and I were talking every day, even if only for a couple of minutes. Marco would never text. He would never even reply to a text. It would always be a conversation on the phone. I asked for his advice, and he suggested that I could come back to London.

What road should I go down? What did I want? I didn't realise it at the time, but I really, really wanted to open my own place. That was where fulfilment lay, but it took some time for it to click.

As soon as you close one door another few doors usually open, and that has always been the case for me. I got a call from Oliver Dunne, the talented chef, who was opening a new restaurant in Malahide. It was to be called Bon Appetit, and he asked me if I wanted to be his restaurant manager. I thought, *Do I really want to drive out to Malahide every day?* Then I had this notion that maybe we could move to Malahide. There were three months of preparation involved before the place actually opened, and I was given a small share of the restaurant to set up the service. They gutted a whole Georgian house and extended it to make a bigger kitchen and brasserie downstairs – the refurbishment ran for ever. I think it overran by six months.

I got really excited about that project because it was a new lease of life for me. It was a new restaurant and a new set-up, which I love. I really got the buzz back at the thought of sourcing stock, having an input into developing the whole package. I even got to do the logos, the menus and everything like that. It was very involved. I got on well with Oliver Dunne. He was very much of the old-school sort of mentality about food and was obsessed by Michelin stars. I was a bit more relaxed than that because I had done that scene. All I wanted to do was create a beautiful restaurant.

I was also asked if I would be interested in doing consultancy for the businessman Tony Ryan, who was opening the Village at Lyons in County Kildare. He was interested in making Richard Corrigan the face of its restaurant. So I went to meet with them as well.

Coming up to the middle of 2007 was a really, really good time for me. I was spending more time with the kids, and I had all these creative juices in my head. I was painting again and was feeling really happy. Settled. I had been offered the general manager's job at the Village by Tony Ryan, and since I really admired Tony and thought I would learn more, I took the job just as the Village opened.

Then Marco got in touch to talk about a little TV project called *Hell's Kitchen*. How could I refuse the opportunity? I handed in my notice to Tony and started a brand new adventure.

EGOS, SOUFFLES AND TANTRUMS

TURNING UP THE HEAT IN HELL'S KITCHEN

Marco had been approached many times before to do *Hell's Kitchen*, but before 2007 he didn't feel ready for a television commitment. Of course, he's made for television: the persona, the look, the intimidating aura. When I heard that he was to be involved in the series and that he wanted me on board, I was very excited. We did speak on the phone every day, but considering I'd been working in Ireland for years and had been out of his team for a very long time, I was quite chuffed to be asked. I think that the *Hell's Kitchen* project was a step into the unknown for him and he wanted people he could trust around him.

I wasn't the only long-term associate of Marco's who was on the show. Three sous-chefs who'd worked with him also joined the team: Matt Brown, Roger Pizey and Tim Payne. Marco chose his team wisely because they were workhorses; they knew how a kitchen functioned, knew the repertoire and could be trusted.

Marco asked me to be *maître d'* on the show, and I was thrilled, not only because it was a good gig but also because it was a chance to showcase to the public what I did as a career. I was doing consultancy work in Bon Appetit and at the Village at Lyons but decided to leave when they wouldn't give me two months off

199

to do the filming. I thought it would be good publicity for the Village, but Tony Ryan didn't agree as I hadn't been there for long enough. I had to resign, which I was quite prepared to do. I wasn't going to miss this opportunity of a lifetime to be back with Marco and the boys.

The *Hell's Kitchen* reality-TV series had been created by Gordon Ramsay and was already quite the ratings hit for ITV. It involved celebrities pitting their skills and their wits in the kitchen against each other, each trying to be the victor on the final night. After Ramsay left to develop the series in the USA, ITV tried it with Gary Rhodes and Jean-Christophe Novelli as rivals in two separate kitchens and with non-celebrities. It didn't really work. Television producers started courting Marco to get involved. It was easy to see why: as well as being very well known and respected, that long-haired, knife-wielding, volatile chef would make for great television.

Marco never liked to conform.

A lot of preparation goes into a television series that big. A trial run with non-celebrities was planned in Luciano's in St James's, one of Marco's London restaurants. The idea was to meet up with the ITV crew and see how we all performed on camera. We would have to serve thirty covers while the cameras followed us around. It was essentially to be an audition, a screen test. I was really nervous because I hadn't done any television before – apart from a quick interview for a programme on Conrad Gallagher called *True Lives: Conrad Gallagher – A Flash in the Pan?* It would be a great platform for me to go and do something new – but first I had to impress the producers.

I arrived in London the night before we were to do the trial filming run. I wanted to be fresh the next day, but it turned out to be one of the craziest nights of my life. I met Marco in another of his restaurants, Frankie's Bar & Grill in Knightsbridge, as I was supposed to be staying with him that night. We were having a great laugh, but then it started to get late and I could feel myself getting tired. I actually go a little crazy without my sleep – I can even get the shakes. Marco is a nocturnal beast. I mean, the guy just doesn't seem to need any sleep. It's extraordinary. He's the Margaret Thatcher of the restaurant business.

By the time it got to 1 a.m., I was really fading, and still trying to look on the ball. Marco was in talking mode. We must have had two gallons of tea, the head waiter was waiting to lock up, and I was thinking, *We are supposed to be up at 8 a.m. to go to Luciano's.* So 2 o'clock came, 3 o'clock came, 4 o'clock came. I said, 'Marco, are we ever going home?'

What I didn't realise was that he had had an argument with Mati, his wife, so he didn't want to go home. They had a very volatile relationship, and they even had public rows in his restaurants before their separation in late 2007. I was about to witness one of their legendary fights.

We eventually left Frankie's at 5 o'clock in the morning. We were due to be up three hours later, and I was exhausted. We got back to Marco's place in Holland Park, but when we went in Mati was there with some friends partying the night away.

Marco erupted, understandably. He shouted at Mati's friends, 'What are you doing in my home? My children are in bed.'

I thought, *This is surreal.* I was in the middle of something that I had not anticipated. To be quite honest, I was more worried about the filming the next day. I was thinking, *Why didn't I just check into a hotel?*

Of course all Marco was worried about was what was going on at that moment in his house. It was all very bizarre. The fight became much more heated and ended up outside the house. The door was open, and Marco was ordering the revellers out. Then Mati went crazy. She jumped on him and started pulling at his hair like a wildcat, and the two of them tumbled all the way down the steps in front of the house. I followed them, thinking, *What the fuck is going on here? This is just atrocious.* He screamed at me, 'Nick, get her off me, get her off me.'

She was scratching him and attacking him, and there was me trying to get her hands off. She was tugging at him, and I was tugging at her, and she started screaming at me to fuck off, that I was always fucking loyal to Marco, and so on. Then I managed to pull her hand off him, and a massive lump of his hair came along too. There was a bald patch now in the middle of his head.

Marco yelled, 'Call the police, call the police!'

Then he managed to break free from her and ran off.

There I was, thinking, *What do I do, what do I do?!* I decided to ring the police. Immediately after I did, Marco rang me on my mobile and said, 'Stop the police!'

I said, 'It's too late at this stage.'

All the while, Mati was screaming at me, going, 'He's a fucker!'

The police arrived, and I went into damage-limitation mode, saying that Mati was my girlfriend and that we had just had an argument, and apologising to them, all the while trying to calm Mati down. The police went back to their car but waited around, watching to make sure the fight was over. I was telling Mati to calm down, calm down. All that was going through my head was, *Can you imagine if Marco Pierre White didn't turn up for the*

Hell's Kitchen *audition because we were all in the police station?*
After the police left and Marco came back, the family dog Pluto
was found to be missing. So he went out looking for the dog.
Eventually he and the dog arrived back at the house, then we sat
in the lounge, drinking tea and smoking, trying to digest what had
happened. Mati was still all over the shop, shouting and arguing.

I said to him afterwards, 'Jesus, Marco, can't you see how volatile she is? You know, she is on the edge. It's not healthy for you.
It's not healthy for the children.' Of course he could see that, and I
felt really bad for him. He had to put up with that sort of treatment
when all his work, everything he did, was done for his family.

Mati and Marco had been married for about seven years,
and this was towards the end of their relationship. I think that
fight marked the beginning of the end. They had three children
together, two boys and a girl. I can't really judge their relationship,
but it was a shame how things ended up for them because they
did go so well together in the early days, but it ended up being an
unhealthy relationship for them both.

Finally we turned in, and I got about an hour's sleep on the
sofa. Then we got up and had a wash and some coffee and headed
straight into Luciano's. Marco didn't give a damn about how he
looked, and it didn't matter – because Marco is famous. He's got
money, and he is recognised. He was the main act, and producers
were desperate to have him on the show. I, on the other hand, was
a nobody who needed to make a good impression. I was shaken
and exhausted and hadn't even shaved on the day I needed to look
and behave at the top of my game. I had a shave downstairs in the
gent's toilets and got my head together to perform on camera.

We got through the screen test; it went fine. Marco was in great
form. It was just extraordinary: he had taken the events of hours
earlier in his stride and was telling everybody what had happened
to us – making it sound hilarious. He even showed everyone where

the clump of hair had been pulled out. Later he had to go to his hairdresser's to get it sorted out. That was the start of my *Hell's Kitchen* experience. Reality TV and sulky celebrities were going to be a breeze after spending a night with Marco and Mati.

To this day I still think about that night and how surreal and scary it was. I felt really bad for Marco. It was something that neither of us needed on that particular night. All that kept going through my head was, *What if we were taken to the police station?* Just how unimaginable would it have been had the story come out?

The television executives were happy with what they got on camera, and the series was given the green light to go ahead in September 2007. I was given dates and times, and plane tickets were sent. I was staying at the Hilton in Canary Wharf, and we were picked up daily and taken to the massive set at Mill Studios in the East End, where they filmed the first *Big Brother.* It was like a huge aeroplane hangar with lots of big cameras on the ceiling and a beautifully constructed restaurant on split level, which allowed for seventy covers. There were cameras everywhere, including some hidden behind mirrors. I had always been interested in how television worked, but this was my first opportunity to experience it.

The ratings for *Hell's Kitchen* were up to 6 million people. I never knew which way it was going to go for me. It's not just a question of being self-conscious. How was I going to be perceived? How was I going to be edited? I quickly realised that I just had to be professional and do my job – we were still serving and feeding a lot of people – and try to forget about the cameras. Marco's mantra was 'Ignore the cameras: we are here to do a job,' and that's basically the mindset that we had.

The series lasted for seventeen days. Cameras would film the entire day over a twenty-four-hour period, then a team of editors would work on the day's footage so viewers could see what had unfolded amongst the contestants in the kitchen earlier that day.

When the guests came in to be fed we went into working-restaurant mode, and that was edited and broadcast the following night.

At the start I thought that everything was live, but it wasn't. When presenter Angus Deayton was on camera, that was when we were being broadcast live. It may as well all have been live though, because everything we did was recorded. Our every move was filmed, and it took me a while to get used to the camera angles and how to behave and not behave. Everything we said was recorded too. We used to have our microphones on all day, and we were told to keep them on, except when we were going to the toilet, because the editors wanted to hear what we were saying.

The sous-chefs used to get up at 6 o'clock in the morning to start preparations. Those guys were on another level when it came to long hours: they were like the diehards, the SAS of the kitchen. The three of them were no-nonsense characters, and they just got on with the job. If they weren't happy they would speak their minds. They were there to teach the celebrities how to cook and how to run a station.

Hell's Kitchen was run as a proper restaurant, and the kitchen was staffed by celebrities who didn't have a clue about cooking. Sure, they might cook at home, but cooking covers for seventy people is a completely different ball game. The chefs ran the training in the sections, kept everything tight and made sure the *mise en place* (the organisation of ingredients and equipment) was ready for that night's service. They worked the kitchen as if it was a normal operating kitchen. The meat was to be cut in a certain way. The fish was to be filleted in a certain way. Believe me, there was no scope for make-believe there.

Given that Marco Pierre White is a control freak, it came as no surprise to me that having to work under the control of TV producers gave him a headache. He thought that everyone was against him and that there was some sort of conspiracy going on.

If his gas cooker wasn't working, for example, he would get para-
noid about it. Any time we went out for little talks he'd say, 'Make
sure your microphone is off. I don't want them to listen to what
we have to say. Tonight we are going to do this, and we are going
to make it easier for ourselves to do it this way.' There were always
little game plans going on between us.

Marco started off very tough: no talking in the kitchen. Then
he was told that the show needed to have everyone talking. The
kitchen was surrounded by rows of moving cameras on tracks,
ready to record every single remark and conversation. There was
nowhere to hide, and even a remark muttered under your breath
could be picked up. The no-talking-in-the-kitchen rule was very
short-lived.

People tend to think that reality TV is an oxymoron and that
in fact a lot of string-pulling, set-ups and scripting goes on behind
the scenes. While the show was edited to include the juicy bits
– otherwise, it would just have been boring – there was very little manipulation going on at all. They didn't need to take that
approach because of the kind of show it was. It was a scenario set
in a kitchen and restaurant, so situations just evolved. Pans full of
food got dropped. People burnt their fingers and swore. People
fought. That's what the producers wanted because it made good
television, but these things happen naturally in every restaurant
on any given night of the week, especially if you're working with
inexperienced people, so they didn't need to be contrived.

Having said that, the producers and the show's format did
push us to the limits. The celebrities and professionals were working every day. I got tired, working under pressure from 10 a.m.
until 2 the following morning. Try doing that for seventeen days
in a row and you will have some idea of how I felt.

The celebrities certainly didn't have an easy time of it either.
In Gordon Ramsay's time, they used to start a bit later in the after-

noon whereas with Marco they started at 8 o'clock in the morning and worked all day. They would have an hour-long break in the afternoon to have lunch and then would be back on for the evening service. Marco would do a demonstration and would supervise throughout the day.

The majority of the prep work would have been done behind the scenes, but the contestants learned how to prepare and run the work stations and how to cook. Then they would be put into teams with other celebrities with whom they may or may not get along. They did need to be really strong-minded to get through it. I think some of them got into a mental state where they were hoping to be kicked out, but then often the public would vote them back in – either because they liked their personality or because they wanted to see them suffer and they would only get more and more demoralised. Yes, the celebrities were getting paid and were upping their profile, but it really was very hard work for them. I don't think they realised it was going to be such a tough environment that year.

I had a team of agency staff who helped me with dinner service. Every day I arrived at 10 a.m. I used to polish the plates to make sure the preparation was perfect, then I'd make tea and look after the celebrities. Things would intensify at around 6 o'clock when the first customers arrived. There was a green room where they would have champagne before the service started.

It became a hot table in London for dinner because you could only get tickets if you had connections with or were part of the ITV network. We would also have the invited families and friends of the celebrities who were cooking. Producers were very keen on having well-known or flamboyant personalities at the restaurant to keep the service footage lively, and there was a whole team in the production office ringing up agents to see which celebrity was available to come and eat on any given night.

Because the first show, where Marco asked someone to leave, had such an impact, a lot of celebrities and A-listers were afraid to come and eat at the *Hell's Kitchen* restaurant. They didn't want to be embarrassed or kicked out. The result was that the producers only managed to get the C, D and E list: a lot of soap stars – *Emmerdale*, *Coronation Street*, the usual suspects. I'd say the really big stars were too spooked to come along once they had seen what had happened to the man who complained about the asparagus.

This hadn't been planned, but I knew from the way Marco worked that if someone complained he wasn't going to take any

nonsense. One of the diners, David Minchin, the husband of TV presenter Louise, complained to me that his starter of asparagus was cold, tasteless and bland. I thought to myself, *That's very strange, because the asparagus is served warm, with a very tasty hollandaise sauce.*

I said, 'It is fresh, new-season asparagus, so I don't understand your point. What do you want me to do?'

He replied, 'Get Marco out here.'

I said, 'I'm not prepared to do that. If you want to complain, off you go and complain at the pass.'

He stayed put, so eventually I gave up and went up to the pass to communicate his complaint. I knew exactly what was going to happen. Marco said the customer could either shut up, or leave. That was my signal. So I got a waiter and said, 'Follow me.'

I went back to the table and said, 'There was nothing wrong with the dish, it was perfectly cooked. I think that you have upset your own evening, and we won't be serving you any more food. We would like you to leave the table.'

David went up to the pass to talk to Marco. He was very unhappy at being asked to leave and didn't want to feel he'd lost the argument. Nobody wants to be told off, do they? Marco was prepared because it's something that he has done for years at his restaurants. When David went up, Marco immediately made a reference to his pink shirt, slagging it off. Whatever David came out with next, he was already on the back foot: he was always going to lose. They had a terse exchange of words, and David left with his wife. I don't know whether he had been egged on, if he wanted a bit of publicity or if he was just showing off to his friends. Either way, it made good TV. I have to admit it left me on a high. It's liberating if you can turn the tables on someone who is not there to enjoy himself.

The moment a customer went up the pass he or she was basically dead meat as far as I was concerned. Don't forget, when you walk up to the pass, everything looks enormous, not least Marco. He is in his element there, and he knows exactly what he is going to say. He is in supreme control. People often went up to the pass on *Hell's Kitchen*, probably because they were well known themselves and thought they could take on Marco. Marco would just say something caustic and walk away, leaving them standing there with the cameras rolling.

Now you can understand why A-listers were so reluctant to come on the show. They saw something like that unfolding in the very first episode and thought to themselves, *My God, I'm not going to go through that.*

Other diners on *Hell's Kitchen* were given the table-clearing treatment. John McCririck, an odd man and well-known horse-racing pundit, was making noise from the moment he arrived. He came with his wife, and it was obvious from the minute he sat down that he wanted to create a fuss. He had actually brought a hamper filled with food, including lobster, and when he sat down at his table he placed it next to him. He announced that this was going to be his backup should he not be fed to his liking. He had dined in *Hell's Kitchen* before, when Gordon Ramsay was cooking, and didn't get fed on that occasion. I made a joke about it, gave him a chair for his hamper and added, 'I'm sure we will be serving you on time tonight, Mr McCririck.'

The *Hell's Kitchen* menu was quite simple and always focused on tried and tested dishes. This was typical Marco: simple cooking at its best. There was a mushroom consommé with truffle oil and a puff-pastry case. A lovely soup. When I took the order, John said that he didn't want the puff-pastry case. Marco refused to change the dish because that was the way it was prepared, and, in any case, if John didn't want to eat the pastry top then he could just leave it to one side. When I served the soup, John complained that it looked greasy.

I explained, 'No, it's not greasy. That's the truffle oil.'

He sent it back, and Marco told him to fuck off. John got his desired moment on camera, saying, 'I've been kicked out, and I only had a starter and the starter wasn't even good. Blah blah.'

What I didn't realise then was that Marco and John McCririck are actually good friends – they have lunch together once a month. Marco clearly realised that John was just trying it on.

Those early *Hell's Kitchen* days were odd for me as I was still trying to find my place within the whole reality-TV format, to figure out what was real, what wasn't, and who I could trust. Looking back, I'm sorry I didn't push myself more from early on and treat it as a performance, because that's what others were doing – especially Marco. I definitely went more for the entertainment element down the line, which I really enjoyed, but early on I just did my job on the shop floor.

I've always said that a restaurant is like a theatre. You've got an audience sitting there, and you are performing. When that restaurant is being filmed, it does add to the adrenalin rush, much as you try to forget the cameras are there. I was more fearful of Marco than I was of the cameras, if that makes sense, because he really is the most intimidating man. You never know what he is thinking, and – this is the worst part about it – if you say something he doesn't agree with, he'll just say 'That's stupid! What did you say that for?' It used to make me even more conscious of what I said to him. That was the most draining, tiring thing for me: to try not to say anything stupid. I'm sure it is for most people who know Marco.

As I got to know the crew a little better, we started to have a good deal more fun, fooling around off camera. Unfortunately, this meant that they liked to play pranks on me. At the end of each evening's service, I would read out customer comments on the food, which were given to me on cue cards. I was asked to do it once, and it worked well so I continued throughout the series. I didn't like to read them in advance as I wanted it to sound natural and spontaneous on camera, but I can have difficulty pronouncing some words so I asked the production staff to write them simply, so I wouldn't get stuck midway through a sentence. This they did until they realised it would be much more fun to confuse me and to put in flowery words that they knew I would have difficulty with. I knew then that they were up to no good so I started reading the cards as soon as I got them (usually five minutes before going on air). One night I was handed six cards and told not to read the last one in advance as it was a surprise for the celebs. I smelled a rat of course and decided to read out whatever was on it in my best French accent: *'Nick is fit, is he looking for a chick? I don't like my steak but I'm looking for a mate. I want to move to Dublin to get me some lovin'. I don't like tart but I do like art. The only way I roll is with a large pole.'* Childish? Yes. But funny.

There was a great mix of people in that series. The research team chose very well. There were ten contestants in all: singer

Paul Young; TV presenter Anneka Rice; comedian Jim Davidson; journalist Rosie Boycott; Lee Ryan, the pop singer from Blue; Adele Silva, the former *Emmerdale* actress; model Abigail Clancy; TV presenter Brian Dowling; actress Kelly LeBrock; and boxer Barry McGuigan.

I really liked Paul Young. A good man, but a very shy guy, which surprised me given his showbiz career. It's funny when the persona doesn't match the personality. For him it was all about the cooking. He was obsessed with cooking and was there to learn. Then you had the likes of Adele Silva, very bubbly – she also wanted to prove that she could cook. Rosie Boycott found the going a bit tough, but she took it seriously and was determined to try her best. She impressed Marco. He really got on well with her even though she didn't last long. Then you had Brian, who was just hilarious, a real extrovert. I liked Brian. He brought his colourful persona, and lots of laughs, to the table. He was always so funny with innuendos and that kind of thing. It livens up a day, and, because he's so camp, he can get away with murder. Brian is very full on – too full on for some people, which became very apparent as the show progressed. But I loved that about him.

And then we had Jim Davidson. Jim is a comedian by trade, but in his daily interaction Jim just wasn't funny. The series ended badly for him when he was axed after a series of rows with Brian which turned ugly when he branded gay people 'shirt-lifters', and Brian was very insulted and upset. It caused a huge fuss in the media at the time – and, of course, huge ratings for the show.

Jim was always very respectful to me, always very nice. That's why when that 'shirt-lifting' story came out, I thought Brian might have taken it too far. It's such an old turn of phrase, I think even I would have said it. It's the kind of old-fashioned language Jim Davidson used to use but now, because everything is politically correct, he can't. Is it offensive? I don't know. I think trouble had been brewing between them for some time, and it all spilled over on the night of the shirt-lifter incident.

The editing on a show like *Hell's Kitchen* can make you look bad or good, but the fact remains that you've said what you've said. Even Barry and Paul, who had mixed feelings about political correctness, tried to tell Jim to calm things down a bit. I can't speak for the millions of people who watched it. Everyone will have their take on it. But I think that once Brian said he was offended it had to be investigated.

Sexuality and gay rows aside, I think a lot of the younger contestants just didn't like Jim. You have different generations and different views on what's OK to say and what isn't. I'm sure in a lot of people's minds Jim Davidson was rude and offensive. Brian is an extrovert and maybe mucked about too much in the kitchen for Jim's liking. Jim couldn't cope with that. I believe what happened started with a personality clash and then escalated into Jim saying things he shouldn't have said.

You could see that the producers considered it to be TV gold because the whole story was so drawn out. Let's face it, if you're not getting anything from the main act, you go to the side acts. I do think they might have taken it a bit too far though.

Marco loved Jim, and it even became a running joke in the series – their affection for each other. Again, they knew each other out of the kitchen. I think Jim looked up to Marco, and Marco loved Jim's sense of humour.

I got to know the celebrities more as the nights progressed. What viewers see, obviously, is an edited version of the day, but when you're spending hours and hours in close proximity with people you get to know what makes them tick and what they're about.

The only person in that series who I found difficult to warm to was the young guy from Blue, Lee Ryan. I just didn't understand what his agenda was, where he was coming from. He wasn't a very disciplined chap. To me, he came across as someone who happened to make good with a boy band and who was then looking for a way to survive in the celebrity world. He had such a chip on his shoulder. One day Marco asked him to put his hat on, which is really essential for health and hygiene reasons, and he refused point blank to do so.

Then there was a remark about Travellers which caused a bit of fuss. One night, Marco was talking about service, and he said, 'I don't think it was a pikey's picnic tonight.' Lee became very annoyed about this, saying that he had friends who were Travellers and that he considered the term derogatory. Marco didn't agree with him. We were going through the diners' verdicts when Marco came out with that, and I didn't think it was offensive. But it was blown out of proportion, and it was in the papers the next day. We were even told there was going to be a security alert as there were apparently 250 Travellers coming down to Mill Studios to protest, but that turned out to be a hoax. Lee tried to get Marco to apologise in the office afterwards, but that was never going to happen. They had a very heated row where Marco told Lee he wasn't part of the team, and Lee walked out of the show. A bit silly really, but probably for the best. He came across as being a little angry. I think his agenda was to leave anyway.

I really liked Anneka Rice. She's a lovely woman, very gentle (perhaps too gentle for a show like *Hell's Kitchen*). She worked very hard, but she just couldn't cope with the heat, the demands of service, the stress, the timing, the chaos. Anneka lasted for a good stretch of the show, but when the group got smaller and smaller as people were voted out, the workload got greater and greater, and I did feel for her.

Barry McGuigan brought his world-champion skills with him and ended up winning the show. Viewers were captivated by him. We became good friends. I think we clicked because of the Irish connection. I had been living in Dublin for many years, and he knew the city well. He was interested in my wife's family background too because Denise is originally from Enniskillen and he grew up just twenty-three miles away, on the other side of the border in Clones. Barry is such a good person – I mean, he hasn't got a wicked bone in his body.

Barry was obsessed with getting his mashed potatoes just right. It was hilarious, the level of his fixation. Actually, with foodies, *pommes purée* is a more accurate term than 'mash'. It's a much smoother mixture, made with the right kind of potato and with lots of butter and cream. To make it really fluffy, it has to be continuously whisked to a smooth paste until it's almost dripping off the spoon. It's all in the wrist and arm action.

Barry's mash became famous, and with good reason – oh my God, it was better than Marco's. I'm telling you, everyone who came through the doors of *Hell's Kitchen* wanted to sample Barry's mash. It was a kitchen recipe, but he perfected it to a tee. I think he applied the same focus that made him a world champion into conquering his spuds. Barry used to joke – at least, I think he was joking – that it was harder to do mashed potato for seventy covers than nine rounds in a boxing match. Given Barry's way with spuds, I always thought that he was going to brand McGuigan's Mash after the show. It would have been an ideal platform for him, but he never did it. His wife Sandra is now involved in making cup cakes, and Barry still does his after-dinner speeches and his boxing training.

I didn't get to know Angus Deayton very well, but I thought he was good on *Hell's Kitchen*. He was very deadpan, like the character he played in *One Foot in the Grave*, Victor Meldrew's next-door neighbour. A very witty and caustic man. I liked the fact that he kept a distance and didn't interact with the customers because it felt like he was floating around, detached, overseeing everything. Angus would always stay in his personal trailer until he was ready to come out and would go over his lines meticulously. We never actually got to see him until he came on the set shortly before filming. He was always very polite to me but that was as far as it went. It was a hello-and-goodnight scenario.

Oddly, he never spoke to Marco once. Marco took one of his dislikes to Angus, I have no idea why. Angus used to keep to himself in any case, so their paths didn't cross. They just didn't connect, but I preferred him as a format presenter.

Since *Hell's Kitchen*, I've become known as the *maître d'* who falls over a lot. I never knew I was clumsy and prone to falling over until I started to do it on live television. Honestly, I wasn't known for dropping trays or tripping, but point a camera at me and over I go. Before, I would have the odd incident where I would drop a tray or tumble over a chair. It was only when I started doing it on national television that I realised, *Nick, you are actually quite clumsy*.

I always walk into chairs now – quite bizarre. Or sometimes my feet knock off things and I go sprawling. I think it's that sense of service being like Groundhog Day for me. When I'm doing the same thing, day in, day out, my mind drifts, and that's when objects pop up out of nowhere for me to fall over.

When I first took a tumble on *Hell's Kitchen*, we were having a very stressful service. I think we had just cleared the table of some troublesome customers and had asked them to leave. There was a very busy twenty minutes of madness, the waiters weren't taking the food out quick enough, and I was trying to do some damage limitation by taking orders. In the first series, I did everything myself: orders, clearing, service. I was running that room with a team of staff who were quite young and who we didn't have time to train fully. There was a particular style of service that

I knew Marco wanted: quite detailed, presenting the plate with two hands, elegantly positioned on the table, with etiquette. It couldn't just be, 'Here's your food, bye!'

I remember taking the tray, which held two shepherd's pies. There was a flight of coloured plastic steps, like you'd get in a nightclub, and I was wearing leather-soled shoes. The steps were quite slippery. Honestly they were. As I was trying to position the tray on the stand I completely missed the first step and just went flying. All that crossed my mind was, *Shit, I've just fallen over on national TV.* I remember Jean-Christophe Novelli came up to help me. I was fine – I had just put my elbow in the shepherd's pie. My ego was bruised though – it was so embarrassing. I find it really funny now, but it wasn't at the time. The worst thing was having to go back to the kitchen to ask for two new dishes when they were already under such pressure and were trying to get everything ready.

That incident confirmed that I was quite clumsy, and it has now happened on a few other occasions. The more you think about it, the more you are going to fall over because you become so self-conscious. Some of my more spectacular tumbles have even ended up on YouTube. My comic hero is Tommy Cooper, but maybe it should really be Buster Keaton.

In another Buster Keaton-style episode on *Hell's Kitchen*, I somehow managed to fall over while sitting on a chair. I was in Marco's office for a meeting about the menu or a task, something like that. I knew the chair was a bit wonky, but forgot, and when I leaned back the chair tipped over and I ended up doing this Olympic-style somersault where my legs went over my head and I landed on a pile of bottles.

Marco, being Marco, just looked at me and said, 'Genius!' and we both started laughing. Only later did I realise that there was a stag's-head-style ornament on a shelf just inches from where I went over, and I was very glad I didn't get an antler in the skull.

While I value my profession, I couldn't take myself too seriously while I was doing a show like *Hell's Kitchen*. I did try my best to be an old pro, but I also had to be prepared to have a skit at myself. It didn't bother me at all: in fact, I quite enjoyed it. If you haven't got a sense of humour then what have you? Take, for example, the moniker that still follows me to this day, courtesy of a droll comment made by Angus Deayton. After one of my many tumbles was caught on camera, Deayton remarked, 'Of course in his *Thunderbirds* days his strings would have held him up.' I didn't take offence at all to it – it was a very funny gag – because ultimately it was nice to be acknowledged and recognised. The reference makes sense because of my glasses and the way I glide around. I have been called Joe 90 in the past, after the bespectacled character in the 1960s TV series, but *Thunderbirds* was a first. I still get people referring to the puppets and the falling over and I should have gone to Specsavers and all that kind of stuff, and I play along with that because I quite like it. I mean, why would you be precious about it? It's all fun, and I've always been a slapstick, *Fawlty Towers* kind of guy.

Take, for example, forgetting an order. What's the best thing to do? Sulk about it or go back to the table and make a joke? I like the whole comic side of the job, and, as I get older, I definitely feel the restaurant industry should embrace humour more.

The falling and the *Thunderbirds* thing did lead to me getting an increased profile on *Hell's Kitchen*. They asked me to do a four-minute slot about my role within the restaurant, which was great because one of my reasons for going on the programme was to showcase the service side of things. Angus had picked up on something that I was doing that would appeal to the public. People liked it and found it funny and I couldn't have a problem with that.

Years later, I did a show with Paul Young and Barry McGuigan in Derry called *The Fabulous Food Adventure*. I was asked to come on as a cameo to re-enact our days on *Hell's Kitchen.* It was really nice to see them again and to have a drink afterwards and swap stories. I also did RTÉ's *Afternoon Show.* Barry McGuigan and presenter Bláthnaid Ní Chofaigh were going to play this new Wii boxing game, and as a surprise for Barry the producers asked me to come in to judge. For a laugh, I had a T-shirt printed with 'Barry's Mash Is the Best Smash,' but the producers said they'd rather that I wore a shirt and bow tie to look like a traditional boxing judge.

As I walked onto live television, I hit a shiny surface and slipped. All they wanted was for me to play a distinguished umpire, and there I was, skidding onto set. Bláthnaid and Barry started the boxing contest. I couldn't pronounce Bláthnaid's name, and I was going, 'Bla … een … nee … een.' I was reading off a cue card, and they said to me, 'Don't read the cue card, we want you to read off the Autocue, on the camera.'

I wasn't told which Autocue it was. Because I was nervous, I started reading the first one I clapped eyes on, and when I got to the bit where it read, 'Nick will now present an award,' I said, live on air, 'Nick will now present an award.'

I thought, *What the fuck have I done?* But it was hilarious. Later, friends sent me text messages mostly consisting of the words 'you', 'fucking' and 'idiot'.

The entrance to l'Ecrivain on Dublin's Baggot Street.

BOILING POINT

THINGS GET HOT IN L'ECRIVAIN

By the end of *Hell's Kitchen*, I found myself in the peculiar situation of being a minor celebrity. The show generated huge ratings and media interest, and I was on television every day for seventeen days to an average audience of 4 or 5 million people. It was a huge success, and it certainly upped my profile. It's not that I was thinking, *Oh I'm a big star now*, but when something is successful in that way, it gets you wondering what else might be out there and what other ways can you capitalise on the level of public interest.

Still, I resigned myself to the idea that I would be going back to a safe, regular job as soon as filming ended. At this time, Denise was working as a receptionist at l'Ecrivain, and the owners, Derry and Sallyanne Clarke, expressed an interest in my coming to work for them. To be really honest, *Hell's Kitchen* pays quite well, and I would have loved to have taken a holiday after the intensity of a month of television work, but I wasn't stupid enough to risk a secure job in a top restaurant.

I went to meet the Clarkes at Dublin's Citywest Hotel where they explained that they needed a general manager who would take them to the next level – the next level being two Michelin stars. They had some good ideas about redesigning the restaurant and were prepared to match what money I had recently been on. It all seemed quite straightforward, and Denise thought it was a good move for me, so we shook on it. Little did I know then that it would lead to one of the rockiest periods of my professional career and end acrimoniously within a matter of months.

At first, the more I thought about it, the more I became quite excited by the prospect. It would be good to go for two stars, to work somewhere new, to experience the foodie culture again. I thought it would be quite a good move, and there weren't many jobs flying around at that time.

L'Ecrivain is a very well-oiled machine. It's a success story – it's been going now for twenty-odd years. It has stood the test of time and is in a nice setting in its own little courtyard, on the site of two old Georgian coach houses. Because it's located in a very fashionable part of Baggot Street, off St Stephen's Green, it also attracts a good mix of clientele. The Clarkes have a very good reputation, and, while I didn't know much about the ins and outs of the new job, or the personalities involved, I wasn't hugely concerned about that.

But almost from the off, I struggled to fit in. It was weird. I tried to ignore it and didn't allow it to affect my performance or my job. I put it down to fatigue from doing the television work and that I just needed time to settle in.

Derry and Sallyanne Clarke are themselves extremely well known in Dublin business and social circles. What I wasn't sure of was whether they liked me and my work or liked the fact that I had been on this huge TV show. I think to some extent, l'Ecrivain capitalised on *Hell's Kitchen*. That's fine; it goes with the territory of being associated with a particular programme. Everyone wanted to know what Marco Pierre White was like, and Derry, being a huge fan of Marco (most chefs are) was intrigued, too.

What concerned me was that it was usually brought to the attention of guests that I was the *maître d'* from *Hell's Kitchen* and that they were having an added bonus to their dinner. They wanted to know all about the show. The majority of people coming into the restaurant were intrigued and excited, and that's understandable. If you see someone on TV and then you see them working in a restaurant, that's of interest. One of the most bizarre things for me was that customers started asking me to sign Derry's book, which was on sale in the restaurant. I felt quite uncomfortable because it is his restaurant, and I think it created conflict, although Derry didn't say anything. I just got an awkward feeling. I thought it was quite surreal.

During my time at l'Ecrivain the Clarkes would try to get every single newspaper to report the fact that I was their restaurant manager and that I had been *maître d'* of *Hell's Kitchen*. I was quite happy to go along. I was getting extremely well paid and was conscious of the fact. What I didn't expect, because I had wanted to increase the profile, was that it caused me some anxiety. I felt like, not a performing seal exactly, but the guy from *Hell's Kitchen* who slipped on the floor.

It was very hard for me to get the staff on board when it came to new habits. The Clarkes had told me that they wanted me to change the service and to improve it. But it didn't seem that way in practice. It was a close-knit community, and I felt quite the outsider. I was also trying to ascertain when we were going to go ahead with redecorating the restaurant. I was keen to be involved in creating the look of the place as we had discussed at that first meeting.

There were a couple of incidents which didn't help in my attempts to fit in with the service ethos of the restaurant and settle into my new job. I remember one occasion when the restaurant was hosting a charity lunch and we ended up having a row.

I was working upstairs, preparing for a busy service, when a photographer asked me if I would have my photograph taken downstairs with Sallyanne and Derry. In the photos we are all smiling, and I am standing in between them. I have to admit I felt a bit uncomfortable. Then, to my mortification, the photographer asked them to step out of the way to take a picture of myself and Denise. This gave me an enormous sense of unease. I already felt I was treading a fine line, and in a situation like that it's hard to gauge what's OK and what isn't. Yes, I was happy that *Hell's Kitchen* had enhanced my profile. Yes, the Clarkes were getting good media from my appointment. But ultimately this was their restaurant.

Later on that day, Derry and I had a terse exchange of words about issues with service that left me feeling very upset.

For all that, I knew it would be terrible to just walk away, so I went out and took a few breaths, came back in and tried to get back to work. When I went outside, Stephen Gibson, one of the chefs, was arriving on his bike, and I was able to have a cooling-down chat with him.

After composing myself, I went back into the restaurant. I had given a painting of mine to be auctioned for the charity. A nice piece. Sallyanne was there as well. She was talking to the guests about this picture, and she just handed me the microphone and said, 'You can talk to these people about your piece of art for the charity.' I was in no frame of mind to do it, but I had to stand there with the microphone and talk about the painting.

I will never forget the simmering feelings of tension between the Clarkes and me that day, and I think this was the moment that it began to dawn on me that my position there was not going to last. It just seemed like there was a massive personality clash and for all of my years working with different characters I couldn't see a way forward.

That day when I got home I said to Denise that I felt the Clarkes and I were not going to work out. She said, 'Just stick it out. You need a job. You need the money. Think of your family.'

I tried to stay the distance, but things never really improved from then on. I used to dread going in there. Usually I'm excited about going into work, so this was not a feeling I was used to at all.

Was it a personality clash? Bad timing? The wrong place at the wrong stage of my life? I've played it over many times in my head, and I don't know. I think it was a series of different elements. For example, I believed that Sallyanne was going to be taking a back seat and that I would have an input into where the restaurant was going as they worked towards two stars. Sallyanne was a front-of-house person, and she would turn up whenever she wanted, which, as co-owner, she was entitled to do, but it got me thinking, *Who is in charge here?*

In the end, the decision about whether I could or should stay working at l'Ecrivain was made for me. They let me go two weeks before Christmas. Derry had indicated that he felt it was not working out, and days later, following another acrimonious exchange of words, I realised the situation was hopeless and my days at the restaurant finished within a matter of months of my starting there. It was a stressful, depressing time, but something really good came out of my brief stint at l'Ecrivain: I met and clicked with the talented young chef with whom I would later end up going into business.

As I was leaving, Stephen Gibson said to me, 'I'm really sorry what has happened to you but please keep in contact, and if you ever want to do something, call me.'

The whole thing was hard on Denise because she had been working there for five years before I started. But she too had decided it was time to move on, and she left the restaurant shortly before I did, after having her own disagreement with the owners.

I don't want to sound like I've been harbouring a grudge against the Clarkes all of this time. I really haven't. But I still wonder why the clash was so spectacular. I think the personalities involved were a huge element. The Clarkes were not ready to have a manager come in and offer ideas as to how the restaurant should be run, even though that was what I thought they wanted. What was more, there was a very tightly knit group in l'Ecrivain, and if you don't go along with their train of thought, you can't stay.

In twenty years of working with very different people, I still regard that period as the lowest point in my career. With the benefit of hindsight, I think I committed too soon to l'Ecrivain because subconsciously I knew that I really didn't want to work there. Maybe I was chasing the money, maybe it was because Denise wanted me to go and work there, but I wasn't being true to myself. Perhaps that came across to them very early on. I wanted to do a nice job, enjoy the customers, enjoy the restaurant and maybe improve the service because I very much liked the kitchen staff (Stephen Gibson is, of course, co-owner of Pichet, and another ex-l'Ecrivain guy, Alan, also works there now). It had seemed like the right choice, but then it didn't work out that way. At the time it was a horrible experience, but I'm now glad that I got out of there quickly because it helped reaffirm the long-niggling idea that maybe I should look at opening my own restaurant.

There was a lot of rubbish again when I set up Pichet in 2009, claims that I was deliberately poaching l'Ecrivain's staff, as though it were some sort of revenge. That would be a ridiculous way of doing business. In any case, you don't poach people's staff. They come and work with you if they want to, if the pay's good, if they're interested in where you're going and what you're trying to achieve. Stephen was chef at l'Ecrivain, but we had a shared dream of opening a restaurant together for some time. To say he was poached is daft. He wanted a change and to set up his own business.

I was bound to run into Derry Clarke eventually. I mean, Dublin's city centre is a small place as it is, and when you all work in the restaurant trade you tend to move in many of the same circles. In summer 2009, we met at the food event, A Taste of Dublin. Stephen and I were in the process of setting up Pichet and were there to showcase the restaurant. Stephen was doing a demonstration, and I was helping him to carry the food. As I was carrying things through, I saw Derry there, chatting to him. I just went over and shook his hand, and we started chatting as if nothing had happened, which was a bit bizarre. He has actually come into the restaurant on one occasion since. So I feel we have buried the hatchet. I did it for Stephen and Denise and for the good of the business. You never know when you are going to meet these people again, and you have to put a brave face on it.

No hard feelings. Derry comes to dinner at Pichet.

While it was nice to spend those few Christmas weeks with the kids, I was quite worried. Denise had also given up her job, so times were very hard. I felt at my very lowest in my career and really didn't know what to do. Work offers were coming in, but everything was short term and was trying to capitalise on *Hell's Kitchen*, which I was wary of doing after the l'Ecrivain experience. I have no grounds to complain about that: it was a journey I took and tried to use to my advantage, even if it appeared to have backfired.

One good thing came out of the whole sorry incident. For the first time in my career I had two weeks off in what is normally one of the busiest times – just before Christmas – to spend with the kids. Of course I was concerned about what I was going to do and where money was going to come from, but I had the best Christmas with my family. And I took up my passion for painting again, just to have a creative outlet and to ease the pressure.

I was keen to explore the option of exhibiting and selling my work. It was very, very difficult to break into the art world in Dublin. It's a conservative scene, and it can take years for people to establish themselves. Because I was unproven and was better known for working in restaurants than as an artist, I found it very hard to be taken seriously. Everyone in Dublin said, 'No.' One day, on spec, I walked around the city in the pouring rain, carrying two paintings wrapped in bin bags, and knocked on gallery doors. I must have looked quite mad, and the gallery owners must have thought, *Who is this wet rat arriving in my shop?* The first thing they generally said was, 'Sorry, not today. No, we don't even want to see your art.' It was demoralising.

But a breakthrough came eventually. I used to get my pictures and other photographs framed in Kimmage, by a very old family firm called Gallery 23. I had gone to them because they had a great reputation and decades of experience. I got chatting to the owner, Greg Muldowney. He asked me to bring more paintings and loved them. Greg said, 'I'll represent you, I'll take you on. I love your stuff.'

It gave me huge confidence to be able to show my paintings to people who liked them. The Muldowney sons set up this new gallery in Blanchardstown, in an industrial estate – not the most fashionable location, but it has a terrific gallery space. They started talking about me doing an exhibition.

It was just an amazing feeling, being able to work towards my first exhibition. The idea of showcasing my own artwork excited me beyond belief. I got very nervous and anxious about it because it was so new to me and I was unsure of myself. I thought, *Am I worthy? Am I worthy?* The art world can be so elitist! Before this, the only people who had really seen my paintings were Denise and our friends.

While twenty years' experience in running restaurants gives you an air of certainty, confidence and self-belief, my feelings coming up to my first exhibition were the exact opposite. Even though I had a certain amount of faith in what I was doing, I was ultimately hoping that other people would like my work. I was putting something very personal forward to be criticised. It was a massive step into the unknown.

Barry McGuigan came to launch the exhibition for me, and we sold 80 per cent of the paintings. It was a magical feeling. People were saying that they had bought paintings because they loved them (as opposed to buying them because they just felt sorry for me!), which was fantastic. There's no hiding place in art, you see. It doesn't matter if you're a well-known restaurateur and the fella off the telly from *Hell's Kitchen*. People have to look at those paintings on their walls every day, so if they don't respond

Pulling no punches. Barry McGuigan opens my first art exhibition.

emotionally to a work, if they don't like it, they're sure as hell not going to buy it. So selling so many paintings was a great affirmation.

I remember talking to the painter Guggi about it one night in the Clarence. He talked about how the most amazing feeling you can ever get is when you sell that first painting. 'They can take anything away from you,' he said, 'but if you sell one painting you know that you've done something good and someone wanted to buy it.' His words have always stayed with me.

I reminded Guggi of that conversation when I met him recently, and he said he still feels the same way when someone buys a piece of his work. It was a lovely nugget of advice to be given when I was starting off.

Painting has been a real release for me, and it's a bonus that I have enjoyed some success with it. For four years in a row we went to the Gallery Trail, an art fair in Arundel, East Sussex. Every year, they turn the town into an art gallery. You pay an exhibition fee and someone sponsors you by showing your work in their house. There's a map that people follow to go to different houses and see different artists. I've sold my wares there, then I got into painting T-shirts for kids, which went down very well. I've also done a couple of group exhibitions in Dublin, and slowly word of mouth has built up about my work. People have often asked me to do special commissions. I also used to sell my paintings in Habitat before it closed. It was such a shame; I used to sell a piece a week there. I exhibited again in Dublin at Gallery 23 early in 2010 and was really pleased with the reaction.

Over time, I've been able to do other art-related projects through people I know in the restaurant industry. I did the art-work for the menus for Bon Appetit in Malahide. Brasserie 15 has menu covers I created and a piece of my art on the wall. Ivan's in Howth also has a piece of mine. It's a great feeling whenever my two worlds become linked in that way.

When Stephen and I were opening Pichet it seemed natural to create something to hang in the restaurant. I decided to paint a specific piece which took me three anxious months to complete, but it came out well, and everyone seems to like it. It represents the clatter, the noise, the environment of a restaurant. It's abstract, but if you delve into it you can see different things: it's a bottle, it's a glass, it's a bowl, it's a bunch of flowers. And it fits so perfectly in Pichet. Some customers of ours, who own a gallery, offered me art for the walls, and it was really satisfying to be able to say, 'Thanks, but I do my own painting.'

Pride of place in the Pichet dining room.

LIKE A VIRGIN VODKA ON THE ROCKS

MADONNA'S CHRISTMAS PARTY

After leaving l'Ecrivain, I was feeling quite battered by my experiences and was facing into a very uncertain time in my life. I had been talking to Marco, as a friend and former boss, about where to turn next. Marco wanted me back in London. It just wasn't an option at that stage. Moving back to the UK would have been far too great an upheaval for us. Besides, we were very much settled in Dublin, and I felt very happy there.

It was flattering how much Marco wanted me to return. He even suggested that I commute from Dublin, fly out on Monday mornings, work five days with him and fly back home on Friday nights. Crazy as it now sounds, I briefly toyed with the idea and wondered if I could make it feasible. It would have been a really bad call. It would have been too much of a strain – on me, on Denise, on our family. How long could you sustain that sort of schedule? Would your marriage founder? Would the kids be upset? I quickly realised it was a non-runner, but it was nice to be told that was what was available for me if I wanted it.

Once Marco realised he wasn't going to coax me back, he invited me to come to London for a few days for a one-off gig. The job? To oversee the catering for Madonna's Christmas party. I jumped at the opportunity. Not only has Madonna been the most iconic and powerful woman in the entertainment business for over two decades, but my wife Denise also happens to be a massive Madonna fan.

At this stage, in late 2007, Madonna was still happily married to film director Guy Ritchie. They were spending most of their time in London and wanted to celebrate Christmas there with family, friends and business associates.

Marco was good friends with the couple but had lots going on with his own business empire, so he asked me to organise everything. I was excited but not particularly overawed at the prospect. For me, it was a job – a fun, glamorous job, but a job all the same. I was to be paid £800, and it was also nice to be entrusted with something like that at a time when my morale was quite low.

I got a bit more enthused when I went to meet Madonna and Guy at their home in the Marylebone area of London. The family was living in two huge Georgian townhouses, which had been knocked into one eighteen-bedroom mansion, but in a very traditional and tasteful way. I was struck by the fact that even though the house was right on a public street there wasn't the media presence that you might have expected. I would have thought that paparazzi would have been hanging around day and night but there was no one at all.

Arriving into the hallway, all I could think was, *Wow*. It was very beautiful, a mix of French and English styles. You would know at a glance that the owners of this house were extremely wealthy and successful, yet there was nothing ostentatious about it. Navy-blue silk curtains were draped over double-height windows. A flight of marble steps, covered with a strip of navy-blue carpet, led upstairs. The banisters were traditional wrought iron. I can still smell the gorgeous scent of Christian Dior candles – just stunning. Off to the right was Guy's office area, which looked like something out of a 1960s James Bond film: old-fashioned leather chairs, lots of chrome, browns and silvers. A very clean, very stylish room.

Marco came with me to introduce me to Madonna and Guy and to give me his endorsement. We were greeted by no fewer than seven assistants. They were all milling around, handling different aspects of the lives of their bosses. Madonna pretty much ran her business empire from her home at that time and there was a lot of activity.

My initial meeting with them was very positive. They were nice people, very polite. Guy had a real warmth about him. I always take a peek at people's shoes, as you can tell a lot about a person from their footwear. Guy's shoes were smart, black, expensive. I'd guess, but not overly stylish. The kind of shoes an ordinary, decent bloke would wear. He was holding their boy, David, who they had recently adopted from Malawi, in his arms, while their older son, Rocco, was flying around the place as boys do. Rocco was attending a French school in London so we had a little chat in French.

I've always maintained from serving celebrities over the years that the bigger the star the more courteous they tend to be. Successful people tend to be self-assured and not carry a chip on their shoulder. So it was with Madonna. She was aware that I had travelled over from Dublin and was thanking me for 'coming over especially to look after our little party'. They were very courteous, offered me a drink, and, if I was tense at meeting people who are so much in the public eye, they quickly made me feel relaxed.

What was refreshing was that Madonna and Guy didn't want a formal, sit-down service: they wanted to open their home to their friends and have some fun. It was to be a relaxed affair, and all about their friends – A-list friends, obviously, but good pals nevertheless. After speaking about what they wanted, Madonna left to go back to her office, and we discussed the logistics with her assistants.

My job was to organise the catering, to oversee and manage the party and to make sure the service went perfectly on the night. We were going to lay up tables for an Italian-themed buffet. The food was to be prepared by the chefs at Luciano's, Marco's Italian restaurant, and I, along with my team of three staff from the restaurant, would oversee everything.

There was one panic in the preparations: the drink. Madonna absolutely adored Krug Rosé and specifically asked for several cases to be provided for the party. Krug Rosé is a fantastic, top-of-the-range champagne that's very special. It's regarded as one of the finest champagnes in the world and is presented in a beautiful pink box. Magical. It would retail for about £300 a pop but the problem wasn't money, it was availability. There followed a frantic search of all the wine merchants in London, because there was a shortage of Krug Rosé at that time. Eventually, we managed to get enough for the party. We also had very good Italian red and white wines as well as a selection of spirits. We had a barman from Luciano's to look after the cocktails. Madonna requested two: cosmopolitans and lemon drops. A cosmopolitan is vodka, triple sec, cranberry juice and lime, and has a lovely pink colour. A lemon drop is simply vodka and lemon juice, shaken with ice.

On the day of the party, Madonna, Guy, daughter Lourdes, Rocco and baby David all arrived, and the staff introduced themselves. I told them I was very happy to be serving their party that evening and that we would do everything to ensure that it ran smoothly. I'm the type of character who gets on with the job and doesn't ask too many questions. I wanted to give an air of confidence, not nosiness. There was a lot of work to do in any case. Although the party wasn't taking place until that night, we arrived at about 10.30 a.m. just to make sure everything was going to plan: that the glassware and utensils had arrived, that everything was to hand for laying out the buffet tables. We went away and came back at about 3 p.m. to start organising the tables and glasses.

I was busy with the preparations when Madonna rang through on a telephone intercom. She said, 'Will someone please pick up the phone? There are so many people in this house, and nobody will pick up the phone.' I was the only one in the room so I thought I should pick up. You don't ignore Madonna, right? I picked up and said hello, and she was bemused, saying, 'I didn't expect *you* to pick up.' She asked me to send one of her assistants up to her.

She wanted to feed her kids before things got busy. A private cook had arrived to cook for the family. I've heard over the years that Madonna has a strict diet but all she wanted that evening were some fish and chips. The chef was making the fish in a traditional way, putting the tempura-coated pieces in a pot of oil. She asked me, 'Are you serving the family dinner?' I said I didn't know I was but that of course I would.

The party was being held in a lounge with a dark velvet sofa and Picassos hanging above the fireplace. Do you have to ask whether they were real? I was just fixated by the paintings. It got better – as I turned the corner I saw this incredible painting by Francis Bacon, a figure with a shotgun on an orange background. It was a present from Madonna to Guy in congratulations of the success of his movie, *Lock, Stock and Two Smoking Barrels*. As I am fanatical about art, I was just mesmerised. I think that's when the excitement hit me about where I was, who I was working for. I got these goose pimples as I thought, *Fuck, that's a £3 million painting there on the wall*. Then I felt a sense of adventure. I would have loved to see more of the house but I wasn't allowed anywhere else, which is understandable. I gathered myself and finished laying the table. The whole family came down for dinner and ate together in the kitchen where the chef had prepared the food. Madonna was dressed casually in a black tracksuit; Guy was in jeans and a jumper. After their fish and chips, Madonna and Guy went to put the children up to bed and to prepare for their guests to arrive.

I did a last-minute spot check, did up the glassware, made sure the champagne was chilled and the cocktails were ready to go. The buffet was ready: a feast of Italian food – gnocchi, spaghetti, salad, olives – all laid out in tiers and beautifully presented. The plates were to one side, the cutlery was folded inside the napkins. I did a nice envelope fold and put the knives and forks inside the napkin – just to make it all look polished and upmarket. Then I positioned the champagne where it would be easy to serve.

The guests started to arrive at the front door: show time.

I estimate that we catered for about fifty to sixty people that night. I was again surprised that there were no photographers hanging around as they would have amassed quite a collection of celebrity snaps that evening. There was no security either. It was all very laid back.

Madonna and Guy asked that Marco stay for the party, but Marco, being Marco, declined. His usual quote is, 'It's cooler to be unseen than be seen.' Whatever. He said, 'Any problem, give me a call, Nick,' and off he went.

I am used to serving celebrities, but I will never forget the number of famous people who turned up that night. It was quite extraordinary. I mean, it wasn't just the number of faces, it was their calibre, and the fact that they were all there at the same time. Paul McCartney and his daughter Stella. Sting and his wife Trudie Styler. Jamie Oliver. All of Coldplay, including Chris Martin, and Chris's wife Gwyneth Paltrow. Then you had movers and shakers such as the journalist A. A. Gill and the restaurant designer David Collins. It was like being in Madame Tussaud's, except these weren't waxworks. They were all real. It was very relaxed, and, as is often the case with seriously famous people, there was no celebrity vibe. Madonna arrived in a very beautiful evening dress, and she sat down on a pure blue silk footstool – massive, like a gigantic cushion.

I got into work mode and kept my eye on everyone, especially her. Does anyone need their drinks topped up? Is everyone fed and relaxed? Madonna was drinking her favourite lemon-drop cocktails, and each time she was nearly finished I'd get her a new one. I must have served her ten in the space of a couple of hours, and she was starting to get a little tipsy.

There was a very good vibe. She and her guests were really enjoying themselves, and it was all very relaxed. Stella McCartney was beautifully turned out as always; her dad was wearing trainers. Sting and Jimmy Nail stayed on the sofa chatting all night.

I'd love to tell you some outrageous story, but the truth is that it was very civilised. There was no funny business. Everyone mingled together, talking, having a good time. Drink was flowing, and everyone was standing up chatting.

People spoke with me too as I snaked around the room, moving between guests to top up their drinks. They got friendlier, of course, as the drink flowed, and when they heard I was living in Dublin they started telling me how much they loved the place. I was working, and I had to know my place, obviously, but I found it great fun, although some of Madonna's assistants were quite nervous. The good thing for me was that because Madonna and Guy knew Marco and trusted his judgement, and Marco had recommended me, they trusted me to do their party.

With so many musicians and actors around, you might expect someone to whip out a guitar and start a sing-song, but there was none of that. It wasn't that kind of party, and, let's face it, that would have been as corny as hell. There was no DJ or anything like that, just good music playing on CD in the background.

In the build-up to the party, Denise was quizzing me all the time: 'What's Madonna like? Describe her house. Tell me all about it.' She was very excited and even hinted that she might be available to help on the night should it be required. Actually, you wouldn't really describe it as hinting. She kept going, 'Can I come as well? Ask Marco. Can I come as well?' But Marco only wanted me there, much to Denise's annoyance. I kind of knew what he would say, so I decided to let her down gently by saying that Marco didn't want any women there in case it would offend Madonna. I'm not sure that she bought it.

However, I did make her one promise: that I would bring back some sort of souvenir from Madonna's house. She was adamant. As the night wore on, that was at the back of my mind, and I was thinking to myself, *What can I bring home as a souvenir without being noticed and would it be OK to do that?* I was concerned, but I was on a mission from Denise. She had actually warned me not to come back to Dublin without something. To put it in context, she is a *huge* Madonna fan. Has all the albums. I was more of a fan of the Police when I was younger, so the big thrill for me that night was to meet Sting. Meeting a Beatle was cool as well, obviously. But in my head I was going, *Woah! Don't lose your cool. You are here for a purpose and to do a job, not to hang out of Sting with your thesis about which is your favourite Police song.*

Towards the end of the night, Madonna told us, 'You can pack up now. We are cool. Thank you very much.' It was a natural kind of finish to a perfect party, and I was feeling chuffed that absolutely everything had passed without a hitch.

Obviously we made sure the place was polished to the hilt. As we were clearing and I was congratulating myself on a job well done, one of the waiters picked up Madonna's espresso machine, promptly dropped it, and it came apart in about fifteen pieces. I thought, *Oh my God, here we go. All hell is going to break loose.* I started frantically trying to put it back together and managed to jigsaw it all back into one piece. It didn't appear to be broken, but let's just say I didn't let on that it mightn't necessarily work either.

A slightly shaky end to the evening, and I was still on my mission to find this piece of memorabilia for Denise. Downstairs in the staff toilets were these John Lewis face towels for people to dry their hands on. I thought, *Well that's almost a souvenir, isn't it? We are in Madonna's house after all.* Technically, I could tell Denise that I'd brought her a towel from Madonna's house. Before I got the chance to back out, I took one of the towels and stuffed it down my trousers. If I had put it in my pocket it would have bulged out, so down the front of my trousers it went, and that was the souvenir.

I brought it home to Denise, and she was absolutely thrilled: here was a towel touched by the hand of her heroine, Madonna. I didn't let on that it was actually from the staff toilets until very recently when she took it out while we were having a dinner party. We had some friends over, and there was a great buzz about the towel because all our gay friends are Madonna devotees. They have followed Madonna's life for decades: it's their pop-idol soap opera.

I finally told them all that the towel wasn't actually Madonna's personal one but came from the staff quarters. Denise took it two ways: one bit of her was going, *Ha ha, that's actually really funny that you kept that from me.* The other bit was going, *You bastard!* I tried to explain myself by saying, 'Well what did you expect me to do?' I was sweating when I picked it up anyway, worried about getting caught, thinking I've got to be professional and here I am taking a towel for my Madonna-obsessed wife.

If I had any remaining doubt about what decent people Madonna and Guy Ritchie are, afterwards they sent me a very nice, handwritten card to say thanks for working at their party. I love when people are classy like that. It's just nice when people take the trouble to say thank you, no matter what walk of life they come from. That was my Madonna experience. No diva fits. No tantrums. No unreasonable demands. A lovely thank-you note. And if she missed that John Lewis towel, she never mentioned it. Classy lady.

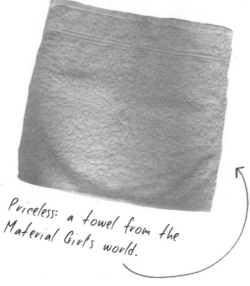

Priceless: a towel from the Material Girl's world.

Be afraid, be very afraid!

HELL FREEZES OVER

HELL'S KITCHEN, PART II

By the time the second series of *Hell's Kitchen* came around, in 2009, I decided that I wanted to put myself forward a little more and to have some fun. Because I was thinking about opening my own restaurant in Dublin, frankly I wanted to increase my profile. I was determined to do my work, for sure, but also to make the show work for me.

In 2008 I got to indulge my love for painting and also to do some consultancy work that helped me forge new and valuable business contacts and to flex my creative muscles. This was to provide lots of extra experience when I finally got to open my own place. I met some lovely people through doing consultancy work for Conor Kenny & Associates. Through this, other jobs came about.

I was contacted by Ian Hyland of the Westgrove Hotel in Clane, with whom I had hit it off when we met previously. He'd heard that I was looking for work and needed somebody to help redo an existing fine-dining restaurant and also to help with training and workshops. This was a lifeline for me, as I'd really enjoyed spending more time at Christmas with the kids and the job enabled me to work during the day and paint at night, as well as to be with my family more.

I was really grateful to Ian for that job, and he then put me in touch with his friend, hotelier Patricia Roberts. She and her husband needed some help on their hotel, No.1 Pery Square in Limerick, a beautiful restored Georgian house overlooking the People's Park on the Tontine. Another great thing that happened was that the Westgrove purchased six of my paintings for their restaurant walls, and Patricia hosted an exhibition of my work in No. 1 Pery Square during my time there. I was also doing some work in Café Leon at this time, so all these projects kept me busy as I prepared for another series of *Hell's Kitchen* and started to make initial plans to open my own restaurant. It was something I had aspired to for years, but I had finally become determined that I should stop thinking, musing and dreaming about it and actually do it. I needed to prove to myself that I could.

I did tell Marco that I had plans, but I was quite cagey about saying too much, because I didn't even have things sorted out in my own head. One morning we had to get up especially early, at 6 a.m., before they closed the roads for the London Marathon. We arrived at the studios and dozed for a couple of hours, sitting around on the chairs. Marco and I were just chit-chatting, about nonsense really, smoking cigarettes and drinking tea. I decided I'd drop my barrier and tell him more about my plans to open my own place. Marco has a tactic of not saying anything when you tell him things. He just stares at you and stays silent, and it's up to you then to give more information. I knew this habit of his, so I didn't go any further.

I had been in Dublin for years at this stage and wasn't even working for Marco, but he's the Don. I had been a loyal member of staff, and often a loyal friend. I made sure that I was always giving 110 per cent of what he expected in his empire, and that's how we got on. Over time, I had been invited to the table to break bread with him. The loyalty, to be fair to Marco, was reciprocated:

Respect the family. Marco could give Don Corleone a run for his money.

if I ever needed something, he would look after me. I never asked for money or anything like that, because I didn't want to feel indebted to him – or to anyone in fact.

But Marco is the Don. While I don't think he would ever place a horse's head in anyone's bed, loyalty is a huge thing for him. It defines him and is basically how he runs his empire. If you upset him, then you will be disregarded. Marco and I were still friends, but I was starting to yearn to do things for myself, both on *Hell's Kitchen* and in my business life. I wasn't feeling as committed to him.

I know I don't create amazing food, like chefs do, but I do create an ambience, and that's where my personality shines. Now that I was used to the *Hell's Kitchen* cameras, I set out to find opportunities to showcase my profession, to have fun and to gain a bit more profile into the bargain. I felt that if I was going to keep making an idiot of myself by falling over on national television, I should try to enjoy myself too.

I've always had a desire to make people laugh. I love spontaneous comedy and prop comedy. Tommy Cooper is one of my all-time heroes. To me, nobody has eclipsed him, though I do like Eddie Izzard and Ricky Gervais. Cooper for me was all about silly, absurd comedy, and that very much reflects my personality. I wanted to bring that out on screen rather than just be the upstanding (or upended) *maître d'*.

At first, there was talk about the producers wanting me to have more input in the show, but the more interested I became in showcasing my job and increasing my profile during my second stint on *Hell's Kitchen*, the more it seemed to me that Marco was resistant to that idea. There were a few times when it felt as though he was trying to keep me in my place.

One of the worst was during a live service when Jonathan Ansell, one of the singers from the group G4, arrived as part of a group of four to dine. I took their order, and his guest asked for the lamb, but when I explained that it would be served pink, she said she wanted meat that was well cooked. I suggested the rose veal to her, because it is well cooked through. I added that because it was rose veal there would be a hint of pink in the middle but that it didn't mean the meat was undercooked. Shortly before their order went out, I had fallen over (yes, again) while carrying a large tray, so I was a bit flustered and stressed.

During service, there are various production staff spotting potential unfolding stories, and when this lady started complaining about her dish, I was dispatched – with the cameras – to her table. Jonathan said that his friend had requested the dish to be cooked through but that it was raw. I said it was not raw, it was cooked through but a little pink in the middle, as I had described it. They weren't happy and wanted to know how I was going to fix it. I said there was nothing I could do about it but if they wished to go up to the pass and speak to Marco, they could.

The mood turned. Jonathan called me arrogant, and I decided to tell them I would no longer be serving them and started to clear their table. He then called me 'an arrogant prick' to camera, which I didn't hear at the time and only saw on the show afterwards. He then went to the pass to speak to Marco, who wanted to know what the problem was. Jonathan said his partner had asked for her meat well cooked, that I was refusing to change the food, and that he found me very rude. Marco said, 'Thank you, how do you want it cooked?' He said he'd cook it whatever way he wanted and told him to return to the table, effectively overturning my judgement call.

Trying to keep calm, I brought out their food and put my hand out to shake Jonathan's as a goodwill gesture. He refused to shake my hand until I apologised. I said, 'Let's be honest, it's a two-way thing. Maybe we should just bury the hatchet here.' He still refused to shake hands until I apologised, which I then did, sarcastically. We never shook hands, and I left them to it.

I was annoyed with Marco. The next day, I thought, *Sod him*, and I took every order well done. I was trying to do what Marco wanted but then he turned it back on me. I was worried about how I was going to be perceived.

There were other little incidents. The producers had planned a pre-recorded afternoon segment where I would show model Danielle Bux how to flambé a crayfish for evening service and she would then do the demo on camera. We had only a tight slot in the afternoon to film it as schedules were really busy in the afternoons before we went to air. Camera shots had to be organised, technical staff needed time to get everything ready, there were mini-rehearsals to be done. All those elements played a huge part in the mechanics of the show and meant there were only certain times of the day when there was free studio time available to film those little extras. And, somehow, Marco made sure there was never time to get them done.

We were set up for the flambé scene and the cameras were ready, but, as we started to film, Marco – who had been watching from the pass – ushered me out of the way and started doing the demo with Danielle himself. It was supposed to be my segment, but, again, I was made to be the sidecar to the motorbike.

On another occasion, the producers planned to have me show the celebrities how to do a steak tartare on the trolley within a few minutes, then getting them to do the same. During the recording of the task, Marco kept heckling from the pass. 'That's not the way to do it. That's wrong. It's all flat. Wrong ingredients.' There was only a very short amount of time to record the segment so it was ruined.

These were Marco's little ways, I believe, of not allowing me to showcase what I did as a *maître d'*. It started to feel like anything I did was going to be gatecrashed.

Then the producers came up with the whole idea that the restaurant floor would become a sort of sin bin. If a celebrity was not performing in the kitchen, Marco had the option of sending them out to wait on tables the following evening. I could see from a TV perspective that it was a great idea, but what annoyed me was that it was turning waiting tables into a punishment, a downgrade, and the restaurant floor into a nasty place to be. I felt really conflicted about it. The TV person in me was thinking, *Good idea.* The *maître d'* in me was thinking, *Hang on a second, what's this about? It's not a sin bin, it's the pitch!*

Angus Deayton didn't return for the second series, and the presenter was Claudia Winkleman this time round. It wasn't that I thought Claudia wasn't any good, it's just that she wasn't Angus. She did bring a different, new approach to the show. She was into mingling and having fun with the customers, which was quite good, quite quirky. But I missed Angus's sarcastic jokes and deadpan delivery.

I didn't think the celebrities in the 2009 series were as good a mix of people as in 2007. I had no idea who was going to be on the show so the first night was as much of a surprise to me as any-one else. TV presenter Anthea Turner and her husband Grant Bovey; model and presenter Danielle Bux; legendary goalie Bruce Grobbelaar; American actress Linda Evans of *Dynasty* fame; Niomi Arleen McLean-Daley, better known as the singer and rapper Ms Dynamite; comedian Adrian Edmondson; and actor Jody Latham.

One of the first items filmed involved the celebrities making their favourite sandwich, something that represented themselves, for Marco. When they arrived on set, they would have been feeling nervous. Their sandwiches were lined up in front of them under silver domes. In those initial moments, the nerves got the better of Danielle. She fainted and had to be given something sweet to raise her blood sugar and to get her back on her feet. After Marco had tasted their sandwiches they were told that they would be expected in the kitchen an hour later. They weren't being given settling-in time and were told to get their chef's whites on and get to work. They had supposed that they wouldn't be doing service until the following night and that the first day would be a famil-iarisation day, but we were actually opening for customers that night. The ante had been upped.

Another big difference that year was that Marco had the ability to sack somebody after service. So that was what he did. In the case of the first four to be eliminated, he would be the one to sack them, and then it was down to the public vote. We hated it because Marco would sit down at midnight, after service, and waffle on for an hour and a half, while we would be sitting there waiting for him to finish, for thirty seconds of television, to see who would be sacked. After service, you are exhausted. You just want to go and take your jacket off, have a beer in the bar and chill out, but we were stuck there. We couldn't leave the set until the Don had spoken.

I thought it was a good idea to bring a married couple into the mix with Anthea and Grant. It was a new idea, and I'm sure the producers were hoping they'd start to squabble. I think, however, that they were very much in love, very much a couple. Grant was portrayed as the guy who had all these multimillion-pound businesses that folded and who was famous because of Anthea Turner. He was very polite, but then you have to wonder if that is just an image he wanted to portray. I think if you sign yourself up to any reality-TV show you try to portray yourself in a certain way. It's like Katie Price going into *I'm a Celebrity ... Get Me Out of Here!* – an acting job. Anthea must have been trying to get a cleaning advert out of it because she used to always have marigolds on and went over the top with the cleaning. I always felt the two of them had an agenda.

I was ambivalent about Adrian Edmondson too. I'd watched *The Young Ones* when I was growing up and didn't particularly find it funny. Even though my sense of humour is quite slapstick and they hit people on the head with frying pans, for me it wasn't really laugh-out-loud stuff. As it turned out, we really didn't click at all. Early on in the series he claimed he didn't understand what I was saying – because I was foreign. Total bullshit. I may be half French, but I was born and raised in England. It was ludicrous and disrespectful, and really annoyed me.

He took the whole thing so seriously. I sometimes wanted to remind him that he was on a reality-TV show, not splitting atoms or saving mankind. I was thinking, *Get over yourself.* Ade had come in with the mindset that he wanted to be a great chef, and he hated his night waiting tables. It was very clear he didn't even want to be in the room. Because he only had half an hour to train to be a waiter and because I could only give him so much information in that time, he got a bit excited. I said to him, 'Don't worry about making a mistake. Enjoy it! It's entertainment.'

He had no regard for what we did. He wasn't even interested. He couldn't understand the role of a *maître d'*. He thought it was a worthless job, basically, which really pissed me off. Let's put it into perspective. Front-of-house person: what do they do? In the eyes of a chef, not a lot. In the eyes of a customer, a hell of a lot. Sure, we don't physically cook the food, but we make or break a customer's experience. We are on the front line. Just because I am wearing a nice suit doesn't mean I'm swanning around.

It was a tough night's service, but Ade blamed his failure on the floor on me, saying he couldn't understand me and that I didn't teach him properly.

Some of the other celebrities took to the job fantastically well. Linda Evans was phenomenal. She was very keen on learning and really got into it. An intelligent woman and a real lady, she took in what was required very quickly. I was really pleased when she went on to win the series.

I didn't know Jody Latham before the show because I don't watch *Shameless*, the comedy drama he was in for four years. A nice guy, but one of those wild horses that needs to be tamed. He was a waiter one night, and he was all fired up. He was like a dog ready to attack. There was this guy on Table 2 who started to say that the food was terrible. So Jody came over to me and said, 'I'm going to kick this fucker out. We are going to get this guy out, Nick. Me and you are going to kick this fucker out, Nick.'

I was like, 'Jody, calm down. Relax. Who is this guy?'

I casually went over and said, 'Is everything all right, Sir? Is there a problem?' Jody was throwing shapes, ready to pounce. This guy was actually complaining that there was too much asparagus in his starter. Ridiculous.

I remember turning to the camera and saying, 'Is he for real?', trying to have fun with him. To Jody's utter joy, I decided to clear his table and asked him to leave. Jody was so happy. He ran into the kitchen and said, 'We have just kicked somebody out!' He was loving the whole scene.

Another time, Claudia was standing at the bar, doing her piece to camera for a live link, and Jody came up behind her, took a bottle of white wine, poured the glass until it was full and slugged the whole thing back on live TV. It was hilarious. I thought he made that year's *Hell's Kitchen* because he had entertainment value. Others were saying, 'We're very serious. We want to cook.' But Jody was being his over-the-top self and trying to cause a little friction along the way. Unfortunately he ended up being portrayed badly, I think. At one point everybody seemed to turn against him, and he made a run for it and tried to jump over the wall. I don't know what other people thought of his persona, but to me he was a genuine guy, very polite, very motivated. He just wanted to succeed.

I found Bruce Grobbelaar very interesting too, and I was sorry he didn't get to stay in the series longer. He had the big, big hands and instinctual coordination of a goalie, so you could count on him not to drop the plates. He had a knack for the job and would make an amazing restaurant manager. Bruce was very passionate about what he did and wanted to be good in the kitchen, but he didn't get a chance to because the producers wanted chaos, which made learning anything difficult. For me, Bruce was cut from the same cloth as Barry McGuigan. He's had his fair share of controversies but remains a sporting icon. The man is a legend in Liverpool. His public image was still intact even though people still joke about the betting stuff. I'm telling you, the number of guests who wanted his autograph above anybody else was phenomenal – everybody wanted Bruce Grobbelaar's signature.

His wife came to dinner one night – a lovely woman. She went up to the pass to give him a kiss, and they spoke in Afrikaans about missing each other, and that's when he decided, 'I'm actually going to quit, going to leave.' It happened that there was an Afrikaans speaker on the crew of ITV who translated what they were saying, so it came up in subtitles. It was a very emotional night, and I was sorry because I wanted Bruce to win. I loved the bloke.

I didn't know Danielle Bux before she came in, but I liked her. She was there for her daughter. She was engaged to Gary Lineker at the time – they married shortly afterwards. He came five times during the seventeen-day stint, just to see how she was getting on. I'd think, *Oh here you are again, Gary.*

The diners who ate at *Hell's Kitchen* in 2009 were a very mixed bunch. I think they tried to get a wider variety of celebrities but obviously we still had the usual suspects, the soap stars. The beauty of that year's format was that there were no separations in the room: the tables were placed much closer together and much nearer to the pass. Whoever was the celebrity of the moment would sit at the centre round table. We had the former pop star David Van Day, with that idiot who brought out 'The Polkadot Bikini Song' – Timmy Mallet. They had both been on *I'm a Celebrity … Get Me Out of Here!* They desperately wanted attention and were trying to be as loud as possible, but the cameramen were taking the piss out of them by filming them and not using the footage.

When one of the contestants was sent to the sin bin, I would have to wait behind to film the scene where I went, 'Welcome to the room. Now I want you to count the laundry,' or 'I want you to wash glasses before you can go home.' The next day, whoever it was wouldn't be working with me; they would be still cooking in the kitchen until the evening service began. They would then get changed, and I would have, say, half an hour before the doors opened to train them how to do the job. To train somebody you need at least a full day, but what would happen was they'd be told, 'You're in the restaurant now. Nick, take half an hour to teach them.' I tried to give them the basics: write the order correctly and clearly, not like a doctor's handwriting. Number the tables and the positions on a table. Go clockwise. Start with a lady. There is all that etiquette involved in the job. If you are passionate about it you do it well. You don't just take an order and then collect the plate. There is a whole procedure about service that not many people could pick up in half an hour.

Although I didn't like the sin-bin tag, I didn't get too uppity about it. I could see the direction the show was going in. The producers wanted chaos, which is fair enough: chaos makes for good TV, and I accept that. I was also prepared, as I've said, to have some fun and not to take whatever was thrown at me too seriously. But I did get the impression in that series that they thought that the waiter was a second-class citizen.

I think some of the celebrities who had to serve on the floor became quite frustrated. The time constraints meant I wasn't able to teach them about service properly, which made for a very stressful experience for them. Danielle Bux and Ade Edmondson both did stints in front of house and hated it, because they were there to learn to cook.

Having inexperienced people on the floor completely messed up the whole service, but I was ready for that. At the same time, we had Marco barking, 'Make sure you don't fuck up and make sure the orders come in quickly.' It was pandemonium, and all the while I'm still trying to be funny because I want to create good TV. It's not that it was overwhelming, it's more that feeling of anxiety that you get in the pit of your stomach. For all my giving out, I did still love working on the show. I was certainly busier and did appreciate that the show was giving more time to the type of work that restaurant staff, not just kitchen staff, do.

I'm not sure how well my sense of humour went down with the producers. Sometimes the jokes I played would end up on the cutting-room floor. One night Chris de Burgh serenaded Claudia Winkleman, and every other female diner in the room, with

'Lady in Red'. When I was being interviewed at the end of service I said that Chris de Burgh's singing was so bad that … then I put on a pair of joke glasses which had fake tears coming down – I'd been waiting for a chance to use them. I thought it was hilarious, but they decided not to broadcast it. Sometimes you made the cut; sometimes you didn't. I was glad the joke-glasses clip wasn't used on the show in the end,

Well they made me laugh!

because Chris actually really livened up the night when he sang. I watched as he grabbed his guitar, and everyone joined in. I have heard 'The Lady in Red' at one wedding too many, but everyone loved it. I recently met Chris in Dublin and we talked about his fond memories of that night in *Hell's Kitchen*.

Another stress factor that year was that the producers introduced a bloody dessert trolley. In the 2007 series, dessert orders were taken and the dishes brought out from the kitchen. Now all the desserts were coming from a trolley. There was a cheese trolley, another one with sorbets and then the dessert trolley. We had to cut from the trolley. Sixty customers, with one trolley feeding sixty people all at the same time? Impossible. It did cause a lot of friction. I would stick it in the middle of the room, get the waiter to take an order and then slice from the trolley, thinking, *Stop giving me all this extra stuff to do!*

I was taking orders for sixty guests, looking after the celebrity waiters and looking after the staff. I had the wine to keep topped up, the customers to look after and the pass to worry about. There was a lot going on. One night, I lost my cool and had a mini-meltdown on camera. There were so many dockets coming in, Marco was making demands, the producers were in my earpiece making demands, and the guy at the pass wasn't coping. Food was being brought to the wrong tables. The whole pass was in chaos, and then Marco made a comment directed at me: 'You couldn't even organise a piss-up in a brewery!'

I was stunned. I wanted to retaliate and to say something but I couldn't because I had to stay cool, for the sake of the service and the customers, and also for my own sake. But when Marco said that, I thought, *What is wrong with you?*

I walked away from the pass and took a deep breath. I had two options: (1) be Mr Moody and not give a damn or (2) get in there and sort everything out. I went for the latter: went back in, told everyone to please move away from the pass, that I'd sort it myself. I got everything organised in five minutes. It was empowering to just be able to clear up the mess and to go on to do my job properly. I took the trays out myself as I had all the dockets.

I did throw a tray stand on the floor, just to get the anger out of my system. Apparently one of the waiters who Marco had brought in to work on the pass stuck two fingers up behind my back. I find that offensive, but whatever. When I was finished, Marco said, 'Well done, thanks very much.' He had definitely been pushing my buttons. After filming, on the way back in the car, he was making a joke out of it, but I was so pissed off I didn't speak at all. I've got a sense of humour, but when I'm trying to be professional I do take remarks like that to heart. Actually, that incident, which came about a week into the series, was a bit of a turning point for me. I wasn't enjoying the show as much as the first series. Denise, whose opinion I trust most, was watching at home and later said it was out of order and seemed designed to make me look bad.

I was well used to Marco's temper tantrums in the kitchen over the years I had worked with him and had learned to take them on the chin. But it's one thing to be lambasted in front of a small group of colleagues and quite another to be shouted at on national television. My friends and family were watching, millions of people were watching, and Marco was saying that I wasn't up to the job in the most derogatory way. It was embarrassing and unfair, and I was incensed by his behaviour towards me on such a massive, public scale. I felt like I'd become the whipping boy. It's OK for a chef. People almost expect you to be fiery. You can throw a pot or slam the fridge door. You can scream at another chef. And people will go, 'Oh, what a genius!' But who was I going to scream at? A customer? They'd think I was loopy. It would be a case of 'Get rid of him! He shouldn't even be working in a restaurant.'

I didn't dwell on the incident too much because I do have that ability to growl a bit, then chill, forget about it and move on. It's just service. My years' experience allowed me to get over it: I would never have survived in a front-of-house position if I was overly sensitive.

For me, *Hell's Kitchen* kind of lost its edge that year. There just wasn't enough drama. You don't want swearing or fighting, but you do want entertainment. Maybe people will read this going, *What was he talking about? It was fantastic.* But I didn't find it that great from the inside. Jody was out, Bruce left, and it just went a bit downhill from there.

I was very happy to be asked to do it again, and it was nice to be invited back. But the whole Marco saga depressed me. It was supposed to be enthralling reality TV, but, by the end, *Hell's Kitchen* just felt like another night's service.

Pichet: a modern take on the classic bistro.

I WANT TO BREAK FREE

FINDING PICHET

I had been doing some consultancy work with Frank Gleeson, the businessman who owns Café Leon, Whelan's and the Village in Dublin, as well as the Brian Boru in Tipperary. I love Café Leon. I always assumed it was thought up by a Frenchman because it was so authentic. I did some work in Leon on Exchequer Street, the branch with the lovely ground-floor room, and briefly worked the floor there. People would be going, 'That's your man out of *Hell's Kitchen!* He is on the floor in a pastry shop!'

It didn't bother me. I loved it because I was in a good environment. I really got on well with Frank, and the more I worked for him the better we got to know each other. He asked me to go and have a look at the branch on Trinity Street which hadn't really taken off. Even though the premises were only a few minutes' walk from Grafton Street, it was slightly off the beaten track – but it had a good shopfront.

The minute I walked into the premises that was to become Pichet, I felt so at home. It had all the attributes of a classic bistro, and I started to get excited – that feeling of, *Wow, I think I've found it*. The room ticked all the right business boxes: the footfall was very good, and the room was a nice size; the smoking area was good. But it wasn't just the practicalities – I kind of fell in love with the room on that very first day. It had high windows that let in loads of natural light, it had a vibe, a personality. But it needed work too, which really excited me because I knew there was an opportunity to put my own stamp on it. I started imagining how it might look. I almost ran home to talk to Denise and to tell her about this room and the thrill it had given me.

I remembered that, as I had left l'Ecrivain on that awful day a year before, the chef Stephen Gibson had said to me, 'If you're ever contemplating doing something, give me a call.' In early 2009, I found myself picking up the phone and taking the first step in the leap of our careers.

'Hi Stephen. Remember you asked me to buzz if I was thinking of doing anything? I think I've found a place.'

We had a chat, Stephen went to look at the premises, and he loved it. Denise knew Stephen much better than I did because they had worked together in l'Ecrivain for five years. Where we hit it off was in our approach to what we did. There was a mutual love for restaurants, food, service and how things should be run. That's where we clicked. We got a great buzz talking about the concept from the first time we put pen to paper. We both had the same ideas and values, and I thought, *That's it – we have to do something together.*

We started putting together a business plan to sublet the place and to develop the restaurant – a journey that took almost eighteen months from conception to opening.

I had toyed with the idea of talking to Marco at one point during the filming of *Hell's Kitchen* but had hesitated. I had nothing concrete in place at that time and felt he would have asked loads of questions about figures and locations. Later on, when the plans were further along, I did ring him to ask for his advice. It was a scary moment because I felt quite nervous about telling him. He had always been helpful in my career but I did have the sense that when it came to going it alone he would dissuade me. I just knew I would be bombarded with questions and he would actually say very little. He has this habit of falling silent on the phone for long pauses. It's a stroke of genius really: if he isn't talking, it makes you speak more and say things that you shouldn't be saying, just to fill in the silence. I believe it's a trick to get information out of people.

Marco always has an agenda, and the scary thing is you may have no idea what that is until after the event. It's not really possible to have a normal conversation with him. This is his planet, and you're just living in it. It's not like a normal friendship where you have a relaxed, two-way chat. You've always got to be alert because he uses that silence tactic to trip you into saying things you shouldn't say or revealing things about yourself that you may later regret. It can be really draining.

Marco wasn't the right person to ask for advice at that time. He wanted me to keep working for him and said I could make better money that way. From his point of view, he wanted me to help him run his new restaurant franchise on Dawson Street in Dublin. In the months leading up to this I had used my business contacts to help Marco get a foothold in the Irish market after he had asked me to help him sell his franchise in Ireland. I introduced him both to the Fitzpatricks, who run the Fitzers chain, and, later on, to businessman Harry Crosbie. First off, I met with the Fitzers Group to discuss their going into partnership with Marco in a rebranding of their Dawson Street restaurant. I did the homework, portfolio, menu concepts and financials, and introduced them to the Marco Pierre White empire. At that time, they decided not to follow up on the project.

Marco was still keen, so I met with Harry – who I've known for years. He was interested: he was looking for a flagship restaurant

Harry and Rita Crosbie with Denise and me at the Taste of Dublin festival 2010.

for the Point Village and thought that Marco fitted the bill. Marco came over to Dublin for meetings, and I arranged a night out on the town to bring him out, to introduce him to some people who worked in the trade and to show him a good time. I had done some consultancy for Ivan's in Howth, and they were having their opening party that night, so I invited Marco along. He said he wasn't interested but I explained I had the whole evening planned, we could go to the launch and then come into town for dinner. I'd even arranged a car for us.

He was in a funny mood that day. TV3 rang me when they heard he was in town and asked if he would do an interview for *Exposé*, but he refused. They were at the Ivan's launch, and he was quite rude to them, actually.

After the launch we went to Dawson Street where we met the Fitzpatricks. Marco was on the terrace being mad as a brush, telling jokes, completely zany. An old colleague of mine had been at the launch party, and she texted me and said, 'My God, Marco Pierre White is fantastic – I want to meet him.' For fun, I showed him the text. Bad idea. He took my phone off me and started texting her. I was trying to get him to go as we had a dinner reservation, but he said, 'Oh, don't worry about your fucking dinner.'

I had arranged a meal for seven people at Balzac. I had invited Domini Kemp and her sister Peaches, who are such great company and had met Marco before. Karen Noble, who is a veteran of the restaurant scene, was a big fan of Marco's, so I invited her to join us. Robert Scanlan, the General Manager of Balzac, came too, and myself and Denise made up the mix.

When we arrived for dinner, Marco – already in an unhinged mood – literally went quite nuts. I was happy just to have got him there but he was determined to make some more mischief. We got to the front bar in the restaurant, where everyone was waiting for us, to have pre-dinner drinks. There was a boat-shaped bowl of peanuts on the bar counter. Marco was being crazy and was at the stage where he would do anything for a laugh. Exclaiming, 'Look at those lovely nuts!' he proceeded to grab the bowl and pour the contents down his trousers before shouting, 'Come on girls! Sniff that! Marco's nuts!'

Karen Noble was meeting him for the first time and was quite shocked. Others who knew him? Well, they weren't fazed in the slightest. Me? I went into nervous-laughter mode, trying to pretend that this was completely normal – which it was, when you were in Marco's company. It was just another escapade in what was a zany, zany night. He was enjoying himself, and loving having a new audience to play up to.

When we eventually went in for dinner, everything was a problem. He didn't like the restaurant, he didn't like the food. He then proceeded to walk around pouring drinks for everyone as if he owned the place. He threw some money onto the table to pay for a bottle of champagne and asked a girl to show him her boobs. Mad stuff. It was still just about funny at that stage, but I knew he was in an unpredictable mood, and I was concerned, trying to contain him. Then my friend arrived in, and Marco left the table, went to the bar and spent the whole evening talking to her, ignoring

me and our guests. The moral of the story: celebrity chefs may be scary in the kitchen, but they're much scarier on the restaurant floor. I was relieved the next day when he left.

Some time after this, the Fitzers Group came back to the table. I thought that Marco was going to do a deal with Harry, but, unbeknownst to me, he was also meeting with Fitzers. He basically just went and did his own thing, which upset the Crosbies and made me look bad. I felt like a scapegoat and was worried because I was still living and working in Dublin – a small place, where business dealings get talked about. When you're doing consultancy work, your reputation is very important. I'm not the big shot. I thought I was doing everybody a favour, and I didn't get anything out of it, just grief. I didn't even know what was going on behind the scenes.

I did work for a brief period at the Marco Pierre White Steakhouse and Grill on Dawson Street, to show the Fitzers people Marco's way and to help with the set-up. Obviously Marco doesn't cook there: he lends his name and has devised a menu. As plans for my own place came together, I went through a nervous time because I had to tell Geraldine Fitzpatrick, the owner, that I was leaving. Then I rang Marco to tell him – this was about four months before we opened in July 2009. It was one of the last conversations we had.

I like to think of myself as a pretty shrewd judge of character, and my job has helped me keep my bullshit radar finely tuned. But I am still baffled by Marco Pierre White. I've known him for fifteen years, have worked with him on and off for nine years, and, at the height of our friendship, even when I moved back to Dublin, we would speak on the phone several times a day. I think what hurts most is that the loyalty I had shown to him for many years wasn't reciprocated. It came as a huge disappointment to me that Marco was not only unenthusiastic about me opening my own restaurant but started to cut ties as soon as he heard about it.

I've known him for long enough to know that striking out on my own could spell the end of our association. Marco likes to be in control, likes to pull strings with even the most trusted associates. And if you leave the Family, he gets all *mafioso* about it.

It was described as a dramatic bust-up in food and media circles, but, really, we just stopped talking. I know it was because I had gone against his number-one rule by deciding to forge my own path in the restaurant world. It's not that he felt threatened, it's more that he doesn't want his people to do their own thing, because then he loses control. He seems to consider it a betrayal.

While we were filming the TV3 series *Nick's Bistro*, about the opening of the restaurant, and preparing to open, I thought it would be nice if Marco came down to have a look, but he kept fobbing me off. He was over for the weekend with Oasis, who were playing Slane. I thought it was a good opportunity to show him around because I was really quite proud and I wanted him to see the restaurant. I really respected his opinion – I mean, not only is the guy one of the most talented chefs of his generation but he *knows* restaurants. His feedback really mattered to me. But it didn't happen. I felt quite deflated. I just wanted him to have a look, if even to take the piss out of me – which is his way – or just to say, 'Fair play to you,' as a friend. I worked with him and for him for years. I felt he could just come down and have a look at least. He didn't have to be filmed, that was fine. I could understand that he wouldn't want to appear to be advertising my place. But it wasn't about that. His lack of interest felt a bit strange, especially when he was in town. After working to make money for other people all of my life, it still bothers me that he couldn't just be happy for me. It's infuriating, but mostly it's just sad.

Some time later I was with my son in the Toy Store on Dawson Street, and when I came out I saw Marco across the road on his phone. I went back in and bought my boy a present, hoping that when we came out he would have gone back inside. I didn't want him to see me. But there he was, with Geraldine and some other people. They saw me, so I had to go over. Marco was very casual towards me, playing it cool. Geraldine kindly invited me along to a drinks reception that night, but I was very busy with the opening, and it just felt awkward.

Then Marco said, 'My phone is broken. I couldn't call you.'

I mean, please. I just said, 'It's nice to see you all,' and that was the last time we ever spoke. I was so disappointed in him, and hurt, but resolute. Marco was a wonderful mentor and boss for a decade of my career, but once I decided to do my own thing, he was gone.

After that, I decided to work independently and to keep Marco at a distance. It has been hard because when someone is in your life every day for so many years it can be tricky to walk away from that. But his lack of interest in what I was doing made it a hell of a lot easier. People I know are baffled that we don't communicate any more. They keep asking me if I have spoken to him. I say I haven't spoken to him, why would I? I'm busy. He is busy. He is looking after his affairs and I am looking after mine.

I tried sending out a few olive branches. I've let him know that he's welcome to come to the restaurant. I mean, I would love him to see it – it's my baby. I'm open over a year now and not one word from him. Ultimately, if he was a mate, he would just come and enjoy what I have done. The longer our rift goes on, the more I am at peace with it. I don't feel the need to ring him only to be asked how many covers I'm doing and how much gross profit I'm making. I no longer want to go down that road.

It's still hanging in the air though. There have been well-meaning friends who tried to mediate. Callum Watson, who worked for Marco for years and helped set up Dawson Street, said that Marco was asking for me and suggested I make the first move. I know how stubborn I look. People have said, 'Why don't you just call him. Life is too short.' But what can I say? I am a stubborn man.

A colleague of the tennis player Greg Rusedski recently contacted us because they were hosting a charity dinner and wanted Marco's number.

Denise said, 'Why don't you ring Marco and give him the details?'

I said, 'No, you ring him.'

So Denise rang Marco, and they had a chat. The first thing he said is, 'How are the children and how is Nick?'

She said, 'He is sulking as he normally is!'

Denise is right – that's basically how it is at the moment. I can't pinpoint why I'm not ringing him, why I don't just pick up the phone. I may do one day, when I'm ready. I don't want anything to spoil what I'm doing at the moment, and maybe not having to answer to him, to explain my business, is liberating after a decade of being his employee. I did nearly ring him one day, and then, later that same day, a journalist I know said he'd interviewed Marco, and that, while he wasn't quite being derogatory about me, he wasn't being nice either. I don't even know what was said, but I decided to shelve the phone call.

My instinct is telling me to steer clear. I have a gut feeling that if I let Marco Pierre White back into my life then my life will become a little more complicated. I'm running my own shop now. I'm independent. If the Don can't understand that, it's not my concern. Working with him was good for me. The association with him helped my career. But I earned that through my work too, and now I'm standing on my own two feet.

Off to a flying start: a busy service at Pichet.

STARTERS' ORDERS

OPENING THE DOORS

We almost lost the Trinity Street premises because the landlords were concerned that we weren't tried and tested enough in the business world. Then we considered opening a gastropub in the Pembroke near Baggot Street, but the room was much too big, and the rent was very high. Even though we were keeping our options open, I had my heart and soul set on Trinity Street, and, as time went on, I knew that was the site I really wanted. We had to decide if the location was right for what we wanted to do. I felt it was.

Securing the finance we needed to open was really difficult, a huge challenge. We might have had the best ideas in the world, but if we didn't have the money to execute them we would be lost before we'd even started. We had to pay a premium for the lease as well as the rent, and, although we were able to negotiate a good deal, it was still very costly in Dublin city centre. It was a huge stretch, and neither Stephen nor I wanted to put our houses up as collateral. We scrimped together some savings, but we also needed a bank loan, which was very difficult to secure.

If you use your will and determination there is always a way to get funds, but we were trying to do so without it costing us a fortune in terms and interest rates. We went to several banks but by this time Ireland was already in recession. I had been an AIB customer for eight years, and my bank manager was always helpful to me. But at the time I was trying to secure the loan he was on sick leave, and I had to deal with somebody else, who treated me as though I was a new customer and said no. Then we went to this other business that offers loans to small companies. So many bank lenders said no to us. It was mad. Those days you could still go on the Internet and get a car loan for €16,000 in no time. We were looking for €25,000, but it was so difficult to find somebody willing to lend it to us. Where's the logic in that? Eventually we managed to secure funds for the lease and some of the rent just a couple of weeks before things got really bad with the economy. We couldn't get all the money together so we had to renegotiate with Frank Gleeson so that we could pay him half now and half later. He saved our bacon because without those terms we just wouldn't have been able to go any further.

We estimated we would need another €40,000 for the set-up, which was a very tight budget for what we wanted to do. It was Denise's charm that enabled us to get the loan for that. She went to Ulster Bank one morning and got on like a house on fire with their loans officer. They loved the whole *Hell's Kitchen* thing, which must have helped, and invited us to come back the following week to discuss things in more detail. We put a business plan together, which was tricky, because how could we anticipate how many people were going to come through our doors once we were open? It was all speculative: we might have had a fantastic business plan but still not have made any money. However, we needed it to show that we knew a bit about the financial side of running a restaurant. On the day of the meeting, I sat there and blagged my way through all the questions, and we got our loan of €40,000 with a €5,000 overdraft, which we thought was massive at the time but which actually is nothing.

The most important thing for us was that we managed to get what we needed without putting up our homes as collateral. Whatever about taking chances and working every hour to set up a new business, losing the family home was not a risk I was willing to take.

There was one figure that was pretty clear, and it was one that kept me awake, staring at the ceiling, for many nights. We knew that our overheads were going to be €26,000 per week – a huge sum. And that was what we needed to take, week in, week out, just to break even. We used to wonder what we would need to sell to make that figure, that enormous amount. It was really frightening actually. It played with my head, that figure. It made me ask, *Are we doing the right thing? Can we break even? Are we going to survive?* Then I would try to calm down and put things into perspective. I'd say to myself, *OK, if the restaurant doesn't work, we'll have the coffee shop, and that will save us.* Then the voice inside my head would come back and bellow, *Hah! Maybe, but will the coffee shop be enough to pay the rent and the loans?* It was a vicious circle, and that voice in my head actually drove me a bit berserk.

Once we got the scary financial stuff organised, we were able to move on to the fun elements. We originally thought about making Pichet a coffee shop by day and a restaurant in one area and tapas bar in the other by night. We knew from Café Leon's experience that there was potential as a coffee shop, because of the footfall. There was a constant flow of people coming in for cups of coffee, sandwiches and cakes, and we thought to ourselves, *We shouldn't lose what has been created here.* If the restaurant was slow to take off, the coffee shop could be the bread and butter of our business.

Seating was something we had to take a close look at. In the coffee-shop area at the front, there was seating for twenty-five people. At the back in the main restaurant area, we could take forty-five. Then there were nine tables in the patio area, so we could fit twenty-five out there. The premises were the right size in terms of our ambition to do between fifty and 100 covers a night, but when it came to making €26,000 every week to break even, that size became quite daunting.

A huge factor was the kitchen, which was tiny. We had to create a menu that would be suited to that small kitchen. This was a mistake, because soon after we opened we realised we couldn't cope with demand and had to extend the kitchen. The refit ended up costing much more than we'd budgeted for – double the amount – which was quite scary because we just didn't have the money. We underestimated the amount it would cost. You can be the most experienced person in catering and still get the maths wrong.

If you had carte blanche to design your own restaurant and menu, what would you do? Where would you start? For me, it was like hosting the biggest-ever house party where I got to plan every detail from the food to the music to the ambiance. Very exciting.

I had spent years working out exactly what I wanted from a restaurant. Michelin-star food is like cooking by numbers, and it can get really boring. It's all about consistency, ticking certain boxes to please inspectors. When we started to dream up Pichet, Stephen and I were yearning for a bistro environment and the sensuality that brings: the clatter of cutlery, glasses clinking, chatter, laughter. An electric atmosphere, without the quietness of high-end places. Relaxed, but with great food. We thought it would be great if we could employ the best things about upmarket dining, like the good service, with that relaxed vibe you get in a more casual restaurant.

Stephen and I loved many of the same eateries: the Arbutus and Wild Honey, both in London, whose ethos we adored. We liked the fact that they sourced quality products, made them into something special and presented them in a very relaxed environment. We toyed with the idea of calling our establishment a 'bistro' or a 'brasserie', but neither seemed the correct fit. Then we came up with 'a modern take on the classic bistro', which has worked very well in defining what we are.

It was very important for us to be clear on who we were because then we would be able to talk with confidence about what we were doing. For example, the Tea Rooms in the Clarence would have made a great brasserie but they wanted it to be fine dining, and – partly because of the location – it suffered from an identity crisis. Restaurant Patrick Guilbaud, on the other hand, is in the right location for a fine-dining restaurant, and they have thrived for years because they know what they are.

We were confident about what we were doing, but we weren't so confident about the market for it. There aren't many authentic French bistros in Dublin, which has always surprised me. There are elements of Frenchness in several restaurants, but very few of them are straight-up bistros – they tend to be more high end.

Masters at work: Stephen and sous chef John Dwyer.

There is one, Peploe's, which I think is amazing, and a very well-oiled machine. I would say that Peploe's is the closest thing in Dublin to a true French restaurant.

Denise came up with 'Pichet' as a name one night, as we were talking over dinner. I wanted something short, sweet and precise and had been racking my brains for the right word. When I heard it, it sounded perfect for what we were doing. From the minute Denise said it, it just stuck. We rang Stephen to see what he thought, and, being Mr Calm, he just said, 'Yeah. Go for it.' The

dictionary meaning, which spooked me a little, is 'an earthenware jug of cheap wine'. We wanted to sell wines by the *pichet*, but we didn't want people to perceive them as cheap. In the end it wasn't an issue because it's not one of those words that's widely used here; 'carafe' would be more common. I love what the word conjures up: a sharpness and coolness, those Gitanes-smoking Parisians from the 1950s and 1960s. It's very slick, cool but not self-consciously so, quite understated. That's what I wanted.

I think 'Pichet' works for us because it's almost become a brand name. When we opened, people coming in didn't realise who owned the restaurant and thought it was a franchise. Because the place really looked very 'London' and very generic, they thought of it as a roll-off concept that could have been designed anywhere in the world. That was actually really exciting and flattering, and it might be something we will explore in the future.

My dad always said to me, 'You need a gimmick to sell.' For me, the gimmick is the word *pichet* because it is still quite an unusual word in this part of the world. That's why we now have Pichet lighters, pencils and pens. It's nice to be able to give something to a customer, and it's also a way of reinforcing your brand.

Once we had the name, I knew in my head what colours and visuals I wanted. I needed something classic that would last for ever because we couldn't afford to keep changing design over and over. This was our one shot. So I focused on colours that never go out of fashion: black, silver, blue. The shade of blue we used is Paris to the very core. I'm in love with metro signs, art deco, that whole romantic side of Paris and the fact that it hasn't lost its sense of tradition, even though it's a massive cosmopolitan city. I knew that I wanted enamel signage like the old French ones and spent hours on the Internet trying to source what I was looking for. I found a French company that cooks the enamel signs in ovens; they are made in Romania. I rang and asked for a sample, and as soon as I saw what came back, I said, 'That's it.' Even the sample was perfect. There was no need to modify it. I showed it to a few good friends, who loved it. It was the perfect shade of blue, the blue I was looking for, the blue of the building numbers in Paris streets.

We wanted the atmosphere to be quite casual too. Linen table-cloths were a definite no-no. I wanted everything to be totally, totally relaxed, with knowledgeable, efficient staff and great food at reasonable prices. The way the staff dressed would help project that relaxed atmosphere too. I now get to wear jeans at work after years of dressing in suits, which is great.

Sourcing comfortable seating for the restaurant was very, very important to me. I hate a place where the chairs mean you can't relax or you want to get out of there as soon as you've eaten. It surprises me how little thought goes into such a crucial element. I hate uncomfortable seating because I've got a bony arse myself, and I despise sitting in hard wooden chairs or uncomfortable chairs that make me sit bolt upright. I wanted seating that would fit the contours of the body and where people could feel relaxed for a couple of hours, comfortable. We also felt that the chairs could provide a 'wow' factor if we got them right. We reck-oned that if we did something really special with the chairs that they could become a talking point for the restaurant in terms of both design and comfort. We wanted people to see them through the windows and be chatting about them before we even opened our doors. Much budgeting was done to see how much we could afford to spend on seating, and I took to the Internet.

Little did I know that I was about to embark on a seating dis-aster we now refer to as Chairgate. I had drawn a rough sketch of what kind of chair we were looking for. A former colleague had bought furniture for his hotel in China and was very impressed by it, so we decided that we would do the same because it would save us a fortune and we would get the exact size and style that we wanted. Big mistake.

We gave them the measurements. We gave them the style. We told them what shade of blue we were looking for. We met with an Irish agent who had been importing furniture from China. For ninety chairs the estimate was coming in at €8,500. A bargain for the type of chair we wanted. The only problem was, we couldn't afford a sample. The agent sent us a photo by email, and we thought it looked fantastic, let's go for it. We didn't have a swatch of the shade of the leather; we just went by what we saw on the email. In hindsight that may seem like a bad call, but our opening date was looming and the chairs were going to take three or four weeks to be manufactured and transported, so we had to commit.

Next, the agent wanted us to pay the €8,500 up front, which we thought was odd. Stephen asked me, 'Are you sure this is the right thing to do?' and I said, 'Of course it is, we have to get on with it.' So we paid the money. We hoped for the best. We had everything planned and measured to a tee. Fifty centimetres by forty, so that the knee is nicely supported, the back is comfortable, and the seat curves in to the back, kind of like a bucket seat in a sports car.

We got emails from China that we couldn't decipher, all in bad English: they were either going on holiday or they had some days off. Concerned that everything would be just right, we asked the Irish agent to send us a sample photo of the chair. When the email arrived, we didn't know whether to laugh or cry. There was a photo of a Chinese girl, very petite – she couldn't have been more than size 8 – squeezed into the chair. It was immediately apparent that the chairs were being manufactured for Chinese bums rather than Western ones, despite our having sent detailed dimensions. We looked at the photo and thought, *What the fuck has gone wrong here?*

We'd paid this money up front, we were due to open in two weeks, and here was this tiny girl squeezed into the chairs that we needed for our Irish customers a fortnight later.

I thought I was going to cry, and Stephen said, 'I told you, we shouldn't have paid the money. I had a bad feeling about this from the start.'

We rang the agent, and we went for a meeting. It was horrific. They didn't want to know. They were trying to tell us that the measurements we gave them were the ones they had used. I explained that they absolutely weren't and that we wanted our money back, but they refused to acknowledge that they were at fault. They tried to tell me I'd signed off on the chairs. I had signed off on the measurements I'd sent them, not the chairs they were actually making me – two different things. We are in litigation with them at the moment.

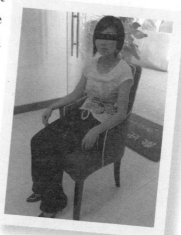

Chairgate. We were opening a restaurant in Dublin, not Beijing!

Your table is ready ... with Irish-sized chairs for Irish-sized bottoms!

It caused a massive panic for us and arguments that we didn't need. We were two weeks from opening, our seating was supposed to be our wow factor, and we had no chairs. Where on earth were we going to get seating in time for the opening, with a dwindling budget? It was unbelievably stressful, and we were very fortunate to find a knight in shining armour. Paddy Traynor, a furniture-maker in Castleblayney, stepped up to the mark. What a wonderful man. We met up with him, and he did us an amazing deal. He knew the whole story. He felt bad for us and made the most amazing chairs, which saved us from the embarrassment of opening without them. Paddy and twelve of his staff made the ninety chairs in two weeks. They arrived the night before we opened, on the back of a lorry. They are the most exquisite chairs you will ever see, and we should have gone to him in the first place.

Looking back, there was no guarantee that the chairs in China would have sustained the voyage on the ship or the humidity. If one got broken where would we have got it repaired? Now if one of the chairs is split or the stitching comes out Paddy comes down and takes the chair away and gets it fixed. We should have stayed with Irish furniture-makers and with people who knew what they were doing. We thought at the beginning that we would do the legwork and save ourselves a few bob, but it didn't work out that way.

We had to borrow money from Stephen's mother to pay for the chairs. It's a talking point forever more, and people love hearing the story, but it was an awful, awful time. I was obsessed with getting the chairs just right, and we did in the end, but not without a lot of grief. As far as I know, the mini-chairs are still in China. It would have been nice to auction them off for charity because of their novelty value – that was one idea we were toying with. But it's nice to be able to just forget about them now and move on, even though we are still trying to get our money back.

Once Chairgate was sorted, there was still a lot more to organise in the final weeks before opening. We were putting a lot of thought into the ambiance of the restaurant, and a huge factor in that – for all of us – was the music. Taste in music is so subjective, but we were keen to use music to try and demonstrate what we were about. Everyone has a horror story about being stuck in a confined space with pan pipes or tinny supermarket music, and we really wanted to avoid the kind of stuff that drives people to distraction. It's something we needed to put a bit of thought into. If we had a lot of classical music then we would be setting the tone for something quite formal, which was just what we were trying to avoid. Neither could the music be too intrusive or too loud. Timing comes into it as well – what works at 10 p.m. on a Saturday night isn't necessarily what you want to hear at lunchtime on a Tuesday. The beginning of the evening is a quieter time. Everyone's in from work and settling down. By eight o'clock there's more of a buzz. The louder the music the louder people will speak and the louder the atmosphere. Then when the restaurant slowly winds down towards the end of the night, around 10 o'clock, you need a different type of music. What we wanted was music we've always loved ourselves and that would be very much of our generation: the 1980s, the 1990s and some of the new stuff in the charts. Depeche Mode, the Pet Shop Boys, Duran Duran and Sade are on the playlist by consensus. (And, of course, Madonna for Denise.) I like French 1960s pop music – Serge Gainsbourg, France Gall – so we put that in too, because we thought it contributed to the fun Gallic feel we wanted in the restaurant. We used an iPod and downloaded loads of music from iTunes, which was great because that makes it a continual work in progress.

We got an awful lot of positive comments from customers from the word go about the music, which was really great feedback to get. We had a review that mentioned the fact that the music was so good. It can help motivate staff too. I've been stuck in enough restaurants for hours on end knowing what time it was by the playlist to know that variety is a motivator.

As we prepared for opening night, that €26,000-a-week-to-break-even figure was weighing heavily on my mind. We had already gone over budget, and the recession had well and truly kicked in in Dublin, with even established and highly regarded restaurants being forced to close their doors. I had the idea of doing a fly-on-the-wall documentary about opening a new business during the recession. I pitched it to a couple of places, but it didn't really take off. Then I mentioned it to my friend, the journalist and TV presenter Donal MacIntyre, and he thought it was a great idea. Donal introduced me to Ben Frow, Director of Programming for TV3. I went with the attitude that it would be nice if it happened but that if it didn't work out then that was fine too. Ben loved the idea, and after that things happened really quickly. We started filming the following day, when we received the keys to the restaurant, and continued for the next four months whilst doing up the place. It was an in-house production filmed by the fantastic director, Fintan Maguire. TV3 took a huge gamble on us and were concerned as to whether they'd have the manpower needed to document the opening over a period of time. Fortunately we managed to secure sponsorship from Bewley's, who were very forward-thinking about getting involved.

I wasn't afraid of bringing the cameras in to witness the highs and lows, because I had worked on *Hell's Kitchen* and had developed a sense of how television worked. I loved that people would get to share in what was the highlight for me: the setting up of a new restaurant. I actually felt it was quite fun to do even though it was adding to the stress. We were juggling so much already, and it was another pull on our time.

The other guys were more apprehensive because they hadn't done anything like that before. I reassured them about how they would be edited. It was a gamble I was willing to take. Yes, the cameras can portray you in a certain way – nasty, impatient, eccentric – but ultimately if you don't swear and don't kill anybody you can get over that. People know they're seeing you at your most stressed when you're opening a business. What was captured on camera was real life, and I'm really glad we did it.

I felt the TV show would showcase Stephen and his talent. Stephen is a very modest man, not very forward, and I thought it would be a nice way to do it. Obviously, it would promote brand awareness as well. Most of all, it would be a bit of fun. The others didn't actually believe it was happening and thought it was another one of my crazy ideas. It was only when the show was given the green light that they started to take me seriously.

The half-hour show aired for six weeks and got an average viewership of 130,000–140,000 people, which we were all delighted with. The week of the final show we had an influx of customers who had been watching TV3 and believed the restaurant had just opened, not realising we had been up and running for four months.

It was hugely labour-intensive at an already busy time but I think what we managed to capture was that it's possible, even in the current climate, to do what you've always dreamed of doing. People loved that connection between seeing us on TV and being able to eat in our restaurant. To come in and sit on the chairs that weren't made for Chinese bottoms.

CLEAN PLATES

CUSTOMERS, CRANKS AND CRITICS

It's easy to make the opening of Pichet sound like a huggy happy story now, but it was a massive shot in the dark for me, Stephen and our families and staff. By the time we came to opening, we had run out of money. There was literally none left – but there were plenty of debts and loans to pay. We couldn't even afford to have a launch or an opening night. We just didn't have the cash. It was all spent. We had to get everything finished fast and open as soon as we possibly could, just to generate some cash flow.

It was about a month before we realised we were on to something. The buzz gradually grew, and more people started coming through the doors. The amount of goodwill was really uplifting. People said we should be really pleased with ourselves to have opened a restaurant in a recession as other places were closing and town was quiet. It was very special – and a challenge too, to keep the momentum going.

When it came to the menu, I completely trusted Stephen. He happens to be a genius chef. He can take something quite basic and turn it into a wonderful, delicious dish, just by tweaking it. That's what's at the heart of his enormous talent. He's very instinctive and will add just a touch of another flavour to a dish and suddenly it blows you away. At the moment, we are doing a rib-eye with shimi mushrooms, but the mushrooms are not served hot. They are marinated in vinegar and olive oil, *à la grecque,* and it gives the dish an added sharpness. The coldness from the mushrooms kicks against the hot meat. A simple rib-eye steak and mushrooms, given a fresh twist.

Even though the restaurant is quite casual, it's still foodie food. It's the dishes people love, but with a bit of a flourish. We opened with quite a small menu, and, because we managed to get some good cash flow much earlier than we could have hoped for, we have been able to extend the menu. It's always evolving. At the moment we are into using micro-herbs. They have an intensity that really brings out the flavour in a dish, rather than just being there for decoration.

Stephen wanted to play around with dishes. He is fanatical about eggs, and his crispy hen's egg became an instant hit with customers. It's a poached egg wrapped in Serrano ham and coated with breadcrumbs, deep fried but still runny in the centre, with frisee salad, lardons, capers and leeks in a vinaigrette dressing, with aioli and mustard grain. It's become the star attraction. I think if we ever took it off the menu there would be uproar. Another hit is veal bolognese: rigatoni pasta with red veal that has been braised overnight, all crumbly, with no fat, and mixed with the tomato sauce into the rigatoni with parmesan cheese.

The perfect signature dish.

We took that off the menu for two weeks and had to put it back on because people were complaining they'd actually come to the restaurant especially to have it.

Stephen is as far removed from your clichéd hot-headed chef as it's possible to be. I mean, the guy is so calm: Mr Zen. A lot of chefs play up to a fearsome image or persona by throwing things around and shouting at people. They can be quite nasty, just so they're perceived as some sort of temperamental genius. Others become hot-headed because of their working environment. The heat, the atmosphere and the pressure build up and up until those frustrations explode. But Stephen has control of his pressure valve. He's like that character out of *Scooby Doo*: Shaggy – completely unflappable. He doesn't get fazed, because, while he's a quiet guy, he is quite an intellectual person, a thinker. He is very self-contained.

Stephen likes pots. Trays suit me better.

A real winner for us has been the dessert menu, which several customers have described as orgasmic. We never imagined that we would sell so many desserts. That's all down to Natasha McGowan, who is Stephen's fiancée and our pastry chef. The *crème brûlée* has been a bit hit. Again, it's a classic recipe but with different flavours going through it, like a hint of raspberry. And the shortbread biscuits are homemade too.

Stephen and Natasha met in l'Ecrivain when he was Head Chef and she was Pastry Chef. When we started getting Pichet together, we did it almost as a partnership between two couples. Natasha looks after the pastries, the coffee shop, the cakes. Stephen does the food. Denise does the bulk of the paperwork, reception and reservations. I look after the PR and the service. We all play to our strengths. The four of us always clicked. There

Our genius
pastry chef,
Natasha
McGowan.

wasn't a question of 'I want to do it my way' – it was very collabora-
tive. Everyone wanted the same thing, which was quite refreshing
because there was no fighting and we were able to focus on the
job. It was very free and easy because we were all on the same
wavelength. We would have a weekly meeting in the house so we
could all feel part of it. It also meant we were all on the same page.
It's been an amazing ride, and we never, ever hoped we could
achieve what we've achieved in such a short space of time. We've
all had our moments of anguish and anxiety but we're happy. All
of us bring different strengths to the table, and I think that is what
has made opening this restaurant so special.

I feel very comfortable working with Denise. There's no nonsense, no bringing it back home. Of course we have the odd argument, but nothing really important. When we were setting up
Pichet, there was the stress of trying to get ready for the opening,
doing too many things in one go, getting sidetracked instead of
being meticulous and working through what we had to do. It was
stressful, but, like anything when you're involved in a set-up, you
also have so many other things to think about – family, school,
home. We work together as a team, but we're also quite individual
in our approaches to how things should be run. Denise will sometimes agree with Stephen on something if she thinks that's the

Denise, the
Queen of
Calm.

best solution. We're inde-
pendent-minded in that
regard.

The beauty of it all is
that we are doing what we
love and doing it our way.
Stephen is cooking the
food that he likes, and the
public seems to love it
too. Hand on heart, the
food that we do is the same standard as you
would find in a Michelin-star restaurant. That's all I can say: the
quality of products we are using, the techniques we are using and
the knowledge behind the kitchen are exactly the same as you
would find in a Michelin-star restaurant.

Everything is fresh. We make eight apple tarts per service,
and if we run out we cook them to order. It does take fifteen minutes, but the customer knows their slice is fresh out of the oven.
We do have a tendency to run out of items, but I think that is a
good thing because it means that stuff isn't left in the fridge.

Recently we nearly lost a very sizeable booking. It was a party for
twenty-one, and one of the ladies rang up to cancel. I asked why
because I thought it was odd for such a big group, and she said,
'To be honest with you, we read your menu online and you've only
got three vegetarian options.'

life never tasted sweeter.

I said, 'Can you give us the opportunity to rectify that?'

She said, 'I didn't think you would be able to.'

I said, 'Well, if you don't ask the question how would you know?' I inquired further: were they vegetarian or vegan? Did they eat fish? We offered some extra options and kept our booking for twenty-one. Everyone was happy.

Vegetarians often feel they are penalised by restaurants because of their food choices. Most restaurants have a problem with knowing exactly what a vegetarian wants – sometimes because they don't put enough thought into it. They act as though vegetarians don't exist; maybe they have an adverse reaction to them. I know some chefs do. I have little time for that, just as I have little time for a chef who wants to cook steaks rare regardless of what the customer would like. If the customer wants the steak they're paying for well done, give it to them. Do it.

People often ask me if critics wield power over the restaurant scene in the same way as, say, a scathing review from a theatre critic can kill a show on Broadway. The answer is, yes: food critics matter. In all the various places I've worked over the past two decades, I've experienced hundreds of reviews, and they definitely matter. But I never realised how much until I opened my own place.

The main critics in Ireland are Paolo Tullio; Tom Doorley; Katy McGuinness; Hugo Arnold, who has written for numerous publications here and in the UK, and has also written several books; Ross Golden Bannon, who writes for the *Sunday Business Post*; and Lucinda O'Sullivan. They are the main people that we look out for and who would be the most respected in food circles. But there are always new kids coming on the block, who want to make a name for themselves.

With critics, it's all about doing your research and knowing what they like. They are like any other customer: some of them want to be fussed over, some of them want to be left alone. Understanding their needs, likes and dislikes is half the battle, as it is with any customer.

Most critics tend to book under a pseudonym, or the name of their guest, so that they can get an authentic customer experience and give a fair review. But lots of restaurants, including Pichet, keep mugshots of critics, from their byline photographs in their newspapers, so staff have a better chance of recognising them if and when they do come in. Marco's restaurants didn't, but we always knew who was who.

Do critics like to be acknowledged? I think so – everyone has an ego. Do they get special treatment? It's a tricky one. I would like to say that they don't, but, even subconsciously, we would be aware of critics because we know they are in the restaurant for a purpose. We have to be so careful: if we are too conscious of them or, worse, fawn over them, we can quite easily mess up the service. So I try to avoid preferential treatment – that would be my stance. I think you should have enough confidence in your business to serve critics in the same way as other diners. Not only is that the just and professional approach – everyone is entitled to the same level of service – it also means that if a customer reads a positive review and decides to dine with us based on that review, they can expect the same, or similar, experience to the reviewer. And why shouldn't they?

I've heard of some places who would offer to comp a meal for a critic, and I just think that's wrong. It's really dodgy territory. You're effectively paying them to give you a good review. And it could be counterproductive, because a journalist who's serious about their job should still be negative about you if they've had a negative experience, whether they've paid for their meal or not.

We were aware that it was possible we would be bombarded with reviewers in the first number of weeks and tried our best to be prepared for it. New openings in Dublin were thin on the ground because of the recession so the critics were probably going to come in to us. I avoided taking time off in case anyone visited as it was really important to me that I was there, to represent our restaurant to the best of my ability.

Lucinda O'Sullivan came in on our second night. She writes for the *Sunday Independent*, and also writes guidebooks on where to stay and eat in Ireland. She is hugely influential, very good at what she does and a tough cookie. Lucinda likes to be recognised, likes to be hugged and looked after. She loves a cocktail before dinner. That is the type of customer she is. She is a wonderful woman, who likes attentive service.

Stephen and I were signing the final papers in the solicitor's office when we got the call that she had come in. We jumped into a cab and got there just as she was given the main course. Honesty is the best policy, so I explained to her where we had been and what we had been doing and hoped for the best, and it worked in our favour. Katy McGuinness, whose brother is U2 manager Paul, wrote a glowing review for the *Sunday Tribune*. The critic who made me most nervous in those early days was Aingeala Flannery from the *Irish Independent* – a very good, quite edgy writer. The main fear for me was that I didn't really know her so I didn't know her quirks as well as I would have with some of the others. The night she came in, she was sitting outside on the terrace, and our alarm started going off. I couldn't shut the fucking thing up. It was going *wewewewewe!* for ages, and I was running around in a panic trying to turn it off. An alarm, as everyone knows, is as irritating as hell. I went out to Aingeala and tried to make a joke of it. I said, *Typical,*

Here I go again ...

isn't it, you have to be in on the night – do you want some ear muffs? That broke the ice, and I moved her and the other customers inside. Something like that can throw you and ruin your entire service, but we got the alarm to shut up after about half an hour. Aingeala seemed to have a great night all the same.

A few positive reviews put Pichet on the radar, but it was Tom Doorley's review for the *Irish Times* that really had an impact. Tom, the former restaurant critic for the *Irish Times*, is a restaurant god in Ireland. There is no other word for it. I cannot exaggerate the response on the Saturday that Tom's review came out. I would estimate that we took about 300 phone calls that day in bookings and enquiries. I couldn't keep up – everyone wanted to book. The phone did not stop hopping, and in the weeks that followed we must have gone from 600 to 1,200 covers a week, solely based, in my view, on that write-up.

I had never experienced the power of one review to that extent before. I think it was the type of review we got, too. With reviews, there is usually a hint of negativity. Someone loves the food but not the ambiance. Someone else loves the atmosphere in the restaurant but there's a mix-up with their order or their bill. But Tom's review was exceptional, glowing, and that was partly, I think, what provoked such an overwhelming response.

Sometimes you can take reviews too personally. Paolo Tullio, who writes for the *Irish Independent*'s Saturday magazine, came in to the restaurant. I thought we had an excellent service that night, but he only gave us eight out of ten for service. I thought, *What do you mean, eight out of ten? Why didn't we get a nine?* I can get overly protective because the whole thing – especially the service – is my baby. I am passionate about what we are doing. I'm sure some of my colleagues would say, 'You idiot, Nick, you should be happy with eight.' But I'm not happy with an eight. I want a nine or a ten. And if I sound mad because I'm not content with an eight, it's because that makes me fight to be the best.

No restaurant should be solely setting out to impress critics, that's not what's it's about, but I'd be lying if I said it wasn't

When the chef is Mr Zen, it's safe to seat customers in earshot of the pass.

relevant to our business. Within two months, everyone had been in. I knew instinctively to be on my guard for that time because reviewers aren't all that sympathetic to teething problems – they assume that you are professional enough to hit the ground running, and if you're opening to paying customers, you should be ready for action. But the flurry of good reviews those first few weeks was incredible. In my experience, you always get a reviewer who wants to go against the grain or be more controversial than others but fortunately for us that didn't happen. Over the following weeks, things got even better – I counted nine good reviews in a row from various publications.

That doesn't mean we can rest on our laurels. We might get reviewed again down the line, and critics will be looking out for any signs of dropping standards, so we really have to stay on top of things. We have to do that anyway, for the customers who come through the doors every night.

To my absolute amazement and to all of our relief, we started breaking even by early September two months after opening. I was totting up the till at the end of service and thought to myself, *That can't be right.* I did the maths again. It was right. It was an amazing feeling. Vindication. Relief. A massive, massive release of stress. I had actually lost weight from the stress of thinking about breaking even, and here we were, within six weeks, doing what we thought would take far longer to accomplish.

No more sleepless nights thinking about the €26,000, and no more worrying about whether we could keep on the staff who came to work with us. In fact, we were looking for more people.

Success can be a fickle friend. You start to think, *Will it always be this way? How do we sustain it?* Restaurants go in and out of fashion all of the time. So while the early success has been a huge relief, we have to be very careful to avoid complacency. I just don't want to let it into my life because that's when you start to lose everything you've built up.

One thing we could never have prepared for is the frustrating side of our success from a customer's point of view. Because we have enjoyed a lot of demand and advance bookings, and because we are a relatively small restaurant, I've noticed a growing frustration from people who can't get a table on the night they want or who have to book far in advance. This is a massive concern for me because I know if people get tired of trying to come to us they will go somewhere else.

We do have a certain number of tables for people who just walk in. We might have cancellations. People might turn up half an hour late. We are constantly juggling with the small number of tables. My biggest fear is that trade will dip and people will perceive us as the restaurant you can't get into without booking well in advance.

We do our best to stay recession-proof. We don't take the mickey, but everything is relative. We keep our gross profit, our mark-ups, at textbook level. For example, we buy our steaks from a reputable source from Northern Ireland, which is tagged, sealed and numbered from Hereford cattle. We pay a premium for that. There is a certain mark-up on that dish because we are adding on fries, mushrooms, salad. Then we have to take the electricity, the gas, the rates, the rent and the staff costs into the equation. I think we are very good value.

Has the business given Denise and me security? It has certainly given us much more freedom. We don't have to worry about the whims of some other boss. Working for yourself is very motivating because it's you who is responsible. I wouldn't say we're financially secure yet but if we keep going the way we are going we should do quite well out of it, and, after all these years, it's a really exciting position to be in.

My aspiration when I opened the door of Pichet was, it's going to be bohemian, it's going to be relaxed, it's going to be cool. We are those things to some extent, but you can't contrive an atmosphere: it might be your baby but it grows its own personality, and that comes down to the clientele. We have had to tweak the business accordingly. The big surprise for us was how many fine-dining customers came through the doors. They were people who knew me or Stephen from more upmarket restaurants. At first we were concerned that some of them would want the fine-dining experience they were used to elsewhere. Thankfully, most of them understood what we were trying to do.

Having read my little rant about Valentine's, you'll probably assume I hate the Christmas party season. Actually, I really enjoy it. You get groups of people hell-bent on having a good time, and, while sometimes it can get a tad wild, there's usually a great atmosphere. You get a whole mixed bag of people, which keeps service lively. Christmas party groups are there for the fun and excitement, and the free drink, obviously. Yuletide parties are all about the release of pent-up anxiety throughout the year. It's the buzz. It's the booze. Alcohol plays a massive part in people's perceptions and their behavioural patterns, never more so than at Christmas.

As a people-watcher, I also love having the vantage point of being at work, sober, observing how people interact when they're at their merriest, cutting loose. I have seen it all. The arc of how an evening goes is fascinating to watch. Generally, early on everyone is on their best behaviour and minding their manners in front of the boss. Very glammed up. By the end of the evening, they are at various stages of dishevellment. It's just so much fun watching how people interact as the drink flows. Girls in particular. They come in like Carrie from *Sex & the City* – high heels, fab new outfit, not a

We're more than prepared for the party season.

hair out of place. By the time they leave, some of the gals are more like Bridget Jones after too much chardonnay.

You can spot the body language of the bloke from Accounts who's desperate to snog Imelda from Marketing. It's just hilarious, you know – then they start pinching your bum as you walk past. The girls, not the guys. I have to admit, at the risk of sounding like I'm seeking cheap thrills, that I find the butt-pinching very amusing. Not because I like having my butt pinched, I hasten to add, but because groups that are being giddy and silly in that way are there to have fun. If it's good-humoured, I laugh it off. That's what any restaurateur wants – to see their place full of happy people.

Party groups always forget what they've picked from the menu, and when the food comes out, chaos briefly reigns. 'Did I order – what did I order – the risotto? No, I didn't order the risotto. Did I? Oh, mushroom risotto? That's me.' Eventually you get the right dishes to everyone, they're eating away, and it's all calm, for a time.

You see, when people are sitting and chatting, they don't know how much wine they're having because they're distracted. Two glasses. Fine. Three glasses. OK. Most people after the third or fourth glass lose their inhibitions. Another bottle of wine comes but at that stage they've had a bottle each. Then comes the cackle.

The first sign of impending madness is the cackle – that loud, group belly laugh that signals to waiting staff that the party's getting started. Before then it's all chatter: 'How. Are. You?! Your hair is gorgeous! I love your shoes!' And that's just the guys, ha ha.

I enjoy every bit of it, because I have been down that road myself. And it's just so funny to watch it all unfold when you're stone-cold sober. I don't tend to eavesdrop because I am just too busy, and when I'm in service mode I'm in my own world. Having said that, sometimes I'm walking by and I hear little snatches of conversation that make me go, *Woah!* The zanier the group – and the juicier the chatter – the better.

Sometimes, unfortunately, people will go overboard, forget the fact that they're in a restaurant and think they're in a nightclub. When you call last drinks you can get customers who say, 'OK, we'll have four bottles of wine.' There's give and take involved in that situation. You don't want customers who've paid good money to feel they're being rushed, or to be mean-spirited with people on their big night out. But you have to keep the number of late drinks within reason because if your staff are working into the night, every night, they'll get to feeling tired, grumpy and resentful.

What I usually do is give people one more drink but tell them we're closing and need them to be leaving in about twenty minutes. Most people are happy with that, and a deadline usually works. Other than the 'have you no homes to go to?' stage of the night, Christmas parties are a laugh.

><

I often get asked by people I know if I could reserve them a table. There's just one problem: I am a terrible man for saying, 'Yes we can squeeze you in on Friday night,' and then promptly forgetting all about it. We work with a good old-fashioned bookings diary rather than one of those new-fangled computerised reservations systems. It works well for us. Most of the time. What sometimes happens is that people call me, I say yes, then I forget to write it

Booked up. Thankfully, the restaurant is always busy.

in the book. I have often received a call from a puzzled member of staff on my day off asking, 'Did you book a guy in called John? He said he spoke to you and you took his booking.'

I remember one Saturday night we had 100 people booked in and were absolutely stuffed. Next thing, a group of eleven women turned up at the door. You get an 'Oh dear God' feeling when something like this happens.

They said, 'We booked with you, Nick.'

I said, 'No you didn't.'

They said, 'Yes we did. We spoke on the phone.'

I said, 'Oh no, you didn't.'

I was praying that they were chancing it, as people occasionally do. You often get people ringing on a busy day, going, 'I just want to confirm my table for two for Delaney.' If people know they can't get in, they will chance their arm and wing it. If a member of staff can't see it in the book and doesn't want to be rude, they will say, 'No problem. 8 p.m. We have it.' It's only later that they might say it to the manager, who has no record of the booking.

Then you get the guy who rings up and says, 'I just want to let you know I just got engaged,' or tells you that it's his wife's birthday. You know damn well that it is bull. The first thing I check when they come in is the ring on the girl's finger, or I wish her a happy birthday. And, indeed, sometimes there is no ring, or she just looks puzzled at my birthday wishes. You get a lot of that. There are always going to be mistakes made and discrepancies on the phone, and there are always going to be chancers. Sometimes it might even be a case of people booking the wrong restaurant or turning up at the wrong place.

But on this occasion I knew that the chancing-it scenario was unlikely for such a large group – you're not going to wing it when there's a large gathering at stake – and I started getting that prickly feeling at the back of my neck that I sometimes get when I fear a fuck-up. I looked through the book again. There, in the right-hand corner, in the tiniest of handwriting – my own handwriting – was 'Booking for eleven.' All I could think was, *Where am I going to put this group?*

Time for some serious juggling. There was a table for eight coming in after 9.30. These women turned up at 9 o'clock. So, I thought, let's get these eleven people seated and then try to figure out what to do when the party of eight arrives. The worst bit was having to go up to a chef who's already under pressure and go, 'Hi! How's things? Playing a blinder tonight! Fabulous! Eleven more people have just showed up and we have to take them.' Then I retreated very quickly from the kitchen.

I am no expert at chess but I had to start moving pieces around the board, and fast. It is understandable that people get upset when they're sitting comfortably and are then asked to move. In my experience it's the one thing that really pisses people off. I was quite lucky that night as three couples obliged me without any fuss at all, but one couple were quite annoyed. I had to go into charm overdrive, offer them a complimentary drink. I had that painful sensation of over-niceness I get when I've made a colossal mistake and I'm relying on the goodwill of people to get me out of trouble. The eleven people were great: they were just happy to sit down, I think. But that couple was deeply offended because first they had to move and, second, the noise level went right up. Their whole experience and comfort zone had been altered. I got away with it, but … I know that I upset them. I could tell from the grimaces on their faces, and no one wants unhappy diners.

I'd love to tell you that that was the only boob of my professional career, but there have been many. Think of a front-of-house job as being like an air-traffic controller: I'm directing people all the time, timing their orders so they wait a comfortable period between courses, trying to squeeze in an extra sitting on a busy night to make up for the quiet nights and to reach my financial targets. Sometimes it goes belly up. And, often, it's my fault.

It's wonderful running my own place after more than two decades since I first donned a commis uniform and started cleaning the loos all those years ago. I still absolutely love what I do – and, to be honest, you'd need to. Let's face it, the restaurant business is colourful and creative, but mostly it's insane. Late nights, split shifts, heat, tension and tempers are all part of my average day,

Still smiling. Stephen and me outside our restaurant.

and that's assuming I don't trip over. Working sixteen-hour days in this environment brings out the most interesting traits in people. It's certainly not for everyone, but it's the world I know and adore. And it's been a blast.

At the finish line: I made it!